China and Global Value Chains

President Trump has raised the intriguing question of bringing the manufacturing of companies like Apple back from China to the U.S. This book, however, argues that in this age of the knowledge-based economy and increased globalization, that value creation and distribution based on knowledge and innovation activities are at the core of economic development. The double-edged sword of globalization has transformed China's economic development in the past few decades. Although China has benefitted from globalization and is now the second largest economy in the world, having become a global manufacturing power and the biggest exporter of high-tech products, it continues to be highly dependent on foreign sources of capital and technology.

This book will explore the core of the Chinese economy from the perspective of the Global Value Chain (GVC), combining analysis of inward investment, international trade, Science and Technology and Innovation (S&TI) and economic development. Specifically, it investigates China's evolving role in GVCs with some innovative Chinese companies emerging in the global market and China's ongoing efforts to become an innovation-driven economy. China's impressive economic record and experience provides an impressive role model for other developing countries.

Yutao Sun is Professor at the Faculty of Management and Economics, Dalian University of Technology, China, and Marie Currie Research Fellow at the University of Nottingham. His research interests focus on S&T and innovation management and policy. He has published several articles in international journals, including *Science*.

Seamus Grimes is Emeritus Professor at the Whitaker Institute for Innovation and Societal Change, National University of Ireland, Galway. His research in recent years has focused mainly on foreign investment in both Ireland and China. He has published more than 70 papers in international journals.

Routledge Frontiers of Business Management

For a full list of titles in this series, please visit www.routledge.com/series/rfbm

China and Global Value Chains

Globalization and the Information and Communications Technology Sector

Yutao Sun and Seamus Grimes

Routledge
Taylor & Francis Group

LONDON AND NEW YORK

First published 2018 by Routledge

2 Park Square, Milton Park, Abingdon, Oxfordshire OX14 4RN

52 Vanderbilt Avenue, New York, NY 10017

Routledge is an imprint of the Taylor & Francis Group, an informa business

First issued in paperback 2019

British Library Cataloguing-in-Publication Data
A catalogue record for this book is available from the British Library

Library of Congress Cataloging-in-Publication Data
Names: Sun, Yutao, author. | Grimes, Seamus, author.
Title: China and the global value chain : globalization and the information and communications technology sector / by Yutao Sun and Seamus Grimes.
Description: Abingdon, Oxon ; New York, NY : Routledge, 2018. | Series: Routledge frontiers of business management ; 18 | Includes bibliographical references and index.
Identifiers: LCCN 2017045763 | ISBN 9781138289079 (hardback) | ISBN 9781315267418 (ebook)
Subjects: LCSH: Information technology—Economic aspects—China. | High technology industries—China. | Industrial policy—China. | Technological innovations—China. | China—Commerce.
Classification: LCC HC430.I55 S865 2018 | DDC 338.4/70040951—dc23
LC record available at https://lccn.loc.gov/2017045763

ISBN: 978-1-138-28907-9 (hbk)
ISBN: 978-0-367-37474-7 (pbk)

Typeset in Galliard
by Apex CoVantage, LLC

China and Global Value Chains

Globalization and the Information and Communications Technology Sector

Yutao Sun and Seamus Grimes

Routledge
Taylor & Francis Group

LONDON AND NEW YORK

First published 2018 by Routledge

2 Park Square, Milton Park, Abingdon, Oxfordshire OX14 4RN
52 Vanderbilt Avenue, New York, NY 10017

Routledge is an imprint of the Taylor & Francis Group, an informa business

First issued in paperback 2019

British Library Cataloguing-in-Publication Data
A catalogue record for this book is available from the British Library

Library of Congress Cataloging-in-Publication Data
Names: Sun, Yutao, author. | Grimes, Seamus, author.
Title: China and the global value chain : globalization and the information and communications technology sector / by Yutao Sun and Seamus Grimes.
Description: Abingdon, Oxon ; New York, NY : Routledge, 2018. | Series: Routledge frontiers of business management ; 18 | Includes bibliographical references and index.
Identifiers: LCCN 2017045763 | ISBN 9781138289079 (hardback) | ISBN 9781315267418 (ebook)
Subjects: LCSH: Information technology—Economic aspects—China. | High technology industries—China. | Industrial policy—China. | Technological innovations—China. | China—Commerce.
Classification: LCC HC430.I55 S865 2018 | DDC 338.4/70040951—dc23
LC record available at https://lccn.loc.gov/2017045763

ISBN: 978-1-138-28907-9 (hbk)
ISBN: 978-0-367-37474-7 (pbk)

Typeset in Galliard
by Apex CoVantage, LLC

Contents

Figures

Tables

Acknowledgments

This work has been supported by the National Natural Science Foundation of China (71673035) and the EU 7th Framework Programme – Marie Curie International Incoming Fellowship (302303/911303). The authors have benefited from data collection and format setting by Tong Yin and Yifan Zhang, two graduate students of Dalian University of Technology. Fieldwork for company interviewing since 2009 has been extensively supported by Professor Debin Du of East China Normal University, Shanghai through financing visiting professorships.

Abbreviations

AAAS	American Association for the Advancement of Science
ATP	Advanced Technology Products
BCG	Boston Consulting Group
BOM	Bill of Materials
BRICS	Brazil, Russia, India, China, South Africa
CAS	Chinese Academy of Sciences
CAST	China Association for Science and Technology
CCCPC	Central Committee of the Communist Party of China
CECC	Congressional-Executive Commission on China
CFIUS	The Committee on Foreign Investment in the U.S.
CNR	China North Locomotive and Rolling Stock Corporation
COEs	Chinese Owned Enterprises
CRRC	China Railway Rolling Stock
CSR	China South Locomotive and Rolling Stock Corporation
E7	Emerging 7 (China, India, Brazil, Mexico, Russia, Indonesia and Turkey)
EAR	Export Administration Regulations
EMSs	Electronics Manufacturing Services
EST	Education, Science and Technology
FDI	Foreign Direct Investment
FIEs	Foreign Invested Enterprises
FTE	Full-time Equivalents
G7	Canada, France, Germany, Italy, Japan, UK and the U.S.
GCCs	Global Commodity Chains
GCR	Global Competitiveness Report
GCS	Global Communication Semiconductors
GDP	Gross Domestic Product
GERD	Gross Domestic Expenditure on R&D
GIN	Global Innovation Networks
GMV	Gross Merchandise Volume
GPA	General Procurement Agreement
GPNs	Global Production Networks
GTAP	Global Trade Analysis Project

Acknowledgments

This work has been supported by the National Natural Science Foundation of China (71673035) and the EU 7th Framework Programme – Marie Curie International Incoming Fellowship (302303/911303). The authors have benefited from data collection and format setting by Tong Yin and Yifan Zhang, two graduate students of Dalian University of Technology. Fieldwork for company interviewing since 2009 has been extensively supported by Professor Debin Du of East China Normal University, Shanghai through financing visiting professorships.

Abbreviations

AAAS	American Association for the Advancement of Science
ATP	Advanced Technology Products
BCG	Boston Consulting Group
BOM	Bill of Materials
BRICS	Brazil, Russia, India, China, South Africa
CAS	Chinese Academy of Sciences
CAST	China Association for Science and Technology
CCCPC	Central Committee of the Communist Party of China
CECC	Congressional-Executive Commission on China
CFIUS	The Committee on Foreign Investment in the U.S.
CNR	China North Locomotive and Rolling Stock Corporation
COEs	Chinese Owned Enterprises
CRRC	China Railway Rolling Stock
CSR	China South Locomotive and Rolling Stock Corporation
E7	Emerging 7 (China, India, Brazil, Mexico, Russia, Indonesia and Turkey)
EAR	Export Administration Regulations
EMSs	Electronics Manufacturing Services
EST	Education, Science and Technology
FDI	Foreign Direct Investment
FIEs	Foreign Invested Enterprises
FTE	Full-time Equivalents
G7	Canada, France, Germany, Italy, Japan, UK and the U.S.
GCCs	Global Commodity Chains
GCR	Global Competitiveness Report
GCS	Global Communication Semiconductors
GDP	Gross Domestic Product
GERD	Gross Domestic Expenditure on R&D
GIN	Global Innovation Networks
GMV	Gross Merchandise Volume
GPA	General Procurement Agreement
GPNs	Global Production Networks
GTAP	Global Trade Analysis Project

GVCs	Global Value Chains
HDDs	Hard Disk Drives
HTDZs	High Tech Development Zones
I6	China, Korea, India, Indonesia, Thailand, and Poland
IB	International Business
IBM	International Business Machines Corporation
IC	Integrated Circuit
ICIO	Inter-Country Input-Output
ICT	Information and Communications Technology
IDP	Investment Development Path
IMF	International Monetary Fund
IP	Intellectual Property
IT	Information Technology
ITSR	Iranian Transactions and Sanctions Regulations
JV	Joint Venture
LQ	Location Quotient
M&A	Merger and Acquisition
MIIT	Ministry of Industry and Information Technology
MLP	Mid- to Long-Term Plan
MNCs	Multinational Companies
MOST	Ministry of Science and Technology
NAFTA	North American Free Trade Agreement
NDRC	National Development and Reform Commission
NGO	Non-Governmental Organizations
NIS	National Innovation System
NSFC	National Natural Science Foundation of China
OBMs	Own Brand Companies
ODM	Original Design Manufacturer
OECD	Organization for Economic Co-operation and Development
OEM	Original Equipment Manufacturer
OFDI	Outward Foreign Direct Investment
OLI	Ownership-Location-Internalization
P4P	Pay-for-Performance
PC	Personal Computer
PCB	Printed Circuit Board
POE	Private-Owned Enterprises
PRD	Pearl River Delta
R&D	Research and Development
RBV	Resource-based View
RCA	Revealed Comparative Advantage
S&T	Scientific & Technological
SCI	Science Citation Index
SEZs	Special Economic Zones
SIPO	State Intellectual Property Office
SMEs	Small Middle Enterprises

SNA	Social Network Analysis
SOE	State Owned Enterprise
TD-SCDMA	Time Division Synchronous Code Division Multiple Access Standard
TFP	Total-factor Productivity
TFT-LCD	Thin-film-transistor-crystal Display
TIS	Territorial Innovation System
TPP	Trans-Pacific Partnership
TSMC	Taiwan Semiconductor Manufacturing Company
U.S.	United States
UK	United Kingdom
UNESCO	United Nations Educational Scientific and Cultural Organization
VAS	Value-Added Services
VIE	Variable Interest Entity
WIOD	World Input-Output Database
WOFEs	Wholly-Owned Foreign Firms
WTO	World Trade Organization
YRD	Yellow River Delta

1 Introduction

A Chinese landscape in the age of globalization

The starting point of our story is President Trump's intriguing question about whether Apple and other companies could bring manufacturing back to the U.S., particularly from China. Our basic argument is that, despite its ongoing dependence on foreign technologies and IP, China has been upgrading its ICT sector through participating in the GVC. Specifically, this chapter investigates China's open economy, high-tech industries and indigenous innovation. Finally, it describes the objectives and organization of this book.

Background and viewpoints

Trump's promise

On January 18, 2016, in a campaign speech at Virginia's Liberty University (a private, Christian school), Donald Trump, Republican Presidential candidate, tangentially promised that he would force Apple to manufacture its hardware in the United States (U.S.) instead of looking to overseas labor (The Washington Post, 2016). When American companies moved manufacturing to China, it was all about cost, according to Trump. China's wages were amongst the lowest in the world and its government provided subsidies and turned a blind eye to labor abuse and environmental degradation. Now, only the Mac Pro is currently assembled in the U.S., in a factory located in Austin, Texas. Apple otherwise relies on manufacturers in China for most of its products, both because of cheap labor and because decades of previous outsourcing has allowed the American manufacturing industry to shrink.

But now, cost competitiveness is changing worldwide. BCG's report – *The Shifting Economics of Global Manufacturing*, published in 2014 – indicates that China's estimated manufacturing-cost advantage over the U.S. has shrunk to less than 5 percent. The *2016 Global Manufacturing Competitiveness Index* published by Deloitte Touche Tohmatsu Limited and the Council on Competitiveness in the U.S. indicated that China was ranked as the most competitive manufacturing nation in 2016, but that the U.S. is expected to take over the number one position from China by 2020. Meanwhile, one of the first executive orders of the new U.S. President was to end the United States' participation in the Trans-Pacific

Partnership (TPP), while at the same time to begin renegotiating the North American Free Trade Agreement (NAFTA). By seeking to fulfil his campaign promises by bringing manufacturing jobs which were lost through offshoring back to the U.S., Trump raises the intriguing possibility of pressuring companies like Apple to reshore jobs from China.

China and the U.S.

In the wake of the financial crisis, China must face the reality that the world is now characterized by the de facto G2 of China and the U.S. These two major economies must find ways of collaborating, both in their own interests and to solve global problems and realize that trade protectionism and economic nationalism pose major threats to the global economy. Labor, real estate, and energy costs in the eastern urbanized regions of China have increased to the point that they are now comparable to some parts of the U.S., while China's other advantages are also being eroded with the result that China is currently a more expensive manufacturing location than Indonesia, Thailand, Mexico, and India. At the same time, there is no evidence that Apple wishes to leave China, which is its second largest market. While its May 2016 investment of $1 billion in Didi Chuxing – a China-based company and Uber's main rival – may have influenced Uber selling its China business to Didi Chuxing in August 2016, Apple clearly saw an important market opportunity. It also suggests a willingness by Apple to further contribute to China's development.

Meanwhile, China is no longer content to be merely a global manufacturing base and the largest market. China is seeking to move to 'Created in China' from 'Made in China'. The objective is to become an innovation powerhouse by 2020, according to the newly adopted *13th Five Year National Plan on Scientific & Technological (S&T) and Innovation (2016–2020)*. The plan aims to substantially improve China's technology and innovation capabilities and lift the national innovation capabilities into the world's top 15 (The China Daily, 2016). Apart from adding 'innovation' to the title, three points in the latest plan are worthy of note. First, China will continue to implement major S&T and innovation projects. The plan called for efforts to accelerate the implementation of major national scientific and technological projects and launch the scientific and technological innovation 2030 project. It puts research emphasis on areas that will contribute to China's industrial upgrading and new economy, including modern agriculture, clean and efficient energy and fifth-generation mobile telecommunication (The State Council, 2016).

Secondly, China emphasizes innovation localization. The country should support Beijing and Shanghai to build scientific and technological innovation centers with international influence, set up a batch of innovative provinces and cities and regional innovation centers, and promote the innovative development of national indigenous innovation demonstration zones, as well as new and high-tech development zones.

Finally, China also stresses innovation globalization. The plan also urged the building of a Belt and Road innovation community aiming to improve the country's ability in the allocation of global innovation resources and to fully participate in global innovation governance. While the Trump administration seeks to bring job opportunities from China to America though trade protectionism and economic nationalism, the Chinese government plans to improve its innovation capability and upgrade its industries.

Our arguments

Indeed, whether Apple could bring manufacturing back to the U.S. or move its manufacturing out of China may not be the right question. This action depends not only on China and the U.S., but also on the whole ecosystem of production and research in East Asia. In a more globalized economy, gross domestic product (GDP) and trade exports do not completely reflect a country's competitiveness. More attention needs to be paid to explaining how a country like China has increased its involvement in global value chains (GVCs) and the extent to which it has contributed to and benefitted from this involvement.

In particular, this book seeks to investigate China's involvement in GVCs from the perspective of the ICT sector. To what extent does China continue to be dependent on key foreign technologies, and how can China make greater progress in acquiring intellectual property (IP) ownership, more influence in the technology trajectory and greater value-added in GVC functions within China? Is GVC participation helping China to transition its economy from the low value-added tasks of being the 'world's factory' to greater levels of indigenous innovation, and greater technological autonomy? How difficult is it for a latecomer nation like China to achieve upgrading within high-tech sectors such as semiconductors, which are global in nature?

Our basic argument is that, despite its ongoing dependence on foreign technologies and IP, China has been upgrading its ICT sector through participating in the GVC

While we would suggest that our argument presents a moderate view of recent developments, it also reflects what has been the de facto situation in China for some time. Although it can be argued that China's ICT industrial output and exports have increased rapidly, and that China has become the largest global base for ICT manufacturing, this does not reflect the complete picture of China's innovation capabilities and competitiveness. While others argue that China's ICT development, in the absence of core competence, has been largely based on foreign equipment, technologies and IP, this does not preclude the fact that Chinese firms, through their involvement in GVCs, have acquired significant knowledge from foreign companies.

China's open economy

Since initiating market reforms in 1978, China has shifted from a centrally-planned to a market-oriented economy and has experienced rapid economic and

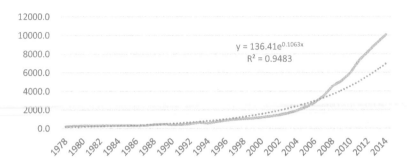

Figure 1.1 China's GDP growth since 1978 ($ billion)

social development. GDP growth has averaged nearly 10 percent a year – the fastest sustained expansion by a major economy in history. China's GDP reached USD 10 trillion in 2014, valued at the prevailing exchange rate, and it has become the world's second-largest economy, having passed the industrial economies of the United Kingdom (UK), France and Japan since 2011 (Figure 1.1).

Globalization, a necessary context of China's economy

An extensive literature has developed seeking to explain how Chinese economic reforms have led to rapid growth. Lin et al.'s (2003) book provides background on the Chinese economic system under Chairman Mao and then explores in detail why the reformed system is better suited to China's labor-rich, land-scarce resource endowment. The book is also unique in that it provides a balanced picture in several respects, explaining for example how both rural and urban reforms have permitted China's comparative advantages to emerge in response to market signals. Wu (2005) provides a systematic discussion and comprehensive review of China's economic reform through 2002. Among the topics explored in the book are the origins of central planning, problems that emerged and the gradual evolution of the reforms, with particular reference to rural reform, state-owned enterprises (SOEs) reform, the development of non-state sectors, the reform of the banking system, the development of the financial markets, fiscal and taxation reform, and reforms related to trade and foreign direct investment. The section on 'opening to the outside world' discusses the role of trade development strategies and foreign direct investment in China.

Naughton (2006) argues that China's economic development can be traced to two incomplete transitions. First, China is still completing its transition away from bureaucratic socialism and toward a market economy. Second, China is in the middle of the industrialization process, the protracted transformation from a rural to an urban society. These two transitions are both far from complete, and so China today carries with it parts of the traditional and socialist, the modern and the market, all mixed up in a jumble of mind-boggling complexity. The book analyzes the reforms in several aspects: the rural economy (rural organization, agriculture, rural industrialization), the urban economy (industrial ownership and govern-ance, technology policy and the knowledge-based economy), China and the world economy (international trade and foreign investment), and macroeconomics and finance (trends and cycles, financial system). Naughton's work is also valuable for his explicit discussion of the two distinct phases of the reforms – the 'reform with-out losers' phase until about 1993 and the 'reform with losers' phase since then.

Indeed, these books contributed significantly to understanding how and why China has succeeded in many ways. Lin et al. (2003) focuses more attention on reform rather than opening-up. Both Wu (2005) and Naughton (2006) refer to the opening of the Chinese to varying degrees. Since China was only begin-ning to participate in globalization at that stage, it had limited impact on the world economy. But now globalization is an inevitable aspect of China's eco-nomic development. On the one hand, many multinational companies (MNCs) have moved their production bases into Mainland China, which helped to pro-mote China's rapid economic growth. On the other hand, China has become an important location for global production networks, with Chinese firms partici-pating in the global value chains of various industries. In this sense, globaliza-tion is an important part of the context of China's rise, and it provides a useful approach for understanding China's economic growth.

WTO: the accelerator of China's globalization

After accession to the World Trade Organization (WTO) in 2001 and particu-larly since the international financial crisis in 2008, China emerged as a leader in the world economy, moving gradually towards an open economy. At the early stage of opening-up, China's economic development depended very heavily on inward FDI and on exports. China's uniquely gradualist reforms produced high levels of inward FDI, while both GDP and export growth in turn impacted on outward FDI and imports. Since 2001, China has gradually become a more open economy. Yet, according to the OECD FDI regulatory restrictiveness index (FDI Index), China's index was the highest of the 58 countries measured at 0.39, compared to 0.05 for Japan, 0.06 for the UK and 0.09 for the U.S. Despite this, however, China ranked number two on the 2016 AT Kearney Foreign Invest-ment Confidence Index at 1.82 after the U.S. at 2.02.

China's increasingly liberal attitude toward inward investment resulted in extremely high rates of inward FDI, substantially higher than rates achieved by other economies in transition. Even in per capita terms for a country with over one billion inhabitants, China achieved inward FDI of $18.20 per capita for 1989–1995 (Liu et al., 2005). In 2014, China overtook the U.S. as the top destination for FDI for the first time since 2003. Foreign firms invested $128 bil-lion in China, and $86 billion in the U.S. in 2015 (UNCTAD, 2015). Generally, China has garnered considerable attention for attracting global direct investment since the 1990s, with its share of FDI increasing to 9.0 percent of the global total in 2012 from 2.9 percent in 2000 (Rosen, 2014, 144). Certainly, the main-stream of existing studies suggests that the role of FDI in Chinese economic development has tended to be strongly positive. Recent research shows that FDI in China has indeed promoted economic development by improving allocative efficiency, but it has also had unfavorable effects, such as worsening productive efficiency (Lo et al., 2016).

More recently, China became a major source of outward FDI (OFDI) (Table 1.1). Chinese levels of OFDI were insignificant before 1985, but in the 1990s they averaged $2.3 billion per annum. While the scale of China's OFDI is comparatively small compared with the U.S., the trend is steeply upwards, and China's peak annual OFDI of $116 billion in 2014 was second only to $317 billion for the U.S. (UNCTAD, 2016). An important aspect of China's OFDI strategy is the acquisition of key technology capabilities in areas such as semiconductors. The Committee on Foreign Investment in the U.S. (CFIUS) has been quite active recently in preventing a number of attempted acquisitions in the U.S. by Chinese companies, including Fairchild, Micron, Global Communication Semiconductors (GCS), Lumileds, Western Digital and Aixtron. There is a widespread fear in the U.S. that the acquisition of such high-tech companies by Chinese firms could result in a significant loss in technology leadership by the U.S. (Atkinson, 2017). Meanwhile, China's rapid growth of OFDI has attracted the widespread attention of the international community. The big fear is that Chinese state-controlled owners will end up absorbing key technologies and know-how, leading to a hollowing out of the industrial base of their Western competitors (Kynge, 2016). Indeed, there is no need to worry about this issue. First, China's six percent of OFDI in the global total was smaller still in 2012, but bigger than 0.1 percent in 2000 (Rosen, 2014, 144). This is an inevitable trend in Chinese economic development. As the second largest economy in the world, China has had the largest foreign exchange reserve for a long time, which is a basic driving force of OFDI. Second, China's non-state owned enterprises' number has accounted for more than half of the total overseas mergers and acquisitions (M&A)'s number in the last five years. The M&A amount of non-SOEs accounted for 75.6 percent in 2015 (Mofcom NBS and SAFE, 2016).[1] Third, during the period of structural economic transition, Chinese enterprises, particularly private enterprises, have to make the best of international markets and resources by becoming more integrated into global innovation networks, manufacturing networks and market networks. Finally, China's public policy has strongly promoted the rapid growth of OFDI. For example, in 2014, the Ministry of Commerce upgraded *Measures on Investment Abroad*, published in 2009. The new *Measures* adopted the management model of filing mainly and approving secondly, which facilitates investment abroad. China's 'Belt and Road' initiative also plays a significant role in guiding and implementing OFDI.

Indeed, China has developed into the largest exporter of manufactured goods and services, with the value of exports reaching $2524.2 billion in 2014. With the value of its imports reaching $2261.6 billion in 2014, China had a trade surplus (Table 1.1). SOE reform has also had an important impact on trade. According to China's trade balance by enterprise ownership, SOEs are net importers, not exporters; Chinese–foreign joint ventures (JVs), wholly foreign-owned, private and other firms are, on the other hand, net exporters (Rosen, 2014, 153–154).

Table 1.1 China's opening economy landscape ($ billion)

Year	GDP	FDI inward	FDI outward	Import	Export
1978	214.2	0	0	–	–
1979	263.2	0	0	–	–
1980	306.5	0.057	0	–	–
1981	293.9	0.3	0	–	–
1982	295.4	0.4	0.044	18.9	23.6
1983	314.6	0.9	0.093	20.7	23.2
1984	317.4	1.4	0.1	26.7	26.7
1985	309.1	2.0	0.6	40.8	28.2
1986	304.3	2.2	0.5	37.2	29.6
1987	329.9	2.3	0.6	38.9	39.2
1988	413.4	3.2	0.9	50.0	45.9
1989	459.8	3.4	0.8	52.8	47.8
1990	404.5	3.5	0.8	46.7	57.4
1991	424.1	4.4	0.9	54.3	65.9
1992	499.9	11.0	4.0	73.8	78.8
1993	641.1	27.5	4.4	98.3	86.9
1994	582.7	33.8	2.0	111.6	119.2
1995	757.0	37.5	2.0	135.3	147.2
1996	892.0	41.7	2.1	154.1	171.7
1997	985.0	45.3	2.6	164.4	207.2
1998	1045.2	45.5	2.6	163.6	207.4
1999	1100.8	40.3	1.8	190.3	221.0
2000	1192.8	40.7	0.9	250.7	279.6
2001	1317.2	46.9	6.9	271.3	299.4
2002	1455.6	52.7	2.5	328.0	365.4
2003	1650.5	53.5	2.9	449.2	485.0
2004	1944.7	60.6	5.5	607.1	658.3
2005	2287.2	72.4	12.3	712.3	836.9
2006	2793.2	72.7	21.2	852.8	1061.7
2007	3504.4	83.5	26.5	1034.2	1342.3
2008	4547.3	108.3	55.9	1233.0	1581.8
2009	5105.5	95.0	56.5	1112.9	1329.5
2010	5949.8	114.7	68.8	1523.3	1742.2
2011	7314.4	124.0	74.7	1898.1	2076.4
2012	8229.4	121.1	87.8	2021.2	2251.4
2013	9181.2	123.9	101.0	2194.7	2428.2
2014	10066.7	128.5	116.0	2261.6	2524.2

Source: United Nations Conference on Trade and Development (UNCTAD) Statistics

Note: U.S. dollars at current prices and current exchange rates in billions

The role of SOEs as major importers of raw materials is in processing those imports. Rosen (2014, 154) suggests that 'a shift in China's trade structure from state to private firms makes trade politics a little less contentious, but there is no reason to expect it to become less so in general'.

The question is what factors determine the significant growth of China's exports? Certainly, abundant low-cost labor, reforms of domestic institutions, free trade based on WTO accession, and the exchange rate regime all contribute to rapid growth in exports. Meanwhile, GVCs as a vehicle for Chinese exports entering international markets played an important role. Half of China's manufacturing exports are assembled with imported parts and components, and most are so-called 'Made in China' products rather than being a 'Chinese creation'. Nevertheless, China has participated in and helped push forward the reform of the global economic governance mechanism.

The impact of WTO and globalization on China

According to official sources, since the reform and opening-up policy was initiated, China's foreign trade system has completed its transformation from mandatory planning to giving greater significance to the fundamental role of the market – from state monopoly to greater openness, and from indiscriminate egalitarianism to giving enterprises discretionary management power and making them responsible for their own profits and losses (The Information Office of State Council, 2001). On December 11, 2001, China became the 143rd member country of the WTO after 16 years of negotiations. To honor its commitments upon entry into the WTO, China agreed to expand its opening-up in the fields of industry, agriculture and services trade, and accelerated trade and investment facilitation and liberalization. When China became a WTO member in 2001, it committed itself to joining the WTO's General Procurement Agreement (GPA). But, China has not yet signed up to the WTO public procurement agreement on services. China is not a GPA party, and its public procurement policy is inconsistent with the GPA (EPRS, 2016). After 15 years, the Congressional–Executive Commission on China (CECC), an independent agency of the U.S. government, expressed their concern about the Chinese government's failure to honor 'many of its WTO commitments to the Office of the U.S. Trade Representative (USTR), for example raising the issues of internet censorship, failure to embrace the rule of law and the passage of China's law governing foreign Non-Governmental Organizations (NGO) activity in China and so on (CECC, 2016). On the other hand, Chinese officials claim that China strictly honored all its commitments to open the market and create favorable conditions for foreign goods to enter China, and China's development provides a huge power source for the global economy (Ge, 2016). According to the WTO's *Trade Policy Review*, in 2016, the State continued to play a very active role in China's economy, providing domestic industries (including those controlled by SOEs) with various support measures, such as credit (WTO, 2016). Obviously, two distinct views about these developments are being presented.

China has undergone considerable globalization in the past 15 years and has come to play a significant role within the global economy. Rather than taking power away from the nation state, globalization and increased competition between MNCs have strengthened the role of the nation state in national development (Sun and Grimes, 2016). The state is the significant unit for comparing levels of economic activity internationally, with the national interest being of prime importance within global governance. The nature of the nation state for development does not change. For example, the Buy American Act passed in 1933 by Congress and signed by President Hoover, required the U.S. government to prefer U.S.-made products in its purchases.[2] Other pieces of Federal legislation extend similar requirements to third-party purchases that utilize Federal funds, such as highway and transit programs. China's indigenous innovation policy – issued in 2006 – is a new version of the Buy American Act. China, however, needs to be more concerned about value creation, value-added and value distribution, and the GVC is a more useful framework for analyzing the benefits to China's economy than that provided by traditional investment, production and trade statistics in a more globalized economy.

Indeed, in the history of modern capitalism the State has not only fixed market failures, but it has also actively shaped and created markets (Mazzucato, 2013). Mazzucato (2013) argues that American economic success is a result of public and state funded investments in innovation and technology, rather than a result of the small state, free market doctrine that often receives credit for the country's strong economy. In this sense, China is following the American development path. The Chinese government launched a series of initiatives to create and shape the market.

In addition to providing benefits, however, globalization has required extremely painful adjustments by China. Employment in state enterprises declined from 110 million at the end of 1995 to 66 million in March 2005. Those who think there has been a simple transfer of U.S. manufacturing jobs to China may be surprised to know that manufacturing jobs in China have declined from over 54 million in 1994 to under 30 million today. Even these striking numbers understate the adjustments China has had to accept due to greater international competition, and more recently from WTO membership (Overholt, 2005).

China's high-tech industries

Every country in the world is exploring the best way to obtain economic benefits on a global scale from the rapid development of innovation. Likewise, the Chinese government, in realizing that high-technology is an important driving force for sustainable development, has introduced many policies to promote high-tech industries.

A simple overview of high-tech industries

The starting point of China's high-tech industrial development was the *Long-range Outline on the Development of Science and Technology (1956–1967)*, issued in 1956. The Outline promoted the development of technologies in six innovative and high-tech fields – nuclear power, rocket and jet technology, computers, semiconductors, automation and precision machinery (Sun and Liu, 2012). This policy document produced the first generation of high-tech researchers and laid a foundation for high-tech research in China and the development of corresponding industries. Since the 1980s, developed countries have invested large amounts of human and material resources in an effort to occupy the commanding heights of technological development. Examples include the Strategic Defense Initiative (SDI or "Star Wars") proposed by the U.S. in 1983, as well as the Eureka plan launched by the European Union (EU) in 1985. With the beginning of economic reform and opening-up in 1978, China's high-tech industries entered a new era of development.

China's National Science and Technology (S&T) Programmes contain four programs related to high-tech industries (Table 1.2). The earliest of these was the 'National Key Technology R&D Program', launched in 1983. In March 1986, four fellows of the Chinese Academy of Sciences (CAS), Wang Dayan, Wang Ganchang, Yang Jiachi, and Chen Fangyun, wrote a letter to the Central Committee of the Communist Party of China (CCCPC) suggesting that China should develop high-technologies in order to catch up with the rest of the world. This proposal was affirmed by Deng Xiaoping, the main leader of CCCPC. Soon after, more than 200 scientists and engineers collaborated in drawing up a development strategy for China's high-tech sector, which then contributed to the successful implementation of *The State High-Tech Development Plan*, or the '863 Program'. The 'Torch Program', designed to develop new high-tech industries in China, was approved by the State Council in August 1988. Implementation of these programs is now the responsibility of the Ministry of Science and Technology (MOST) (formerly the State Science and Technology Commission). All of these programs have played a powerful role in promoting the further development of China's high-technologies.

In the early 1990s, China attained several world-class achievements in S&T and high-tech industries, in such areas as electronics, space exploration, fine chemicals and instruments, thus establishing a firm basis for development. Despite these achievements and China's all-round effort to catch up with the developed world in S&T and economic development, the country continued to suffer from such adverse circumstances as a lack of capital and talent, fragmented investment and a weak investment environment. In order to meet the challenge of the new S&T revolution by accelerating the development of high-tech industries, China's State Council approved a motion in 1991 to establish 26 national high-tech industrial zones in medium and large intellectual resource-intensive cities, 25 of which were approved in 1992.

In August 1999, a National Technology Innovation Conference, organized by the CCCPC and the State Council, was held in Beijing to look into the implementation of the *Decision on Strengthening Technology Innovation, Developing High and New Technology, and Accomplishing Industrialization*. In January 2006, the National Science and Technology Conference issued the *Mid- to Long-Term Plan Outline for National Science and Technology Development (2006–2020)* (MLP). In order to put this MLP into operation, MOST, along with the NDRC, the Ministry of Land and Resources, and the Ministry of Housing and Urban-Rural Development issued a document entitled, *Several Opinions on Promoting the Further Development of National New & High-tech*

Table 1.2 Main high-tech research programs in China

Program	Time	Objects	Sponsored fields
National Key Technology R&D Program* (Keji Zhicheng)	1983	Facing the national economic and social development needs, resolving the major scientific and technological problems in economic and social development	Agriculture, ICT, energy, resources, biology, environment, medicine and health.
863 Program (State High-tech Development Plan)	1986	Promoting innovation ability of high-technology, especially the international competitiveness of strategic high technology	Biological technology, information technology, aerospace, laser, advanced materials, advanced manufacturing and automation technology, energy technology, agriculture.
Torch Program	1988	Picking winners: the projects are selected and organized to develop new and high-technology products and related industries, meeting international standard of high-technology products	Electronics and information technology, biotechnology and new medicines, new materials and their application, mechatronics, new energy, high-efficiency energy conservation technology and environment protection technology.
National Key R&D Plan	2015	Big social commonweal research, big scientific problems, big generic key technology and products	Agriculture, energy and resources, ecological environment and health.

Note: *The National Key Technology R&D Program (Keji Zhicheng) is directed to the implementation of the *Mid-to Long-term Plan Outline* for National Science and Technology Development (2006–2020) (MLP) and deals with national economic and social development needs facing China. It mainly focuses on important scientific and technological problems in the process of economic and social development, which are based on the old National Key Technology R&D Program (Keji Gongguan).

Source: Ministry of Science and Technology. www.most.gov.cn

Development Zones and Enhancing Indigenous Innovative Ability, which suggested that 'a new undertaking be started' for enhancing innovation within national high-tech industrial zones.

The development of China's high-tech industries has largely followed the course laid down in government plans. In the mid-1990s, China's high-tech industries were still in their initial stage of development. *The Ninth Five-Year Plan for the Scientific and Technological Development of China and the Outline for 2010* proposed that high-tech industries of all kinds should be developed in parallel. With the advent of the information revolution and the Internet, electronic information and computer-related industries have developed more rapidly. *The Special Plan for High-tech Industrial Development in the Tenth Five-Year Plan for S&T and Education Development*, issued in 2000, proposed the development of new industries such as software, communication equipment, digital products, biomedical products and biological chips. In *the Eleventh Five-Year Plan for High-tech Industrial Development*, electronic information, biological and aerospace industries were named as focuses for development. The information technology industry is more mature and on a larger scale than the others, and the biological and aerospace industries have potential for future development. In *The Twelfth Five-Year Plan for Strategic Emerging Industrial Development*, plans were developed for seven new industries, including new energy, new energy vehicles, high-end equipment manufacturing, energy saving and environmental protection, new generation information technology, biopharmaceuticals and new materials.

In 2015, the Chinese government launched an important reform document, *The Scheme on Deepening Management Reform of the Central Fiscal Science and Technology Plan*. The *Scheme* integrated National S&T Programmes into five parts: National Natural Science Foundation of China (NSFC) Programmes, National S&T Major Projects, National Key R&D Plan, Technological Innovation Guidance Specialized Programmes and Specialized Projects for Base and Talent. The reform integrates the 863 Program, the 973 Program, the National Key Technology R&D Program and other programs under the Ministry of Science and Technology (MOST); Industrial Technology Research and Development Funds under the National Development and Reform Commission (NDRC) and the Ministry of Industry and Information Technology (MIIT); the Special Scientific Research Fund of Public Welfare Profession under the Ministry of Agriculture, National Health and Family Planning Commission and another thirteen departments into a new National Key R&D Plan (Zhongdian Yanfa Jihua). In other words, the National Key R&D Plan deploys the central government's budget resources on S&T and innovation. The goal of this reform is to break barriers among central agencies and between basic, applied and development research. Cao and Suttmeier (2017) argued that this integration of programs raises many new questions, such as arbitrary assignment, unnecessary churn and uncertainty, polarization in funding sources. Maybe this reorganization just 'put "old" wine into a "new" bottle', not fundamentally changing the way government funds high-tech fields.

The role of ICT sector in high-tech industry

The construction of national high-tech zones and a series of policies aimed at encouraging innovation have enabled China to make dramatic gains since the 1980s, although these gains have been made in spurts. The high-tech sector is playing an increasingly important role in industrial development, and its production has increased sharply since 1995 (Figure 1.2). According to official statistics, in 2013, the gross revenue of 114 national high-tech industrial zones and the Suzhou Industrial Park (excluding Xiangtan and Taizhou) was RMB 19.96 trillion, and they had a gross industrial output value of RMB 15.14 trillion and a net margin of RMB 1.24 trillion, and paid more than RMB 1.1 trillion in taxes. In 2014, the revenue from the principal businesses of China's high-tech industry exceeded RMB 12 trillion, nearly five times that of 2004 and more than 30 times the 1995 total. The rapid growth of the high-tech industry prompted a readjustment of the industrial structure and made it a new pole for national economic growth.

Although the scale of high-tech industry has increased sharply, its contribution through profit and tax has varied over time (Figure 1.2) The profit-taxation ratio (profit and tax divided by revenue from principal business) of China's high-tech industry increased from 8.32 percent to 10.29 percent between 1995 and 2000; it decreased to 6.16 percent in 2005, and began to show an increasing trend again in 2006 and 2007. The ratio increased to 9.57 percent in 2014, reaching a peak value of 10.29 percent. Sun and Liu (2012) indicated that China's high-tech industry was less profitable than other industrial sectors before 2008. However, China's overall industrial profit-taxation ratio increased to 7.68 percent, which was lower than the high-tech industrial ratio in 2014 according to the Statistical Yearbook of China. This indicates that China's high-tech industry is now more profitable and contributes more taxation than other industrial sectors.

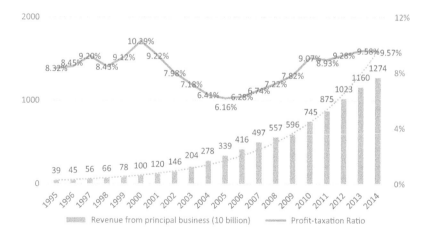

Figure 1.2 The development of Chinese high-tech industries (1995–2014)

Source: China Statistics Yearbook on High-technology Industry (1996–2015)

According to a *Notice on the Classified Catalogue of Statistics on High-tech Industries,* issued by the National Bureau of Statistics in July 2002, China's high-tech industries include the pharmaceutical manufacturing industry (PS), aerospace plane manufacturing industry (AS), electronic and telecommunication equipment manufacturing industry (ETE), electronic computer and office equipment manufacturing industry (COE), and medical equipment and instrumentation manufacturing (MEM) (Table 1.3). Of these, ETE occupies a dominant position among China's high-tech industries, accounting for 50 percent of gross output value (around 53.26 percent in 1995 and 53.06 percent in 2014). The fastest-growing industry is COE, whose share of high-tech output value has increased from 8.65 percent to 29.45 percent between 1995 and 2007, then decreased to 18.45 percent in 2014. Practically, ETE and COE, referring to Information and Communications Technology (ICT), accounted for more than 70 percent of high-tech industries in China. This indicates that the ICT sector represents a large part of the high-tech industry sector, and the development of

Table 1.3 The development of Chinese high-tech industries by sector (RMB 100 million)

Industries	PS	AS	ETE	COE	MEM	Total	ICT share %
1995	961	269	2182	354	331	4097	61.90
1996	1151	286	2504	581	386	4909	62.84
1997	1262	313	3172	797	427	5972	66.46
1998	1373	323	3847	1121	447	7111	69.86
1999	1497	333	4709	1203	474	8217	71.95
2000	1781	388	5981	1677	584	10411	73.56
2001	2041	469	6900	2200	653	12263	74.21
2002	2378	535	7948	3479	759	15099	75.68
2003	2890	551	10217	5987	911	20556	78.83
2004	3241	502	14007	8692	1327	27769	81.74
2005	4250	797	16867	10667	1785	34366	80.12
2006	5019	828	21218	12511	2421	41997	80.31
2007	6362	1024	25088	14859	3128	50461	79.16
2008	7875	1199	28151	16493	3369	57087	78.20
2009	9443	1353	28947	16292	4394	60429	74.86
2010	11741	1598	35930	19823	5617	74709	74.63
2011	14942	1913	43559	21135	6884	88433	73.16
2012	17338	2330	52799	22045	7772	102284	73.17
2013	20484	2853	60634	23214	8863	116048	72.25
2014	23350	3028	67584	23499	9907	127368	71.51

Source: China Statistics Yearbook on High-technology Industry (1996–2015) www.sts.org.cn/sjkl/gjscy/index.htm.

Notes: The development indicators of Chinese high-tech industries changed in Chinese statistics: between 1995 and 2011 the indicator used was gross industrial output, and this changed to revenue from principal businesses between 2012 and 2014. PS: Pharmaceutical manufacturing industry; AS: Aerospace plane manufacturing industry; ETE: Electronic and telecommunication equipment manufacturing industry; COE: Electronic computer and office equipment manufacturing industry; MEM: Medical equipment and instrumentation manufacturing.

high-tech industries also reflects trends in the ICT sector. PS and MEM have also grown fast, but their values, particularly in the case of PS, as percentages of the total for high-tech industries, have fallen. The value of AS as a percentage of the high-tech total is lower and has dropped from 6.56 percent to 2.38 percent, due to a relatively slow growth rate.

China's indigenous innovation

In a knowledge-based economy, innovation is critically important for generating higher value added and higher paying jobs. Currently, China is striving to shift to this next stage, to an economy mainly driven by innovation, in order to address the slowdown of its previous growth model.

A major question of S&T development in China

Having seen that the earlier policy of market access for technology transfer had undermined China's technological independence and security without significantly benefitting China's R&D capacity, there was a decisive shift to indigenous innovation (Zhou et al., 2016). Improvements in innovation capability, especially in its industrial sectors, are considered essential for China's sustainable economic growth in the future. Like the rest of the world, the importance of innovation for economic growth in China means that innovation should not be treated by policymakers merely as an economic residual, but rather as a key instrument for transitioning China's development (Yu et al., 2013). It could be said that China's S&T and innovation began to be internationalized in 1978.

After the reform and opening-up policy was introduced in 1978, the Board of Directors of the American Association for the Advancement of Science (AAAS) organized a three-week visit to China to promote cooperation between the AAAS and the China Association for Science and Technology (CAST). A subsequent issue on *China in Transition* which looked at education, science and technology (EST) was published in *Science* after the visit. While not being an academic analysis, the editor of *Science* provided useful insights into the state of China's S&T sector in 1979. At that time, most research was carried out in institutes affiliated with the Chinese Academy of Sciences, while a smaller amount was conducted in Chinese universities (Abelson, 1979). Scientific leadership in China depended on foreign-trained Chinese, and those educated in the U.S. were particularly prominent. Chinese rulers had little experience with the effective integration of advanced research and development into major industrial complexes (Abelson, 1979). A major question raised by this publication was, 'Why hasn't China developed faster and more extensively?'

A possible answer to this question, based on China's development, can be attempted three decades later. In relation to China's development path of innovation, 'believers' claim that China is out-innovating the West' while 'doubters' claim that China is lagging on the innovation front (Steinfeld, 2010, 34). Zhou and Leydesdorff (2006) indicated that China had become the fifth leading nation in terms of its share of the world's scientific publications; the citation rate of papers with a Chinese address for the corresponding author also exhibited exponential growth. More specifically, China had become a major player in critical technologies, like nanotechnology. Abrami et al. (2014) believe that the West is home to creative business thinkers and innovators, and that China is largely a land of rule-bound rote learners – a place where R&D is diligently pursued but breakthroughs are rare. In reality, as a leading country in S&T and innovation, China had increased its level of innovation with increased globalization, but also faced many challenges in terms of quality and value (Fan, 2014).

The effort on S&T and innovation development

Although Table 1.4 indicates that China has become a powerhouse in research and development (R&D) spending, the structure of R&D spending needs to be optimized. China was the second-largest performer ($368.73 billion) in 2014 accounting for about 20 percent of the global total (NSF, 2016). China's gross domestic expenditure on R&D (GERD) as a percentage of GDP (GERD/GDP) reached 2.05 percent in 2014. It continues to exhibit the world's most dramatic R&D growth pattern, more than tripling since 1995 (Sun and Cao, 2014). China will outpace the U.S. as the world's leading R&D spender by around 2019, reaching another important milestone in its endeavor to become an innovation-oriented nation by 2020 (OECD, 2014). But China spends relatively little of its total R&D budget on basic research – just 4.68 percent compared with 24.1 percent in France, 17.6 percent in the U.S. and 12.6 percent in Japan in 2013. Indeed, for a long time, China's R&D spending on basic research hovered around 5 percent, which was an obstacle for original innovation. The share of GERD financed by government has decreased from 33.41 percent in 2000 to 20.25 percent in 2014, and the share of GERD performed by the business enterprise sector has increased from 39.82 percent in 1991 to 77.30 percent in 2014. This is due to the Chinese policy of building an enterprises-centered innovation system, but it is a little exaggerated.

According to the Global Information Technology Report 2016 (Baller et al., 2016), China, while being firmly among the leading emerging and developing Asian economies, also lags significantly behind more developed regions. In network readiness, it ranks 59th compared with Singapore in first place, Hong Kong in 12th and Taiwan in 19th place. Its ranking for political and regulatory environment is 83rd compared with Singapore in first, Hong Kong in fourth and Taiwan in 29th place. China is ranked 104th for business and innovation environment compared with Singapore in first, Hong Kong in second, and Taiwan in 14th place. The report notes the need for China's businesses to embrace digital technologies and innovative processes, and despite the increase in patenting activity, it had a low ranking compared with advanced economies.

Second, China has become the world leader for number of researchers, but the intensity of researchers needs to be increased. Since 2011, China at 19.1 percent has overtaken the U.S. at 16.7 percent, as predicted by the UNESCO Science

Table 1.4 China's landscape of S&T and innovation

Year	1 R&D expenditure					2 Research personnel		3 SCI papers		4 Triadic patents	
	1.1	1.2	1.3	1.4	1.5	2.1	2.2	3.1	3.2	4.1	4.2
1991	9.15	0.73	4.66	–	39.82	0.72	1.02	0.93	15	12	0.04
1992	10.74	0.73	4.50	–	41.80	0.71	1.02	0.85	17	15	0.05
1993	11.96	0.70	4.79	–	41.70	0.73	1.04	1.25	15	17	0.06
1994	12.50	0.63	5.52	–	43.13	0.82	1.16	1.29	15	19	0.06
1995	12.78	0.57	5.18	–	43.67	0.77	1.10	1.32	15	22	0.06
1996	14.17	0.57	5.00	–	43.25	0.79	1.17	1.59	14	23	0.06
1997	17.86	0.64	5.39	–	46.05	0.84	1.19	1.84	12	42	0.10
1998	19.72	0.65	5.25	–	44.83	0.69	1.07	2.12	12	49	0.11
1999	24.99	0.75	4.99	–	49.59	0.74	1.15	2.51	10	63	0.13
2000	33.04	0.90	5.22	33.41	59.96	0.96	1.28	3.15	8	87	0.16
2001	38.55	0.95	5.33	–	60.44	1.02	1.31	3.57	8	152	0.28
2002	48.06	1.06	5.73	–	61.18	1.11	1.41	4.18	6	271	0.49
2003	57.14	1.13	4.28	29.91	62.37	1.17	1.48	4.48	6	356	0.61
2004	70.13	1.22	4.38	26.63	66.82	1.25	1.55	5.43	5	401	0.66
2005	86.83	1.32	4.08	26.34	68.32	1.50	1.83	5.25	5	518	0.85
2006	105.58	1.38	3.90	24.71	71.08	1.63	2.00	5.87	5	561	0.99
2007	124.19	1.38	3.36	24.62	72.28	1.89	2.31	7.00	5	689	1.30
2008	146.13	1.46	3.33	23.59	73.26	2.11	2.60	6.60	4	826	1.63
2009	185.27	1.68	4.66	23.41	73.23	1.52	3.02	8.84	2	1295	2.53
2010	213.46	1.73	4.59	24.02	73.42	1.59	3.36	10.12	2	1419	2.80
2011	247.81	1.79	4.47	21.68	75.47	1.72	3.77	11.1	2	1545	2.94
2012	292.06	1.93	4.84	21.57	76.15	1.83	4.23	12.08	2	1714	3.21
2013	333.52	2.01	4.68	21.11	76.61	1.93	4.59	13.5	2	1896	3.51
2014	368.73	2.05	4.71	20.25	77.30	1.97	4.80	–	–	–	–

Source: OECD Main S&T indicators and China's S&T statistics yearbook

Notes for indicators: 1.1 Gross Domestic Expenditure on R&D – GERD (current PPP $); 1.2 GERD as a percentage of GDP (percent); 1.3 Basic research expenditure as a percentage of GERD (percent); 1.4 Percentage of GERD financed by government(percent); 1.5 Percentage of GERD performed by the Business Enterprise sector (percent). 2.1 Total researchers per thousand total employment; 2.2 Total R&D personnel per thousand total employment. 3.1 Share of the World's Total in papers cataloged by Science Citation Index (SCI) (percent); 3.2 SCI papers' rank in the world. 4.1 Number of 'triadic' patent families (priority year). 4.2 Share of countries in 'triadic' patent families (priority year) (percent). Patents taken in various countries to protect inventions can be linked together to build triadic patent families: a set of patents taken at the European Patent Office (EPO), the Japanese Patent Office (JPO), and the U.S. Patent and Trademark Office (USPTO) that share one or more priorities. Patent families are derived from priority application.

Report 2010. The number of researchers in China is unequivocally the world's highest with 1.48 million full-time equivalents (FTE) in 2013 (UNESCO, 2015). The situation of R&D personnel is similar to that of researchers. It is worth noting that researchers per thousand total employment is relatively small – only 1.97 in China compared with 14.07 in Sweden, 10.47 in Japan and 9.88 in France in 2014, with a very slow growth rate since 1991. Chinese R&D personnel per thousand total employment has increased slightly faster, but it was only 4.8 in 2014, which is still lower than that in the main industrial countries, such as 12.63 in the UK and 13.73 in Japan. Obviously, China's volume of researchers is the largest in the world, but its intensity reflects a big gap with developed countries.

Third, while China has become the main knowledge generator of publications and patents, the overall quality still lags behind. Chinese publications have almost doubled over the past five years to reach 20 percent of the world total, whereas 10 years ago, China accounted for just 5 percent. This rapid growth reflects the coming of age of the Chinese research system, be it in terms of investment, number of researchers or number of publications (UNESCO, 2015). However, papers cataloged by Science Citation Index (SCI), which are regarded as significant scientific publications, accounted for 13.5 percent of the world total, ranking China in second place after the U.S.

China's State Intellectual Property Office (SIPO) received more than half a million applications for invention patents in 2011, making it the world's largest patent office (Cao, 2015). However, the number of 'triadic' patent families is relatively small in China, with only 1896 'triadic' patent families in 2013, compared with 14211 in the U.S. and 16196 in Japan. Accordingly, China's share of the world total of 'triadic' patents is quite low – just 3.51 percent, compared with 26.32 percent in the U.S.

China's S&T and innovation model

The first evaluations of China's progress in innovation notes that a major thrust of policy was to raise the level of indigenous innovation beyond the low profit/ low margin manufacturing platform model for FDI to a more sustainable level because of increasing threats from low-cost locations like Vietnam (OECD, 2008). The technology gap between local and foreign companies was reflected in the fact that only an estimated 15 percent of the value of IT and electronics exports was added in China, and between 50 and 70 percent of the manufacturing costs of a personal computer (PC) manufactured in China represented license fees to Microsoft and Intel. In relation to China's High Tech Development Zones (HTDZs), the OECD report noted that while foreign companies constituted only 15 percent of the total in these zones, they were responsible for 50 percent of production and 85 percent of exports, and that it was misleading, therefore to suggest that the results from these parks were generated by China's S&T potential. McKinsey (2015) investigated the actual impact of innovation – as measured by the success of companies in global markets, which also provides a mixed picture. In the industries where innovation requires original inventions or engineering breakthroughs, such as branded pharmaceuticals and autos, China has small shares of global markets. But in industries where innovation is about meeting unmet consumer needs or driving efficiencies in manufacturing such as appliances and solar panels, for example, China is flourishing. China's massive consumer market and unmatched manufacturing ecosystem give it unique advantages in these sectors.

Perhaps the most striking examples of this success are in e-commerce and consumer electronics, where companies such as Alibaba and Xiaomi are rapidly emerging as top global players. China does have the potential to become a global innovation leader, and while it has not yet seen the payoff, China has made the necessary investments in R&D and education to improve its performance in science- and engineering-based industries. China's success in high-speed rail and telecommunications equipment suggests that, under the right circumstances, Chinese companies can become global competitors in engineering-based industries. The high-speed rail sector, however, provides an interesting case study of how Chinese SOEs such as China South Locomotive and Rolling Stock Corporation (CSR) and China North Locomotive and Rolling Stock Corporation (CNR) acquired core technologies from French company Alstom, Japanese company Kawasaki and German company Siemens in the early 2000s, after they were required to form JVs with the SOEs (Hout and Ghemawat, 2010). In 2015, CSR merged with CNR to form China Railway Rolling Stock (CRRC) Corporation.

In science-based industries such as biopharmaceuticals, Chinese companies are harnessing the scale and speed of the home market to become more nimble and stronger innovators. With the right policies in place to support entrepreneurship, encourage market-based competition in more industries and make China more attractive to top science talent, China has the potential to succeed in other forms of innovation.

An example of innovation based on domestic standards was China's development of the Time Division Synchronous Code Division Multiple Access Standard (TD-SCDMA) for 3G mobile telecommunications. Gao (2014) examined the key strategies used by Datang, a local Chinese company, which played a proactive role in promoting TD-SCDMA, in order to understand how a latecomer country could promote a domestic technology standard. His findings suggest that Datang faced formidable challenges because of latecomer disadvantages and transitional institutions. Datang had limited influence and was not able to play a dominant role in its strategic maneuvering. In many cases, it was not able to attract strong support, and it had to rely on public stakeholders such as scholars to promote this technology. The Chinese government offered important support to TD-SCDMA, but many policies were inconsistent. The government was very supportive of making TD-SCDMA a 3G standard, but it failed to follow up. The development of innovation capabilities and new technologies, therefore, while necessary, are far from sufficient. It is necessary to develop special capabilities to get support from the government and public stakeholders such as scholars.

While delaying the introduction of 3G into China, the development of TD-SCDMA provided experience for both Chinese engineers and telecommunications companies, which could in turn be used for developing the 4th generation wireless technology, allowing China to play a bigger role than heretofore in the development of global standards. However, scholars such as Liu and Cheng (2011) express some skepticism about the relative success of TD-SCDMA, arguing that even major SOEs like China Mobile were reluctant to commit themselves fully to the project, while Breznitz and Murphree (2011) present a more negative evaluation of this experiment as an example of continuing interference by the Chinese state in the market.

The Western capitalist (neoliberal) system is dominated by the role of large corporations, which together account for a huge proportion of internationalized economic activity. Their strategies are based around delivering the highest level of profit to shareholders in the form of dividends. The management of these corporations is incentivized by exceptionally high levels of pay related to the ongoing stock market performance of these corporations. This 'financialization' model has been a significant driver of globalization, as corporations increasingly outsource and offshore different functions to raise profitability. Corporations from the U.S. and elsewhere have been exploiting China's comparative advantage of low costs, especially labor costs, for many decades, delivering high levels of profit to the owners of IP.

China's aggressive approach toward the implementation of indigenous innovation policy suggests that there is a fundamental ideological difference between how the Chinese state sees its role in bringing about 'state capitalism' and the traditional Western model of capitalism supported by global organizations such as the WTO. As latecomers to these organizations, China and other less-developed countries are obviously at a disadvantage in many respects, since they have had little time or experience in developing their own intellectual property. Part of China's 'justification' for not totally falling into line with the WTO rules may be partly a strategy to bring about changes in the rules more favorable to less-developed regions. Many see China's approach as a bargaining stance in which it will try to seek more favorable conditions, even after signing up to existing rules.

Timing will be critical; with slowing GDP growth, an aging population, and declining returns on massive fixed investments, China must find ways to raise productivity. Innovation is key to this sustainable growth path.

Objectives and organization of the book

This book sets out to understand and explain the contributions made and the benefits gained by China through engagement in the global value chain (GVC) of the information and communication technology (ICT) sector during its economic transition.

The organization of chapters

This chapter presents the background to this book, raises the questions it will answer and explains its organization. It first analyzes economic development, foreign direct investment, international trade and S&T development, and it presents the hidden issues behind prosperous development. It argues that China's economic development depends on labor, capital and resource intensity, and exports, and that the GVC is a useful framework to decipher the reasons for China's predominantly lower value-added functions.

The second chapter presents a theoretical framework for the GVC distribution. We argue that, with globalization, a country's competitiveness reflects its participation and role in the GVC, while national innovation capability is a key factor influencing participation in the GVC, and we propose an analytical framework of a nation's role in the GVC at the Macro-, Meso- and Micro-scale.

The third chapter examines the ongoing high level of dependency of China's economy on foreign sources of technology since WTO accession in 2001. We argue that while China's economic activity has become integrated within the GVC, helped by international activities like FDI and exporting, it continues to play a subordinate role in GVCs.

The fourth chapter maps the involvement of China-based companies in the ICT GVC through synthesizing evidence from international trade data. We argue that while China's increasing participation in the ICT GVC is due to modularization, and outsourcing and offshoring of manufacturing, China continues to linger in the low value-added segments of the ICT GVC because of a lack of core IP.

The fifth chapter analyses how one of the world's most significant lead technology companies and its network of suppliers has become increasingly embedded in China's ICT industry. We argue that Apple, albeit one of the most significant ICT companies globally, is but one of many major global technology companies, together with an extensive ecosystem of both foreign and Chinese supplier companies that constitute that part of the ICT GVC which is located in China.

The final chapter generalizes some conclusions based on the above analysis and proposes recommendations for China's future development within the context of opportunities and challenges.

Theory and methodology

The theoretical basis of this work seeks to explain how globalization has impacted competitive advantage and national innovation capability. Our premise is based on making a distinction between 'location' and 'ownership'. Within the classical models of Ricardo and Heckscher-Ohlin, comparative advantage represents a sole factor determining international competitiveness (Xing, 2016). Within the context of globalization, however, arising from transnational investment and trade, the economic activities or exports of a particular country do not necessarily specify either value captured by that country or its competitiveness. In a Schumpeterian world of knowledge-based economic activity and innovation-based competition in an increasingly globalized economy, the approach adopted in this book has greater relevance. Rather than focusing on the volume of trade or gross output, the focus here is on the capacity of a country's companies to create and capture value. In this sense, brands, networks, core technology and innovation assume very significant roles in determining the winners and losers in global competition (Xing, 2016). The trajectory of technology development tends to be controlled by IP-rich companies in IP-rich regions, creating an asymmetrical relationship of power within the GVC, with IP-poor regions like China carrying out low value-added functions such as assembly.

Based on this approach, our main methodological focus is to analyze the GVC at different scales. At the national scale, we focus mainly on the ownership and technological intensity of major exporters. High-tech exporters in China reflect the competitive advantage of their home countries. At the industry scale, we focus on the division of labor of trading companies within the ICT value chain, and particularly on ICT trading companies based in China which we classify as own brand companies (OBMs), component companies and original design/electronic manufacturing services companies (ODM/EMS). Global brand companies and those supplying core components create significant value within the ICT industry and reflect the competitive advantage of their home countries. At the firm scale, the focus is on the division of labor of supplier companies within the company's supply chain, which we classify as core component, non-core component and 'other' companies. Companies supplying core components add more value, which in turn provides greater value capture and wealth for their home countries.

In sum, this book examines China's role in the GVC by focusing on the ownership of, and the value creation and capture by, companies operating in China. Thus, if Chinese-owned companies create and capture more value in the GVC, this means that China will have strengthened its competitive advantage by participating in the GVC.

Data collection

Our research is based on three datasets. The first dataset of trade data at the firm-level is derived from the China Customs (Zhongguo Haiguan) trade database published (in Chinese) as a list of China's Top Exporting Firms and also a list of China's Top Trading Firms (Imports and Exports) for the years 2001 to 2004 by China Customs Magazine. Chapter three uses the data relating to China's top 200 exporting companies and the top 20 exporting firms in 2001 and 2012. Chapter four abstracts all the ICT firms from these listings and examines both imports and exports for 2001, 2005 and 2012.

The second dataset in chapter five is made up of Apple's list of supplier companies, both globally and located in China, with the name and location of each supplier company.

The third data set is comprised of interview data, which we use throughout the book to provide additional insights. Around 100 hours of interviews, lasting about one hour, with senior management of foreign technology companies in Shanghai between 2009 and 2017 were conducted. These interviews covered a range of topics related to the company's operation in the China market, including the impact of China's indigenous innovation policy.

Notes

1 Ministry of Commerce, National Bureau of Statistics, State Administration of Foreign Exchange. 2015 Statistical Bulletin of China's Outward Foreign Direct Investment. Beijing: China Statistics Press, 2016 (9).

2 Under certain conditions, however, the Buy American Act can be waived: for example, if the domestic product is 25 percent or more expensive than an identical foreign-sourced product, or the product is not available domestically in sufficient quantity or quality, or doing so is in the public interest. The President has the authority to waive the Buy American Act within the terms of a reciprocal agreement or otherwise in response to the provision of reciprocal treatment to U.S. producers.

References

Abelson, P., 1979, 'Education, science, and technology in China', *Science*, 203(4380), 505–509.

Abrami, R.M., Kirby, W.C. and McFarlan, F.W., 2014, 'Why China can't innovate and what's it's doing about it', *Harvard Business Review*, 3, 107–111.

Atkinson, R.D., 2017, 'Testimony of Robert D. Atkinson, President, information technology and innovation foundation before the U.S.-China economic and security review commission hearing on Chinese investment in the United States: Impacts and issues for policymakers', Available at www.uscc.gov/sites/default/files/Atkinson_USCCpercent20Hearingpercent20Testimony012617.pdf

Baller, S., Dutta, S. and Lanvin, B., 2016, 'The global information technology report 2016', Geneva, World Economic Forum.

Breznitz, D. and Murphree, M., 2011, *Run of the Red Queen*, New Haven, CT, Yale University Press.

Cao, C., 2015, *UNESCO Science Report 2015*, Paris, UNESCO.

Cao, C. and Suttmeier, R., 2017, 'Challenges of S&T system reform in China', *Science*, 355(6329), 1019–1021.

CECC, 2016, 'China's failure to honor WTO commitments subject of CECC chairs' letter to U.S. trade representative', Available at www.cecc.gov/media-center/press-releases/china's-failure-to-honor-wto-commitments-subject-of-cecc-chairs'-letter. Accessed 03/06/2016.

The China Daily, 2016, 'Li says new plan shows innovation's top priority', Available at www.chinadaily.com.cn/china/2016-07/21/content_26162209.htm. Accessed 08/15/2016.

EPRS, 2016, 'China, the WTO and global trade', Available at www.europarl.europa.eu/EPRS/TD_China-WTO-GlobalTrade.pdf. Accessed 03/06/2016.

Fan, P., 2014, 'Innovation in China', *Journal of Economic Surveys*, 28(4), 725–745.

Gao, X., 2014, 'A latecomer's strategy to promote a technology standard: The case of Datang and TD-SCDMA', *Research Policy*, 43(3), 597–607.

Ge, F., 2016, 'China economic weekly: Accession to the WTO 15 years, China fully fulfill its commitments', Available at http://world.people.com.cn/n1/2016/1221/c1002-28965618.html. Accessed 03/06/2016.

Hout, T.M. and Ghemawat, P., 2010, 'China vs the world: Whose technology is it?' *Harvard Business Review*, 88(12), 94–103.

The Information Office of State Council, 2001, 'China's foreign trade', Available at www.china-embassy.org/eng/zt/bps/t943740.htm. Accessed 08/17/2015.

Kynge, J., 2016, 'Europe needs tougher response to China's state-led investments', Available at http://blogs.ft.com/beyond-brics/2016/06/09/europe-needs-tougher-response-to-chinas-state-led-investments/. Accessed 03/06/2016.

Lin, J.Y., Cai, F. and Li, Z., 2003, *The China Miracle: Development Strategy and Economic Reform*, Revised Edition, Hong Kong, The Chinese University Press.

Liu, X., Buck, T. and Shu, C., 2005, 'Chinese economic development, the next stage: Outward FDI?' *International Business Review*, 14(1), 97–115.

Liu, X. and Cheng, P., 2011, *Is China's Indigenous Innovation Strategy Compatible With Globalization?* Policy Studies No 61, Honolulu, East-West Center.

Lo, D., Hong, F. and Li, G., 2016, 'Assessing the role of inward foreign direct investment in Chinese economic development, 1990–2007: Towards a synthesis of alternative views', *Structural Change and Economic Dynamics*, 37, 107–120.

Mazzucato, M., 2013, *The Entrepreneurial State: Debunking Public vs. Private Sector Myths*, London, Anthem Press.

The McKinsey Global Institute, 2015, 'The China effect on global innovation', Available at www.mckinseychina.com/the-china-effect-on-global-innovation/. Accessed 08/22/2016.

Ministry of Commerce (Mofcom), National Bureau of Statistics (NBS), State Administration of Foreign Exchange (SAFE), 2016, *2015 Statistical Bulletin of China's Outward Foreign Direct Investment*, Beijing, China Statistics Press.

Naughton, B., 2006, *The Chinese Economy: Transitions and Growth*, Cambridge, MA, MIT Press.

NSF, 2016, 'Science and Engineering Indicators 2016', Available at www.nsf.gov/statistics/2016/nsb20161/#/report. Accessed 12/18/2016.

OECD, 2008, *Review of Innovation Policy: China*, Paris, OECD.

OECD, 2014, *Technology and Industry Outlook 2014*, Paris, OECD.

Overholt, W.H., 2005, 'China and globalization, testimony presented to the U.S.-China economic and security review commission on May 19', Available at www.rand.org/pubs/testimonies/CT244.html. Accessed 08/17/2016.

Rosen, D.H., 2014, *Avoiding the Blind Alley: China's Economic Overhaul and Its Global Implications*, New York and Washington, DC, The Asia Society Policy Institute.

The State Council, 2016, 'China to boost scientific and technological innovation', Available at http://english.gov.cn/policies/latest_releases/2016/08/08/content_281475412096102.htm. Accessed 08/15/2016.

Steinfeld, E.S., 2010, *Playing Our Game: Why China's Rise Doesn't Threaten the West*, Oxford, Oxford University Press.

Sun, Y. and Cao, C., 2014, 'Demystifying central government R&D spending in China', *Science*, 345(6200), 1006–1008.

Sun, Y. and Grimes, S., 2016, 'The emerging dynamic structure of national innovation studies: A bibliometric analysis', *Scientometrics*, 106(1), 17–40.

Sun, Y. and Liu, F., 2012, 'Evolution of the spatial distribution of China's high-tech industries: Agglomeration and spillover effects', *Issues & Studies*, 48(1), 151–190.

UNCTAD, 2015, 'Global investment trends monitor No. 18', Geneva, United Nations Publication. Available at http://unctad.org/en/PublicationsLibrary/webdiaeia2015d1_en.pdf

UNCTAD, 2016, *World Investment Report 2016 – Investor Nationality: Policy Challenges*, Geneva, United Nations Publication.

The Washington Post, 2016, 'Trump's demand that Apple must make iPhones in the U.S. actually isn't that crazy', Available at www.washingtonpost.com/news/innovations/wp/2016/05/17/trumps-demand-that-apple-must-make-iphones-in-the-u-s-actually-isnt-that-crazy/. Accessed 08/12/2016.

WTO, 2016, 'Trade policy review: China – concluding remarks by the Chairperson', Available at www.wto.org/english/tratop_e/tpr_e/tp442_crc_e.htm. Accessed 03/06/2016.

Wu, J., 2005, *Understanding and Interpreting Chinese Economic Reform*, New York, Thomason Texere.

Xing, Y., 2016, 'Global value chains and China's exports to high-income countries', *International Economic Journal*, 30(2), 191–203.

Yu, W., Hong, J., Wu, Y. and Zhao, D., 2013, 'Emerging geography of creativity and labor productivity effects in China', *China & World Economy*, 21(5), 78–99.

Zhou, P. and Leydesdorff, L., 2006, 'The emergence of China as a leading nation in science', *Research Policy*, 35(1), 83–104.

Zhou, Y., Lazonick, W. and Sun, Y., 2016, *China as an Innovation Nation*, Oxford, Oxford University Press.

2 A theoretical framework

Global value chain distribution

This chapter presents a theoretical framework for the global value chain distribution. At first, it explains the theoretical background of the GVC. With increased globalization, every country attempts to improve its own competitiveness in the face of international competition. Both comparative advantage and competitive advantage seek to interpret the content and source of international competitiveness, and the GVC is a new framework to interpret a country's international competitiveness. Second, a country's competitiveness is related to its domestic productivity, which is reflected in how it participates in the GVC, while national innovation capability is a key factor influencing participation in the GVC. Finally, we propose an analytical framework of a country's role in the GVC at the Macro-, Meso- and Micro-scale.

Globalization, competitiveness and global value chain

Globalization and comparative advantage

Although globalizing processes have been underway for centuries, the term itself only became current in the 1970s and was rarely used until the 1990s (James and Manfred, 2014). The cost of moving goods, the cost of moving ideas and the cost of moving people are three constraints that limit the separation of production and consumption, but shipping costs fell radically a century and a half before communication costs did (Baldwin, 2017). In 1944, 44 nations attended the Bretton Woods Conference with the purpose of stabilizing world currencies and establishing credit for international trade in the post-World War II era. While the international economic order envisioned by the conference gave way to the neo-liberal economic order prevalent today, the conference established many of the organizations essential to advancement toward a close-knit global economy and global financial system, such as the World Bank, the International Monetary Fund (IMF) and the International Trade Organization.

In 2000, the IMF identified the following four basic aspects of globalization: trade and transactions, capital and investment movements, migration and movement of people and the dissemination of knowledge (IMF, 2000). The IMF concept of globalization refers mainly to the economic dimensions of globalization.

Economic globalization is the increasing economic interdependence of national economies across the world through a rapid increase in the cross-border movement of goods, services, technology and capital (Joshi, 2009). Economic 'globalization' is considered an historical process, the result of human innovation and technological progress. Depending on the paradigm, economic globalization, which comprises the globalization of production, markets, competition, technology and corporations and industries, can be viewed as either a positive or a negative phenomenon (Joshi, 2009).

Five top-line facts that marked globalization's first unbundling included: (a) the developed economies industrialized while the less-developed economies deindustrialized; (b) trade boomed; (c) growth took off worldwide, but sooner and faster in the developed than in the less-developed; (d) the Great Divergence happened; and (e) urbanization accelerated, especially in the developed economies (Baldwin, 2017). In its early state, globalization trends can be largely accounted for by developed economies integrating with less-developed economies by means of FDI, the reduction of trade barriers as well as other economic reforms and, in many cases, immigration. In most cases, developed economies ensure that they benefit substantially from their relations with less-developed economies through free trade, investment, industrial transformation and exploiting their intellectual property. Recently, however, developed economies have also begun to re-think the effects of globalization, such as global trade imbalance, high unemployment rates and so on. In particular, the work of Autor et al. (2016) has called into question the consensus in relation to the overall positive effects of international trade and has highlighted the significant adjustment costs in particular industries and regions of the developed economies arising from the offshoring of manufacturing to six low wage economies, the I6: China, Korea, India, Indonesia, Thailand and Poland. This new globalization of offshoring manufacturing has very large and very different winners and losers than the old globalization of international trade.

A major concern being discussed has to do with defining what the competitiveness of a country is and how to achieve it in a more globalized economy. Comparative advantage, one of the oldest and most important concepts in economics, is the first interpretation. It emerged from international trade. Adam Smith (1776, 12) first alluded to the concept of absolute advantage as the basis for international trade in *The Wealth of Nations*:

> If a foreign country can supply us with a commodity cheaper than we ourselves can make it, better buy it off them with some part of the produce of our own industry employed in a way in which we have some advantage. The general industry of the country, being always in proportion to the capital which employs it, will not thereby be diminished . . . but only left to find out the way in which it can be employed with the greatest advantage.

The principle of comparative advantage is historically tied to the framework of the Ricardian trade model. In 1817, David Ricardo published what has since become known as the theory of comparative advantage in his book *On the*

Principles of Political Economy and Taxation. This is an economic theory about the work gains from trade for individuals, firms or nations that arise from differences in their factor endowments or technological progress (Maneschi, 1998). David Ricardo explains why countries engage in international trade even when one country's workers are more efficient at producing every single good than workers in other countries. This could be called a kind of national advantage or competitiveness. In terms of the theory of comparative advantage, if two countries capable of producing two commodities engage in the free market, then each country will increase its overall consumption by exporting the good for which it has a comparative advantage while importing the other good, provided that there exist differences in labor productivity between both countries. The closely related law or principle of comparative advantage holds that under free trade, an agent will produce more and consume less of a good for which they have a comparative advantage (Dixit and Norman, 1980).

It is common in the empirical trade literature to measure comparative advantage with the help of the Balassa (1965) index of revealed comparative advantage (RCA). This measure reflects the success of exporting of countries relative to a world-wide norm. Exports can result from subsidies or other incentives provided, for instance by exchange rate misalignment. Therefore, the RCA index is more a measures competitiveness than comparative advantage (Siggel, 2006). Comparative advantage is only one interpretation of competitiveness.

From comparative advantage to competitive advantage

It is true that in classical and neo-classical trade theory comparative advantage is established by cost comparison under autarchy and under trade, whereas in international trade the cost advantage is captured when markets have been joined and firms have relocated their plants (Siggel, 2006). Obviously, the RCA index based on comparative advantage can't reflect a country's competitiveness. Accordingly, a large number of concepts of competitiveness have been proposed in the economic and business literature.

The first interpretation of competitiveness is more in line with the concept of comparative advantage. In this view, an economy is deemed to be competitive if it harbors a large number of internationally competitive enterprises and industries. In other words, it must perform strongly in exports. For example, Hatsopoulos et al. (1988) postulate that the competitiveness of economies translates into trade balance with a rising living standard or real income. If export success can always be achieved at the cost of diminished real income, it is then not a reflection of competitiveness.

Second, perhaps the best known version of competitiveness is the World Competitiveness Index, computed and published yearly by the World Economic Forum. Since 2004, the Global Competitiveness Report (GCR) ranks the world's nations according to the Global Competitiveness Index. In the latest report (2015–2016), the WEF defines competitiveness as the set of institutions, policies and factors that determine the level of productivity of an economy, which in turn

sets the level of prosperity that the country can earn (WEF, 2016). Thus, the definition of competitiveness is the level of productivity of an economy, and the WEF measures productivity through its potential determinants. Certainly, it is not a new idea. This idea underlies the concept used by Dollar and Wolff (1993), who proposed to measure it in terms of productivity – both labor and total factor productivity. Similar approaches include the concepts proposed by Hatsopoulos et al. (1988) and Markusen (1992).

Naturally, the more important issue is to identify the factors determining the labor productivity and total factor productivity. The GCR groups these factors into 12 pillars: institutions, infrastructure, macroeconomic environment, health and primary education, higher education and training, goods market efficiency, labor market efficiency, financial market development, technological readiness, market size, business sophistication and innovation. These are in turn are organized into three sub-indexes, in line with three main stages of development: basic requirements, efficiency enhancers and innovation and sophistication factors. The economies are grouped into factor-driven economies, efficiency-driven economies and innovation driven economies.

Third, Porter (1990, 73) proposed the concept of competitive advantage, relative to comparative advantage: 'National prosperity is created, not inherited. It does not grow out of a country's natural endowments, its labor pool, its interest rates, or its currency's value, as classical economics insists. A nation's competitiveness depends on the capacity of its industry to innovate and upgrade'. According to Porter, there are four main determinants of competitiveness: firm strategy, structure and rivalry, the demand conditions they face, the factor supply conditions they encounter, and the conditions of related industries. In fact, it is a multitude of factors that influence the competitiveness of producers, but Porter models them under four facets of a diamond. These facets can be viewed as dimensions along which competitiveness can be measured. Porter's concept has attracted wide interest in the business and political communities, perhaps because of its comprehensive nature (Oral, 1993).

Krugman (1994), on the other hand, famously criticized policymakers for their incorrect use of the term 'competitiveness', confusing the competitiveness of companies, which could be measured in terms of their market share, and that of countries, which he argued was not a zero-sum game, since wealth being created by one country did not necessarily have a negative impact on other countries. Meanwhile, Krugman (1994) pointed out that competitiveness is about productivity, not international competition after all, and the growth rate of living standards essentially equals the growth rate of domestic productivity, not productivity relative to competitors, but simply domestic productivity. However, it is worth noting that the domestic productivity will impact the competition in international markets with increased globalization. Consequently it is quite shocking to learn that in 2015 China's productivity was only 19 percent of that of the U.S., despite the progress in China's productivity in recent years (The Conference Board, 2016).

Fourth, the competitive advantage of a country consists of firms with competitiveness. Scholars have long understood that competitive advantage depends upon the match between distinctive internal (organizational) capabilities and changing external (environmental) circumstances (Chandler, 1962; Penrose, 1959). Although both internal analyses of organizational strengths and weaknesses and external analyses of opportunities and threats have received some attention in the literature, work has tended to focus primarily on analyzing a firm's opportunities and threats in its competitive environment. For example, Porter (1985) thoroughly developed the concepts of cost leadership and differentiation relative to competitors as two important sources of competitive advantage: a low-cost position enables a firm to use aggressive pricing and high sales volume, whereas a differentiated product creates brand loyalty and positive reputation, facilitating premium pricing. Hamel and Prahalad (1994) emphasized the importance of "competing for the future" as a neglected dimension of competitive advantage. According to this view, the firm must be concerned not only with profitability in the present and growth in the medium term, but also with its future position and source of competitive advantage. This view requires explicit strategizing about how the firm will compete when its current strategy configuration is either copied or made obsolete (Hart, 1995).

In the strategic management literature, there appears to be general agreement about the resource characteristics that contribute to a firm's sustained competitive advantage, which is called the resource-based view (the 'RBV'). According to Barney (1991), firm resources include all assets, capabilities, organizational processes, firm attributes, information, knowledge, etc., controlled by a firm that enable the firm to conceive of and implement strategies that improve its efficiency and effectiveness. At the most basic level, such resources must be *valuable*, rare, inimitable (*specific* to a given firm), and *nonsubstitutable* (VRIN). In other words, for a resource to have enduring value, it must contribute to a firm's capability that has competitive significance and is not easily accomplished through alternative means. That is, they must not be widely distributed within an industry and/or must be closely identified with a given organization, making them difficult to transfer or trade (e.g. a brand image or an exclusive supply arrangement).

Moreover, the property rights of resources is a central issue for a firm. First, resources are conceptualized as being composed of multiple attributes for which property rights may be held. Second, a resource owner's ability to create, appropriate, and sustain value from resources depends on the property rights that he or she holds and on the transaction costs of exchanging, defining and protecting them. While transaction costs are a major source of value dissipation, reducing such dissipation may create value (Foss and Foss, 2005). While extant literature focuses on a common lineage between Penrosean theory and the RBV, Nason and Wiklund (2015) explicate that RBV's central tenets concern resources that meet VRIN criteria, while Penrose's theory discusses the versatility of resources. Theoretically, VRIN resources allow firms to exploit unique opportunities, while versatile resources allow firms to recombine resources in novel ways to create growth. Using meta-analytic techniques, they find that versatile resources are associated with higher levels of growth, whereas VRIN resources are not.

However, as Kraaijenbrink et al. (2010) have noted, the resource-based view of the firm, which has been around for 20 years, has gained wide adoption but has also been subjected to criticism. They conclude that the core message of RBV can withstand most of this critique provided the RBV's variables, boundaries and applicability are clearly stated. They also feel that two of the criticisms, which arise from the indeterminate nature of the concepts of resource and value in the RBV, together with the narrow conceptualization of a firm's competitive advantage, are quite valid, and argues that its narrow neoclassical rationality had inhibited further progress in relation to these weaknesses to date.

Competitiveness and the global value chain

The concept of value chain comes from business management and was first described and popularized by Michael Porter in his 1985 best-seller, *Competitive Advantage: Creating and Sustaining Superior Performance* (Porter, 1985). The concept could help to understand how a company creates value and looks for ways to add more value, which are critical elements in developing a competitive strategy. Porter proposed a general-purpose value chain that companies can use to examine all of their activities. The way in which value chain activities are performed determines costs and affects profits, so this tool can help to understand the sources of value for an organization. The value chain describes the full range of activities that firms and workers perform to bring a product from its conception to end use and beyond. The concept of value chain mainly focuses on a firm's value creation.

Indeed, trade in value-added changes the notion of competitiveness. As mentioned above, assessing the competitiveness of a country by indicators related to trade is not appropriate when supply-chain trade is increasingly important (IMF, 2013). This has led to a debate on how to incorporate the effect of GVCs in measuring competitiveness. With the emergence of and the growing importance of the role of GVCs, one way of modification is to move away from a 'goods' world to a 'value-added' world, given that value-added as opposed to gross trade ultimately matters for competitiveness.

Due to product modularization, firm specialization and operation globalization, the value-creating activities in a specific industry form a cross-boundary of organization, region and nation. The activities that comprise a value chain can be contained within a single firm or divided among different firms. The geographical dispersion of value creation has recently begun to play an increasingly important role in the analysis of national competitive advantage. Since the late nineties, international trade and investment have undergone accelerated changes with the emergence of GVCs, which have had important consequences for enterprises and governments, as well as a bearing on the activities of trade and investment promotion agencies (Gurría, 2013). Technology progress, liberalization in trade and investment, cost-reducing and profit-seeking behaviors of MNCs have been driving the emergence of GVCs in recent decades (OECD, 2013). The concept of GVCs can more accurately reflect value-creating activities. Today, GVCs have been extended from manufacturing into business processes and management, such as software development, maintenance and voice services.

Multinational companies (MNCs) now locate different stages and activities across the globe. The process of research and development, design, assembly, production of parts, marketing and branding are no longer concentrated in one firm and one location, but they are instead increasingly located across different countries (Gurría, 2013). Firms develop global value chains, investing abroad and establishing affiliates that provide critical support to remaining activities at home. For example, MNCs offshore labor-intensive activities, such as assembly, to emerging countries characterized by skilled but comparatively cheap labor. GVCs have interconnected national economies through various international activities. The market drives economic integration by means of value chains, which is more stable and effective than what could be achieved by institutions. Thus, GVCs help explain why China has become the largest manufacturer in the world over the past decade. GVCs offer opportunities for enterprises to enhance efficiency and source inputs globally, investing in specific activities where the location factors are optimal for profit. Conversely, activities such as research will often be located in countries with strong universities and a large pool of scientists and engineers. At this time, an important question is how to use low-wage labor in I6 as part of a high-productivity global manufacturing value chain, and this important knowledge is 'owned' by firms headquartered in the G7 (Baldwin, 2017).

In the 1990s, Gereffi and others developed a framework called 'global commodity chains' (GCCs) that tied the concept of the value-added chain directly to the global organization of industries (see Gereffi, 1994). GCCs are the prototype of GVCs which are rooted in transnational production systems, which link the economic activities of firms to technological, organizational, and institutional networks that are utilized to develop, manufacture and market specific commodities. Gereffi (1995, 113) proposed that GVCs have four main dimensions:

> a value-added chain of products, services, and resources linked together across a range of relevant industries; a geographic dispersion of production and a marketing network at the national, regional, and global scales, comprised of enterprises of different sizes and types; a governance structure of authority and power relationships between firms that determines how financial, material, and human resources are allocated and flow within a chain; and an institutional framework that identifies how local, national, and international conditions and policies shape the globalization process at each stage in the chain.

Using these four fundamental dimensions, contributions from Gereffi (1999) and Humphrey and Schmitz (2002) developed an additional element of analysis referred to as upgrading, which describes the dynamic movement within the value chain by examining how producers shift between different stages of the chain.

After many years of research on GVCs, Gereffi et al. (2005) built a theoretical framework to help explain governance patterns in global value chains. It identifies three variables – the complexity of transactions, the ability to codify transactions and the capabilities in the supply-base that play a large role in determining how global value chains are governed and change. The theory generates five types of global value chain governance – hierarchy, captive, relational, modular and market – which range from high to low levels of explicit coordination and power asymmetry. One of the key findings of value chain studies is that access to developed country markets has become increasingly dependent on participating in global production networks (GPNs) led by firms based in developed countries. Thus, the governance of global value chains is essential for understanding how firms in developing countries can gain access to global markets, what the benefits of access and the risks of exclusion might be and how the net gains from participation in global value chains might be increased.

For us, the GVC framework provides a useful guide as we seek answers to questions about the dynamic political economy of industries. GVC analysis highlights three basic characteristics of any industry: (1) the geography and character of linkages between tasks, or stages, in the chain of value-added activities; (2) how power is distributed and exerted among firms and other actors in the chain; and (3) the role that institutions play in structuring business relationships and industrial location. These elements help explain how industries and places evolve, and offer clues about possible changes in the future. The chain metaphor is purposely simplistic. It focuses on the location of work and the linkages between tasks as a single product or service makes its way from conception to end use (Sturgeon and Gereffi, 2009).

Case studies of global value chains based on detailed micro data for a single product or a single sector in industries such as electronics, apparel, and motor vehicles have provided detailed examples of the discrepancy between gross and value-added trade. While enhancing our intuitive understanding of global production chains in particular industries, they do not offer a comprehensive picture of the gap between value-added and gross trade, and an economy's participation in cross-border production chains (Koopman et al., 2014). A growing recent literature, such as Daudin et al. (2011) and Johnson and Noguera (2012) aims to estimate value-added trade in the field of international economics using global Inter-Country Input-Output (ICIO) tables based on the Global Trade Analysis Project (GTAP) and World Input-Output database (WIOD). Most of these papers discuss the connections between their work with HIY (Hummels et al., 2001, henceforth HIY), but they are more closely related to the factor content trade literature. Koopman et al. (2014) proposes a framework for gross exports accounting that breaks up a country's gross exports into various value-added components by source and additional double-counted terms. By identifying which parts of the official trade data are double-counted and the sources of the double-counting, it bridges official trade (in gross value terms) and national accounts statistics (in value-added terms).

Participating in GVCs and national innovation capability

As globalization develops further, it has made production increasingly frag-mented across countries, with roughly two-thirds of world trade accounted by trade in intermediate inputs (Johnson and Noguera, 2012). In particular, out-sourcing and FDI to developing countries have accelerated the 'slicing-up' of the global value chain across national borders. Meanwhile, this also provides good opportunities for developing countries to participate in GVCs, through creat-ing and acquiring value. Further, industrialization became easier for developing countries joining GVCs. It is clear that the know-how necessary to set up single stages is much easier for developing countries to absorb than the know-how that is necessary to set up a whole sector (Baldwin, 2017). GVCs make the sales-scale conundrum evaporate since the MNCs setting up the offshore facilities have already attained global competitiveness.

The gap between gross value and value-added

There is a widening gap between the value of gross exports and the actual value-added that is created in the exporting country (Ma et al., 2015). This is because exports and GDP are measured by different accounting standards. GDP is meas-ured in value-added – a net concept, whereas exports are measured in gross terms containing intermediate inputs, which may cross borders many times before they become final products. In this sense, exports can't completely reflect the coun-try's competitive advantage.

For example, the iPad, a device that is designed and owned by Apple, is assem-bled by Foxconn in China, and its components are manufactured by differ-ent suppliers around the world. The final product is then exported to the U.S. and other countries. In trade statistics, each iPad sold in the U.S. adds $275 to the U.S. trade deficit with China. However, the value-added contributed by China is merely $10, given that most parts are produced outside of China (The Economist, 2012). Hence, although iPads accounted for $4 billion of America's reported trade deficit with China in 2011, the Chinese value-added in the deficit was estimated to be only $150 million (Xing and Detert, 2011). After accounting for foreign content, Johnson and Noguera (2012) showed that the controversial U.S.–China imbalance is about 40 percent smaller than what was reported in offi-cial trade statistics. Indeed, the value added by a nation's indigenous enterprise is essential to understanding its role and contribution in global trade and economic growth. Yet, China can gain value through participating in the iPad GVC, reflect-ing its competitive advantage.

A technology gap in the vertical specialization system

The GVC based on the global production network is a vertical specialization system. Hummels et al. (2001) suggested that a country can participate in verti-cal specialization in two ways: by using imported intermediate inputs to produce exports; and exporting intermediate goods that are used as inputs by other countries to produce goods for export. Exporting is an important way of participating in the GVC. The next question is what determine a country's exports, and in particular the value added in exports. In this time of knowledge-based economics, we have all realized that knowledge, technology and innovation are core factors of national production function and economic growth. For a long time, the academic community has treated technology as one (usually a rather important) element in the competitive struggle between firms and nation-states, knowing that it may be manipulated by appropriate policies, both at the national level and at the level of the firm (OECD, 1978).

As mentioned above, there are several theories of international trade, such as comparative advantage, to explain a country's competitiveness. During the post-war period, the traditional theory of international trade proved incapable of providing a satisfactory explanation of the observed patterns of commodity trade (Freeman, 2004). In 1953, Leontief found that the U.S. – the most capital-abundant country in the world – exported commodities that were more labor-intensive than capital-intensive, in contradiction with the comparative advantage theory (Leontief, 1953). Leontief's paradox shows that the country with the world's highest capital-per worker has a lower capital/labor ratio in exports than in imports. Following this demonstration in 1953 of the 'Leontief Paradox', it became difficult to sustain explanations of the trade performance of such countries as the U.S. and the German Federal Republic, in terms of the relative costs of labor and capital.

In 1960, Posner's seminal work opened the way to the development of an alternative paradigm. Posner (1961) developed a set of concepts which became the basis for various 'technology gap' theories of foreign trade. Posner identified several mechanisms that might tend to maintain this gap for fairly long periods, including the quality and scale of commitment to R&D, the 'clustering' of technical innovation and the dynamic economies of scale. All of them start from the self-evident fact that a firm which introduces a new product may enjoy an export monopoly from the country of origin at least until imitators come into the market. Then came Soete's (1981) systematic attempts to relate international trade performance to some measure of 'technological output' across the board and for a large number of OECD countries. His results demonstrated the crucial role of the technology variable in explaining inter-country variation in export performance in the great majority of industries. Indeed, while the 'technology gap' could explain parts of value-added in international trade, these studies did not build a comprehensive mechanisms or theory to explain the gap.

National innovation system and capacity

Porter (1990, 74) pointed out that 'Companies achieve competitive advantage through acts of innovation. They approach innovation in its broadest sense, including both new technologies and new ways of doing things. . . . Innovation can be manifested in a new product design, a new production process, a new marketing approach, or a new way of conducting training.' Thus, innovation is a core factor in helping companies narrow the technology gap and participate in the GVCs. Accordingly, national innovation determines a country's role in GVCs.

According to recent research, the national innovation system (NIS) is the largest cluster within national innovation studies that attempts to explain a country's technological innovation development (Sun and Grimes, 2016). Most authors agree that the concept of NIS comes from researchers like Freeman, Lundvall and Nelson. The first person to use the expression NIS was Lundvall, who is also the editor of *National Systems of Innovation: Toward a Theory of Innovation and Interactive Learning*, a highly original and thought-provoking book on the subject (Sun and Liu, 2010). Using the concept of 'the national innovation system', Freeman (2004) first analyzes how technological infrastructure differs between countries and how such differences are reflected in international competitiveness and value-added in exports. Technological leadership gives absolute rather than comparative advantage and 'technological leadership will reflect institutions supporting coupling, creating, clustering, comprehending and coping in connection with technology' (Freeman, 2004, 541). Thus, public investment in technological infrastructure and intellectual capital is crucial for successful economic development, and there is a need to combine education, science, trade and industry policy in order to build competitiveness.

NIS is rooted in the historical context through references to Friedrich List's national system and Joseph Schumpeter's innovation theory. There is no single definition of what an NIS is. The concept of an NIS rests on the premise that understanding the linkages among the actors involved in innovation is a key to improving technological performance (OECD, 1997). Thus, an NIS can be seen as a new structural model similar to the technology-push model, the demand-pull model, or that of university–industry cooperation (Sun and Liu, 2010). According to innovation system theory, innovation and technology development is the result of a complex set of relationships among actors in a system. Such innovation actors include enterprises, universities, governments and research institutions. The NIS model focuses more on the relationships and processes between various innovation actors, which emphasize the systemic characteristics of innovation, rapid technological change and globalization.

When it comes specifically to China, the notion of a national innovation system differs from developed countries in the following ways (Sun and Liu, 2010): (1) The context of an NIS. China's innovation system was constructed as part of a transition process from a centrally planned to a market-oriented economy. An enterprise-centered innovation system is a key development aim of policymakers in China. (2) The establishment of an NIS. NISs in different countries have different structures, types and functions. China's NIS has similarities with a construction project, and establishment of such an NIS is dependent upon certain conditions. (3) The content of an NIS. Chinese policy of NIS seeks to build an enterprise-centered technological innovation system with the state spending a large amount to establish labs, R&D centers and other organizations or buildings. (4) The role of state in NIS. China's state plays the leading role in the development, restructuring and performance of innovation systems.

The recent trend in NIS research is to focus on capacity. Furman, Porter and Stern (FP&S) introduced a novel framework based on the concept of national innovative capacity in 2002 (Furman et al., 2002). The national innovative capacity framework draws on three distinct areas of prior research: ideas-driven endogenous growth theory, the cluster-based theory of national industrial competitive advantage and research on national innovation systems. National innovative capacity depends on the strength of a nation's common innovation infrastructure, the environment for innovation in a nation's industrial clusters and the strength of linkages between these two (Furman et al., 2002). Based on the FP&S framework, Furman and Hayes (2004) investigated the factors that enabled such emerging innovator economies to achieve successful catch-up while some historically more innovative countries experienced relative declines in innovative productivity. Hu and Mathews (2005) extended and modified the FP&S approach by applying it to five 'latecomer' countries from East Asia, with their latest work being 'China's National Innovative Capacity' (Hu and Mathews, 2008). Hu and Mathews (2008) found that universities played a strong role in the building of China's national innovative capacity over the last 15 years, and the puzzling apparent lack of contribution by the public sector in reinforcing China's national innovative capacity. In essence, the national innovative capacity is central to a country's participation and value-added in GVCs.

Thus, a less-developed country with weak innovative capacity will find it difficult to participate in GVCs, or it may only occupy a low-end role in GVCs. However, a less-developed country may acquire knowledge spillovers from developed countries. The supply and demand of products within the global value chain results in an interconnected infrastructure involving international marketing and distribution. Buyer-seller links between exporters and overseas buyers provides an important channel for the diffusion and learning of information, technology and knowledge (Egan and Mody, 1992). For companies from a less-developed country, participation in GVCs can facilitate market access, reduce transaction costs and increase information acquisition through knowledge spillovers. For example, Chinese firms involved in GVCs have not only entered the international market successfully, but they have also been freed from concerns about learning from their customers or suppliers (Xing, 2016). In fact, such participation results in a process of upgrading and catching-up. But, the new international movement of knowledge is very carefully controlled by the MNCs that own it, and they make great efforts to see that it stays inside the contours of their global value chains (Baldwin, 2017). As a consequence, the new globalization is transforming only the developing economies that are on the receiving end of the know-how.

An analytical framework of a nation's role in the GVC

In this book, we propose an analytical framework for revealing a nation's role in the GVC at the macro-, meso- and micro-scale. At the macro-scale, the framework seeks to reveal a country's value-added based on its trade system. At the meso-scale, the framework seeks to reveal a country's value-added in the ICT sector. At the micro-scale, the framework seeks to reveal a country's value-added based on a company's supply chain.

Macro

The internationalization of NIS is the new trend in national S&T and economic development within the context of globalization. Internationalization is primarily the way to construct international technology ties and obtain external technology. There are several patterns of internationalization according to the direction of technology flows between developed and developing countries. There are four different patterns of R&D internationalization – traditional, modern, expansionary and catch-up – depending upon the dichotomy of the nations involved in global innovation networks, developed and emerging or home and host (Von Zedtwitz and Gassmann, 2002). The network model reveals the multilateral investment and trade relations between countries. Countries are nodes in the network, while the ties show flows between the nodes (Sun and Liu, 2013). Within the global innovation network, a country is the product and service source and also the product and service receiver though investment and trade (Figure 2.1). The country could introduce foreign products and services through FDI and import trade, and output products and services to other countries through OFDI and export trade. A country's contribution in the GVC is the value-added of indigenous firms as opposed to that of foreign firms or Joint Ventures (JVs).

In the field of international business (IB), Dunning (1981) introduced the OLI (Ownership-Location-Internalization) paradigm more than 40 years ago to explain the origin, level, pattern and growth of MNCs' offshore activities. Over the years, OLI has developed into perhaps the dominant paradigm in IB studies. In the eclectic paradigm, MNCs possess ownership (O) advantages as a result of technological knowledge and/or market power developed in their home countries; host countries offer 'localization' (L) advantages, and between the MNC

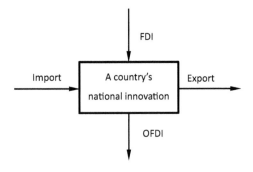

Figure 2.1 A framework of a nation's role in GVC at the macro-scale

and the host economy, 'internationalization' (I) advantages may develop (Eden and Dai, 2010).

Dunning later proposed the investment development path (IDP) theory, which is derived from OLI theory (Dunning, 2003). The IDP theory is based on two premises: economic development implicitly involves a succession of structural changes; and these changes entail a dynamic relationship between their nature and the type and volume of FDI that a country sends and receives. The IDP model consists of five stages. In the first stage, countries receive virtually no FDI, while those that do receive FDI flows are in the second stage. In the third stage, countries are beginning to make investment abroad but still remain net receivers of FDI. In the fourth stage, outward investment is higher than inward investment. Finally, in the more advanced countries, in the fifth stage, on average, FDI outflows are neutralized by incoming investment.

However, economic liberalization and transition to a market economy may therefore, give a massive stimulus to OFDI, with firms anxious to escape for the first time the strictures of local markets previously subject to socialist controls (Svetličič, 2003). 'Leapfrogging' OFDI in transitional economies may, therefore, provide a major exception to the IDP hypothesis, with OFDI driven not by ownership advantages from home and L-advantages abroad, but by L-disadvantages at home (Svetličič, 2003). At the same time, the opposite tendency has been found in developing countries, where OFDI has been found to lag behind GDP-based expectations at each IDP stage (Kuada and Sorensen, 2000). Thus, for a less-developed country, the point is to offer L-advantages for FDI and O-advantages for OFDI. In this sense, the ownership of the firm is central to a country's economic operation.

Investment could restructure ownership of firms in economies, which is reflected in ownership within international trade. More recently, a growing literature emphasizes the vertical structure of global value chains and the nation's role in GVCs. Notably, Koopman et al. (2012, henceforth KWW) propose a formula to compute domestic and foreign content, which takes the differences in using imported inputs by processing exporters versus normal exporters into consideration. Their results are in sharp contrast to those of Hummels et al. (2001), for the latter do not recognize the role of processing trade. KWW show that the share of domestic content in Chinese manufacturing exports was about 50 percent before China's accession to the WTO, and has risen to more than 60 percent since then.

KWW's approach still depends on industry-level statistics and may have a measurement bias as long as different firms within an industry have different imported input intensities. Some scholars attempt to obtain direct measures of the I/O coefficients for processing exports. For example, Cruz et al. (2011) show that domestic value-added accounts for only 34 percent of Mexico's manufacturing exports on average. Using a carefully cleaned sample of processing firms that merges firms' exports, imports and production information from 2000 to 2006, Kee and Tang (2013) study the input choices of processing firms without resorting to the standard input-output data. They found that the average share of domestic value-added in China's processing exports has risen from 35 percent in

2000 to 49 percent in 2006. This trend is very similar to that reported by KWW, which uses industry-level data. Similarly, Upward et al. (2013) obtain consistent results with a more general sample of Chinese firms with trade and production information from 2003 to 2006. However, although firm-level data provide rich information, it may not be applicable to cases with less suitable data.

With the increasing fragmentation of production across production networks and value chains, it is necessary to develop more effective conceptual frameworks such as GPNs and global value chains to determine the particular roles of different regions within production networks, as well as providing a better indication of the added value accruing to those regions (Sturgeon, 2008; Coe et al., 2008). Increased fragmentation of production associated with globalization has resulted in 80 percent of global trade occurring within global value chains, which are typically coordinated by MNCs, with the cross-border trade of inputs and outputs taking place within their networks of affiliates, contractual partners and arm's-length suppliers (UNCTAD, 2013). Obviously, firm-level information is useful to mitigate the measurement bias.

As mentioned above, investment and trade are two kinds of globalization decisions made by firms. When firms are heterogeneous, the optimal choice differs across firms. Antràs and Helpman (2004) formalized how a firm sources abroad either through trade or through FDI. In their model, high-productivity firm's source overseas by engaging in FDI; low-productivity firms acquire intermediates only within the home country. On the other hand, Helpman et al. (2004) analyze the decision to serve foreign markets through exporting or FDI. Their model predicts that only the most productive firms find it profitable to produce offshore by FDI; the firms with medium productivity serve foreign markets by exporting; the least productive firms serve only the domestic market. These theories of organizational modal choice have deepened our understanding of trade and FDI from the aggregate sector level to the fundamental firm-level.

The world is increasingly polarized between developed countries with superior technologies but saturated markets, and less-developed countries with backward technologies but relatively unexplored markets. While firms from developed countries may prefer to export their products to unexplored markets, developing countries will attempt to use their market potential to attract FDI (Qiu and Tao, 2001). FDI by MNCs may raise employment and enhance technology transfer in less-developed countries. This indicates that less-developed countries' exports cannot reflect its indigenous context or value contribution. Because indigenous contribution policies require multinational firms to use a certain proportion of locally made parts and components in their production, employment in the local parts industries is bound to increase. Furthermore, to maintain the quality of their final products, multinational firms must transfer technology to the local parts industries. Thus, indigenous contribution has become a popular form of governmental regulation of FDI in less-developed countries. In order to investigate the indigenous contribution to GVC, a feasible approach is to analyze the ownership profile of importers and exporters at the firm-level.

Relying solely on firm-level information, however, may result in the loss of generality and prevent us from understanding the economy as a whole. We therefore choose to group firms based on their characteristics and integrate the information on firm heterogeneity with industry-level data. We draw information from firm-level data to make the appropriate groupings. To summarize, we developed a framework and an estimation procedure that separately accounts for the production and trade activities of foreign firms, indigenous firms and JVs. Although our empirical investigation is based on Chinese data, our method is also applicable to other emerging economies, such as Mexico and Vietnam that engage in massive trade processing or have significant FDI inflows.

Meso

At the meso-scale, it is valuable to know a nation's role in the GVC of a specific industry or sector. This book focuses on the ICT sector. ICT is an extended term for information technology (IT) which stresses the role of unified communications and the integration of telecommunications (telephone lines and wireless signals), computers as well as necessary enterprise software, middleware, storage and audio-visual systems, which enable users to access, store, transmit and manipulate information. The OECD's evidence shows that ICT has had considerable impact on productivity growth in the second half of the 1990s, and up to 2001 (OECD, 2003). The challenge facing China is enormous, with productivity across industries being just 15 to 30 percent of the average for industries in the OECD countries (McKinsey and Company, 2016). While admittedly a wide range, McKinsey (2014) estimate that the next wave of digital transformation in China could add 0.3 to 1.0 percent to GDP from 2013 to 2025. The logistics sector is an example provided in which digital platforms for scheduling could help make the 700,000 companies in the sector more efficient.

First, in several countries with strong growth performance, notably Australia, Canada and the U.S., investment in ICT has supported labor productivity growth, while the available evidence suggests that these impacts have not disappeared with the slowdown. Second, in a number of countries, notably Finland, Ireland and Korea, ICT production has provided an important contribution to aggregate labor and total-factor productivity (TFP) growth. Third, in a number of OECD countries, notably Australia and the U.S., there is evidence that sectors that have invested heavily in ICT, notably service sectors such as distribution and financial services, have been able to achieve more rapid TFP growth. In order to explain the rapid developments in the ICT sector, scholars have been evolving their conceptualizations, using a variety of frameworks, including the global value chain, the GPNs and global innovation networks (GIN) (Cooke, 2013a, Gereffi, 2014 and Yeung and Coe, 2015). This evolution has been partly related to the shift from a productivity perspective initially to a greater emphasis on the role of innovation more recently, or from a short-term view to a long-term view (Cooke, 2013a).

An important element in this book is the focus on how power and control is exercised by leading firms in the global value chain in order to achieve dominance in the market. Because of their leadership in technological innovation, product design and marketing, major corporations such as Apple play a leading role in the overall trajectory of the sector and in controlling elements of the value chain. Through their control of core intellectual property in operating systems and chip design, leading companies are in a position to dictate the terms of operation for many supplier companies that are positioned further down the value chain (Clelland, 2014). The recent period in the evolution of the value chain has been one of rapid transformation in the internet-driven market with huge growth in the number of users and to some extent an increasingly integrated globalized market. This has also been accompanied by major advances in the technology from the earlier desktop to an increasing emphasis on mobile devices, including smartphones and tablets, and an increasing reliance on cloud computing.

In addition to significant investment in R&D, major companies like Apple also maintain their leadership in the sector by acquiring innovative companies in key niche areas, which will allow them to develop greater convergence between new technological developments. Leading global corporations are engaged in an ongoing battle for supremacy in the internet-related market as they seek to shape the future of how that market will evolve. Some argue that indicators such as market capitalization rather than market dominance *per se* is key to their success, and that financialization of companies like Apple has been a key determinant of its recent period of success, as it places major collaborating companies like Foxconn under considerable pressure to take on more of the risks associated with production (Froud et al., 2014). Some argue that not unlike other sectors, the ICT sector is also engaged in a race to the bottom with the shareholders of major technology corporations putting pressure on management to increase share value and reduce costs, resulting in a wider range of activities being outsourced to the most competitive location.

In Baldwin (2017) 's estimation, the parameters of industrial policy have been overturned as global production has shifted from the 'frown curve', whereby value-added was created by the manufacturer to the 'smile curve' whereby value-added is created by owning (a) raw materials, (b) design, (c) branded distribution and (d) ancillary post-manufacturing services. A smile curve of value creation is an illustration of value-adding potentials of different components of the value chain in an ICT-related manufacturing industry (see Figure 2.2). The concept was first proposed in 1992 by Stan Shih, the founder of Acer, an IT company headquartered in Taiwan. Firms are finding that value-added is becoming increasingly concentrated at the upstream and downstream ends of the value chain (Mudambi, 2007).

Activities at both ends of the value chain are intensive in their application of knowledge and creativity. For convenience sake, the ICT GVC can be divided into three main groupings of companies (Figure 2.2). (1) *Own Brand Manufacturers* (OBMs) mainly refer to R&D and product design, brand, sales and marketing; (2) the component companies mainly refer to R&D and product design,

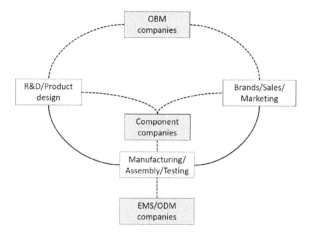

Figure 2.2 Theoretical framework on three type companies in GVC

brand, sales and marketing, and manufacturing of product parts; (3) and *Electronics Manufacturing Services* (EMSs) mainly refer to design, manufacturing, assembly and testing.

Lead or brand names (sometimes referred to as OBMs) are companies like Apple, Samsung, Huawei and so on. In smartphones, Apple continues to be a highly profitable leading brand, although for years now part manufacturing and product assembly have been concentrated in East Asia, especially China. The government-driven initiatives to develop the Korean electronics and IT industries, especially the display and semiconductor industries, have gradually enabled the major brand of electronics products – such as Samsung a world leader in smartphones – to dominate the market.

Component companies have become an important power in ICT GVC due to the modularity design of product architecture. OBM companies depend on component companies, although parts of components are manufactured in-house by some companies, such as Samsung – also a world leader in flat panel and DRAM memory. For example, in the PC sector, semiconductor chips, display, power and storage parts have formed independent sub-sectors with leading companies like Intel and AMD; in the mobile device sector, Qualcomm is the leading company of semiconductor chips.

Generally, EMS companies design, manufacture and assemble products on behalf of OBMs; they also include companies that design, test, manufacture, distribute and provide return/repair services for electronic components and assemblies for OBMs. EMSs could be classified into two types. An *Original Design Manufacturer* (ODM) is a company that designs and manufactures a product as specified and eventually rebranded by OBMs for sale, while an *Original Equipment Manufacturer* (OEM) is a company that produces parts and equipment that may be marketed by another manufacturer. ODMs allow the firm that owns or licenses the brand to produce products (either as a supplement or solely) without having to engage in the organization or running of a factory. ODM and OEM companies can be regarded as suppliers of OBMs, or leading brand companies.

However, in attempting to compile a database of a large number of companies involved in the ICT GVC, this neat classification system frequently breaks down, since the boundaries between different subsectors such as ODM and EMS have become increasingly blurred over time as the ICT industry evolved and company business models responded to change. Also, some companies may be involved in a range of functions, such as Samsung, which is both a major brand name and also a major supplier of smartphone chipsets to Apple. Foxconn, the biggest EMS company in the world, which is Taiwanese with a significant part of its global activity in China, is regarded as an industry in itself because of the range of functions it carries out.

These different categories of companies are related to the outsourcing/offshoring model that emerged in recent decades, whereby brand companies and even component companies have outsourced an increasing range of functions associated with the production of ICT products, with the range increasing in sophistication and complexity. Globalization facilitated the emergence of innovation in outlying regions, creating a global innovation network (GIN) whose development is related to an evolving territorial innovation system (TIS) in which Cross Straits regions, including Taiwan to Mainland China and also South Korea, are playing an increasingly important role (Cooke, 2013b). This evolution has, in turn, forced EMSs to increase their capabilities to the point of being capable of developing their own brands in the process, but then having to face intense competition from their former client companies. To a large extent, the outsourcing model was driven by the desire to reduce the cost of production of ICT hardware because of the increasingly low margins that characterize this sector. But in the process of its evolution, this outsourcing model, with its offshoring to ever more competitive locations, has resulted in major clusters of ICT production in key Chinese locations, which have developed the capabilities of being able to respond rapidly and on a large scale to quickly changing requirements of major brand companies that exercise control over the GVC.

Some researchers have warned of the 'modularity trap' that can face late-developing regions with contract manufacturers being forced to buy highly modular design solutions from companies that are platform leaders, leaving them trapped in the low value segments of the GVC (Sturgeon and Kawakami, 2011). One argument which is somewhat more radical than others, suggests that the Western dominance of the older GVC/GPN model has ended, making it possible for growing an Asian innovation to become more influential in shaping future developments (Cooke, 2013a). According to this view, the new GIN has displaced the preceding GPN associated with traditional desktop PC and laptop production, which had been a successor to a Western multinational-dominated global value chain. The West, however, retains the leading edge in software, systems, services and 'apps', but Asia Pacific dominates hardware, and in Taiwan, South Korea and China, hardware engineering and design were the main innovative applications being exploited.

Somewhat controversially, Cooke (2013a) argues that the increasing significance of innovation, and particularly innovation from Asia, in the more recent stages of the ICT GVC's evolution, heralds the end of a brief period of Western dominance of ICT innovation. Although much of the innovation, technological leadership and market dominance remains within major Western companies, because these companies and their many thousands of suppliers have outsourced and offshored so much of the manufacturing and assembly to Asia in recent decades, the center of gravity of that part of the value chain has shifted eastward. This eastward shift of manufacturing, and China's increased participation in that activity, is the focus of this book. The question arises, however, about the extent to which this increased participation has benefited China, and the extent to which Chinese companies have moved up the value chain.

Micro

At the micro-scale, it is valuable to know a nation's role in the global value chain or supply chain of a specific firm. This book focuses on Apple's supply chain, which is ranked as the best supply chain in the world.[1] Apple is an American multinational technology company headquartered in California that designs, develops and sells consumer electronics, computer software and online services. Its hardware products include the iPhone smartphone, the iPad tablet computer, the Mac personal computer, the iPod portable media player, the Apple Watch smartwatch and the Apple TV digital media player. In a nutshell, Apple purchases components and materials from various suppliers, then gets them shipped to the assembling plant in China. From there, products are shipped directly to consumers who buy them from Apple's Online Store.

Governance, which is seen as a top-down process, is one of the building blocks of the global value chain framework, and it explores how lead companies with a strong market presence exercise power in the coordination of supplier companies within the GVC (Gereffi et al., 2005). Based on Gereffi et al.'s (2005) classification, when the ability to codify – in the form of detailed instructions – and the complexity of product specifications are both high but supplier capabilities are low, then value chain governance will tend toward the captive type. In this sense, Apple's global value chain is a captive value chain. In Apple's case, the suppliers' low competence and Apple's specifications for the production of complex products such as the iPhone encourages the build-up of transactional dependence. Apple seeks to lock-in suppliers because of significant switching costs and monopoly benefits. Captive suppliers are frequently confined to a narrow range of tasks – for example, mainly engaged in simple assembly – and are dependent on Apple for complementary activities such as design, logistics, component purchasing and process technology upgrading.

As mentioned above, the smile curve of value creation within a firm's value/supply chain is similar to the curve in the ICT sector. Activities within a firm's value chain can be broadly grouped into three categories: the upstream (input) end, the downstream (output or market) end and the middle (manufacturing) (Mudambi, 2008). Activities at the upstream end generally comprise design, basic and applied research and the commercialization of creative endeavors. Activities at the downstream end typically comprise marketing, advertising and brand management and after-sales services. Activities in the middle comprise manufacturing, standardized service delivery and other repetitious processes in which commercialized prototypes are implemented on a mass scale.

The global geography of economic activity is influenced by how a firm organizes and controls various parts of the value chain and where it locates different activities (Mudambi, 2008). Lead firms that control the higher ends of the value chain strip out standardized activities to be offshored and maintain their market leadership through high levels of R&D and innovation. Higher value-added activities at both ends of the value chain are usually concentrated in more advanced regions, while those in the middle dealing mainly with production and assembly tend to be in emerging market locations.

Firms in emerging markets are gradually catching up in their competencies, and firms from advanced markets are contributing to spillovers through relocating advanced activities in lower cost locations to benefit from their comparative advantage, while a wider dispersal of functions is creating opportunities for developing value in these locations (Xu and Sheng, 2012). While scholars have pointed to the benefits for emerging economies from integration in GVCs, they also highlight the pitfalls of the low value-added modularity trap, with Sturgeon and Kawakami (2011) suggesting that by 2010 China's handset sector had already fallen into this trap because of its high dependence on external sources of technology. Over time, firms which carry out these lower value-added functions seek to move up the value chain by developing their own brands and marketing expertise.

In Apple's case, by decoupling intangible and tangible functions, it exercises control over R&D intensive activities at one end of the chain and marketing and brand activities at the other end, while outsourcing manufacturing, assembly and testing, and exercising considerable control in coordinating the value chain (Mudambi, 2008). Figure 2.3 illustrates the smile curve of Apple's global value chain, with a range of core, non-core and assembly-related functions disaggregated at different points in the curve and in different global locations. With much of the outsourcing and offshoring involving a significant shift in the locus of production to Asia, and particularly to China, this framework also pays attention to the upgrading challenges facing late-developing countries both in terms of their firms and their technology sector.

The more recent stage of Apple's evolution, particularly with products like the iPhone, suggests a much more sophisticated level of activity between supplier companies and their brand clients than that depicted by the more basic level of activity associated with the earlier production of computer peripherals by Taiwanese supplier companies to their major clients in locations like Dongguan (Cooke, 2013b; Yang, 2007). An increasing number of supplier companies from China, as opposed to the U.S. and Europe, were being used by Apple with each iteration of its iconic products. By tracking the ecosystem developed by Apple in China, this book seeks to evaluate the extent to which Chinese companies have succeeded in

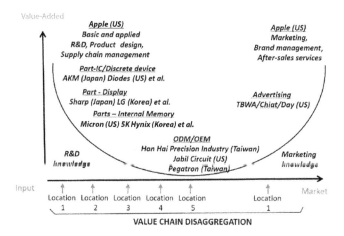

Figure 2.3 Apple's smile curve and GVC (Mudambi, 2007, 2008; Sun and Grimes, 2016)

upgrading their involvement in Apple's supply chain. While Apple is only one of many global technology companies with a significant involvement in East Asia's and particularly China's ICT GVC, it is particularly suitable as a case study for understanding how such companies from more developed regions exploit the comparative advantages of China and the implications for this exploitation for China's own developing ICT sector.

Apple is a leading technology company with an extensive global supply chain consisting in 2015 of 198 companies, many of which are also major global technology companies, whose 759 subsidiaries are involved in supplying Apple with components, or like Foxconn, are primarily involved in assembly of products. 336 of these subsidiaries are located in China and another 115 are in Taiwan, with only 84 located either in Europe or the U.S. Apple's iPad suppliers show that 82 percent of 748 suppliers were in Asia, with 351 in China and with final assembly in 17 plants in 2011 (Clelland, 2014). The network of suppliers included one assembly firm, 20 manufacturers and sub-assemblers of major components, producers of subcomponents used to manufacturer components, subcontractors to these material producers, firms that extracted processed raw materials, and ancillary inputs into production and management processes. While being headquartered in the U.S., Europe, South Korea, Taiwan, Japan and Singapore, the lead suppliers outsourced most of the manufacturing to China.

Hence Apple's global supply chain provides an excellent case study of both the global spread and the major concentrations of supplier companies in China. In the context of China, the power exercised by a lead company may be partly constrained by state policies in relation to foreign investors (Cooke, 2013a). Within the far-flung value chains, facilitated by modularization in electronics, lead companies set performance criteria in areas of price, quality, speed of response and delivery standards for their suppliers. Partly helped by an increasing number of acquisitions, Apple and other companies have been involved in more complex technological convergence than in earlier stages, involving the integration of 'wireless communication, powerful processors, optical systems, music, video, software apps, flat panel display, touchscreens and the various systems controls to implement interactions among these' (Cooke, 2013c, 1331).

Although the center of gravity of innovation, technological leadership and market dominance remains among major Western companies, because these companies and their many thousands of suppliers have increasingly outsourced and offshored the manufacturing and assembly of products to Asia in recent decades, the center of gravity of that part of the value chain has shifted eastward. It is this eastward shift of manufacturing and the increased participation of China in that activity that is the focus of this book. The question arises, however, about the extent to which this increased participation has benefited China and the extent to which Chinese companies have moved further up the value chain.

Note

1 According to Gartner's ranking, www.gartner.com.

References

Antràs, P. and Helpman, E., 2004, 'Global sourcing', *Journal of Political Economy*, 112(3), 552–580.

Autor, D.H., Dorn, D. and Hanson, G.H., 2016, 'The China shock: Learning from labour-market adjustment to large changes in trade', *Annual Review of Economics*, 8, 205–240.

Balassa, B., 1965, 'Trade liberalisation and "revealed" comparative advantage1', *The Manchester School*, 33(2), 99–123.

Baldwin, R., 2017, *The Great Convergence: Information Technology and the New Globalization*, Cambridge, Belknap Press.

Barney, J., 1991, 'Firm resources and sustained competitive advantage', *Journal of Management*, 17, 99–120.

Chandler, A., 1962, *Strategy and Structure*, Cambridge, MA, MIT Press.

Clelland, D., 2014, 'The core of the Apple: Dark value and degrees of monopoly in global commodity chains', *Journal of World-Systems Research*, 20(1), 82–111.

Coe, N.M., Dicken, P. and Hess, M., 2008, 'Global production networks: Realising the potential', *Journal of Economic Geography*, 8, 271–295.

The Conference Board, 2016, 'Total economy database™', Available at www.conference-board.org/data/economydatabase/. Accessed 06/24/2017.

Cooke, P., 2013a, 'Qualitative analysis and comparison of firm and system incumbents in the new ICT global innovation network', *European Planning Studies*, 21(9), 1323–1340.

Cooke, P., 2013b, 'Global production networks and global innovation networks: Stability versus growth', *European Planning Studies*, 21(7), 1081–1094.

Cooke, P., 2013c, 'The ICT-led model of economic evolution in global innovation networks: ICT and eco-innovation as qualitative comparison', In P. Cooke, G.

Searle, K. and O'Connor, ed. *The Economic Geography of the IT Industry in the Asia Pacific Region*, Oxon, Routledge.

Cruz, J., Koopman, R., Wang, Z. and Wei, S., 2011, 'Estimating foreign value-added in Mexico's manufacturing exports', Available at www.usitc.gov/research_and_analysis/documents/Mexico-DVA__Jan5_2011.pdf. Accessed 11/24/2016.

Daudin, G., Rifflart, C. and Schweisguth, D., 2011, 'Who produces for whom in the world economy?' *Canadian Journal of Economics*, 44(4), 1409–1538.

Dixit, A. and Norman, V., 1980, *Theory of International Trade: A Dual, General Equilibrium Approach*, Cambridge, Cambridge University Press.

Dollar, D. and Wolff, N.E., 1993, *Competitiveness, Convergence and International Specialization*, Cambridge, MA, MIT Press.

Dunning, J.H., 1981, 'Explaining the international direct investment position of countries: Toward a dynamic and development approach', *Weltwirtschaftliches Archiv*, 117(5), 30–64.

Dunning, J.H., 2003, 'The eclectic (OLI) paradigm of international production', In J. Cantwell and R. Narula, ed. *International Business and the Electric Paradigm*, London, Routledge, 25–51.

The Economist, 2012, 'IPadded', Available at www.economist.com/node/21543174. Accessed 01/21/2012.

Eden, L. and Dai, L., 2010, 'Rethinking the O in dunning's OLI/eclectic paradigm', *Multinational Business Review*, 18(2), 13–34.

Egan, M.L. and Mody, A., 1992, 'Buyer-seller links in export development', *World Development*, 20, 321–334.

Foss, K. and Foss, N.J., 2005, 'Resources and transaction costs: How property rights economics furthers the resource-based view', *Strategic Management Journal*, 26(6), 541–553.

Freeman, C., 2004, 'Technological infrastructure and international competitiveness', *Industrial and Corporate Change Volume*, 13(3), 541–569.

Froud, J., Sukhdev, J., Leaver, A. and Williams, K., 2014, 'Financialization across the Pacific: Manufacturing cost ratios, supply chains and power', *Critical Perspectives on Accounting*, 25(1), 46–57.

Furman, J.L. and Hayes, R., 2004, 'Catching up or standing still? National innovative capacity among "follower" countries, 1978–1999', *Research Policy*, 33(9), 1329–1354.

Furman, J.L., Porter, M.E. and Stern, S., 2002, 'The determinants of national innovative capacity', *Research Policy*, 31(6), 899–933.

Gereffi, G., 1994, 'The organisation of buyer-driven global commodity chains: How US retailers shape overseas production networks', In G. Gereffi and M. Korzeniewicz, ed. *Commodity Chains and Global Capitalism*, Westport, CT, Praeger.

Gereffi, G., 1995, 'Global production systems and third world development', In B. Stallings, ed. *Global Change, Regional Response: The New International Context of Development*, Cambridge, Cambridge University Press, 100–142.

Gereffi, G., 1999, 'International trade and industrial upgrading in the apparel commodity chain', *Journal of International Economics*, 48(1), 37–70.

Gereffi, G., 2014, 'Global value chains in a post-Washington Consensus world', *Review of International Political Economy*, 21(1), 9–37.

Gereffi, G., Humphrey, J. and Sturgeon, T., 2005, 'The governance of global value chains', *Review of International Political Economy*, 12(1), 78–104.

Gurría, A., 2013, *The Emergence of Global Value Chains: What Do They Mean for Business, G20 Trade and Investment Promotion Summit*, Mexico City, OECD.

Hamel, G. and Prahalad, C.K., 1994, *Competing for the Future*, Boston, MA, Harvard Business School Press.

Hart, S.L., 1995, 'A natural-resource-based view of the firm', *Academy of Management Review*, 20(4), 986–1014.

Hatsopoulos, G., Krugman, P. and Summers, L., 1988, 'U.S. competitiveness: Beyond the trade deficit', *Science*, 241, 299–307.

Helpman, E., Melitz, M. and Yeaple, S., 2004, 'Export versus FDI with heterogeneous firms', *American Economic Review*, 94(1), 300–316.

Hu, M.C. and Mathews, J.A., 2005, 'National innovation capacity in East Asia', *Research Policy*, 34(9), 1322–1349.

Hu, M.C. and Mathews, J.A., 2008, 'China's national innovative capacity', *Research Policy*, 37(9), 1465–1479.

Hummels, D., Ishii, J. and Yi, K., 2001, 'The nature and growth of vertical specialization in world trade', *Journal of International Economics*, 54, 75–96.

Humphrey, J. and Schmitz, H., 2002, 'How does insertion in global value chains affect upgrading in industrial clusters?' *Regional Studies*, 36(9), 1017–1027.

IMF, 2013, 'Trade Interconnectedness: The world with global value chains', Available at www.imf.org/external/np/pp/eng/2013/082613.pdf. Accessed 06/24/2017.

International Monetary Fund, 2000, 'Globalization: Threats or opportunity', Available at www.imf.org/external/np/exr/ib/2000/041200to.htm. Accessed 11/24/2016.

James, P. and Steger, M.B., 2014, 'A genealogy of globalization: The career of a concept', *Globalizations*, 11(4), 417–434.

Johnson, R. and Noguera, G., 2012, 'Accounting for Intermediates: Production Sharing and Trade in Value-added', *Journal of International Economics*, 86(2012), 224–236.

Joshi, R.M., 2009, *International Business*, New Delhi and New York, Oxford University Press.

Kee, H.L. and Tang, H., 2013, *Domestic Value Added in Chinese Exports: Firm-Level Evidence*, Johns Hopkins University, Baltimore, MD, mimeo.

Koopman, R., Wang, Z. and Wei, S., 2012, 'Estimating domestic content in exports when processing trade is pervasive', *Journal of Development Economics*, 99(2012), 178–189.

Koopman, R., Wang, Z. and Wei, S.J., 2014, 'Tracing value-added and double counting in gross exports', *The American Economic Review*, 104(2), 459–494.

Kraaijenbrink, J., Spender, J.C. and Groen, A.J., 2010, 'The resource-based view: A review and assessment of its critiques', *Journal of Management*, 36(1), 349–372.

Krugman, P., 1994, 'Competitiveness: A dangerous obsession', *Foreign Affairs*, 73(2), 28–44.

Kuada, J. and Sorensen, O.J., 2000, *Internationalization of Companies From Developing Countries*, Binghampton, International Business Press.

Leontief, W., 1953, 'Domestic production and foreign trade: The American capital position re-examined', *Proceedings of the American Philosophical Society*, 97(4), 332–349.

Ma, H., Wang, Z. and Zhu, K., 2015, 'Domestic content in China's exports and its distribution by firm ownership', *Journal of Comparative Economics*, 43(1), 3–18.

Maneschi, A., 1998, *Comparative Advantage in International Trade: A Historical Perspective*, Cheltenham, Edward Elgar Publishing.

Markusen, J.R., 1992, *Productivity, Competitiveness, Trade Performance and Real Income: The Nexus Among Four Concepts*, Ottawa, Canada, Minister of Supply and Services.

McKinsey & Company, 2014, 'China's digital transformation: The internet's impact on productivity and growth', Available at www.mckinsey.com/industries/high-tech/our-insights/chinas-digital-transformation.

McKinsey & Company, 2016, 'China's choice: Capturing the $5 trillion productivity opportunity', Available at www.mckinsey.com/global-themes/employment-and-growth/capturing-chinas-5-trillion-productivity-opportunity

Mudambi, R., 2007, 'Offshoring: Economic geography and the multinational firm', *Journal of International Business Studies*, 38(1), 206.

Mudambi, R., 2008, 'Location, control and innovation in innovation intensive industries', *Journal of Economic Geography*, 8, 699–725.

Nason, R.S. and Wiklund, J., 2015, 'An assessment of resource-based theorizing on firm growth and suggestions for the future', *Journal of Management*, 14, 33–46. 0149206315610635.

OECD, 1978, 'The international competitiveness of selected OECD countries', In *OECD Economic Outlook, Occasional Studies*, July.

OECD, 1997, *National Innovation System*, Paris, OECD.

OECD, 2003, *ICT and Economic Growth: Evidence From OECD Countries, Industries and Firms*, Paris, OECD.

OECD, 2013, *Interconnected Economies: Benefiting From Global Value Chains*, Paris, OECD.

Oral, M., 1993, 'A methodology for competitiveness analysis and strategy formulation in glass industry', *European Journal of Operational Research*, 68(1), 9–22.

Penrose, E., 1959, *The Theory of the Growth of the Firm*, New York, Wiley-Blackwell.

Porter, M.E., 1985, *Competitive Advantage: Creating and Sustaining Superior Performance*, New York, The Free Press.

Porter, M.E., 1990, 'The competitive advantage of Nations', *Harvard Business Review*.

Posner, M.V., 1961, 'International trade and technical change', *Oxford Economic Papers*, 13(3), 323–341.

Qiu, L.D. and Tao, Z., 2001, 'Export, foreign direct investment, and local content requirement', *Journal of Development Economics*, 66(1), 101–125.

Siggel, E., 2006, 'International competitiveness and comparative advantage: A survey and a proposal for measurement', *Journal of Industry, Competition and Trade*, 6(2), 137–159.

Smith, A., 1776, *An Inquiry into the Nature and Causes of the Wealth of Nations* (1904 ed.), London, Library of Economics and Liberty.

Soete, L.L.G., 1981, 'A general test of technological gap trade theory', *Review of World Economics*, 117(4), 638–660.

Sturgeon, T.J., 2008, 'From commodity chains to value chains: Interdisciplinary theory building in an age of globalization', In J. Bair, ed. *Frontiers of Commodity Chain Research*, Stanford, CA, Stanford University Press.

Sturgeon, T.J. and Gereffi, G., 2009, 'Measuring success in the global economy: International trade, industrial upgrading, and business function outsourcing in global value chains', *Transnational Corporations*, 18(2), 1–35.

Sturgeon, T.J. and Kawakami, M., 2011, 'Global value chains in the electronics industry: Characteristics, crisis, and upgrading opportunities in firms from developing countries', *International Journal of Technological Learning Innovation and Development*, 4(1–3), 120–147.

Sun, Y. and Grimes, S., 2016, 'The emerging dynamic structure of national innovation studies: A bibliometric analysis', *Scientometrics*, 106(1), 17–40.

Sun, Y. and Liu, F., 2010, 'A regional perspective on the structural transformation of China's national innovation system since 1999', *Technological Forecasting and Social Change*, 77(8), 1311–1321.

Sun, Y. and Liu, F., 2013, 'Measuring international trade-related technology spillover: A composite approach of network analysis and information theory', *Scientometrics*, 94(3), 963–979.

Svetličič, M., 2003, 'Theoretical context of outward foreign direct investment from transition economies', In M. Svetličič and M. Rojec, ed. *Facilitating Transition by Internationalization: Outward Direct Investment From European Economies in Transition*, Aldershot, Ashgate, 3–28.

UNCTAD, 2013, 'World investment report 2013: Global value chains: Investment and trade for development', Available at www.cggc.duke.edu/pdfs/2013_UNCTAD_WIR_GVCs_and_Development.pdf. Accessed 11/24/2016.

Upward, R., Wang, Z. and Zheng, J., 2013, 'Weighing China's export Basket: The domestic content and technology intensity of Chinese exports', *Journal of Comparative Economics*, 41(2), 527–543.

Von Zedtwitz, M. and Gassmann, O., 2002, 'Market versus technology drive in R&D Internationalisation: Four different patterns of managing research and development', *Research Policy*, 31(4), 569–588.

WEF, 2016, 'The world competitiveness report 2015–2016', Available at www3.weforum.org/docs/gcr/2015   2016/Global_Competitiveness_Report_2015–2016.pdf. Accessed 11/24/2016.

Xing, Y., 2016, 'Global value chains and China's exports to high-income countries', *International Economic Journal*, 30(2), 191–203.

Xing, Y. and Detert, N., 2011, 'How the iPhone widens the United States trade deficit with the people's republic of China', *ADB Working Paper*, 257.

Xu, X. and Sheng, Y., 2012, 'Productivity spillovers from foreign direct investment: Firm-level evidence from China', *World Development*, 40(1), 62–74.

Yang, C., 2007, 'Divergent hybrid capitalisms in China: Hong Kong and Taiwanese electronics clusters in Dongguan', *Economic Geography*, 83(4), 395–420.

Yeung, H.W-C. and Coe, N., 2015, 'Toward a dynamic theory of global production networks', *Economic Geography*, 91(1), 29–58.

3 China's dependence on foreign technology in the GVC

A macro view

This chapter examines the ongoing high level of dependency of China's economy on foreign sources of technology since accession to the WTO in 2001. Although China's economic activity has become integrated within the global value chains of major corporations helped by international activities, like FDI, and exporting since the reform and opening and particularly with accession to the WTO, it continues to play a subordinate role in GVCs. This dependence is a major cause of concern for China's leaders and policymakers, and they have sought to shift the direction of the economy, particularly since 2006, toward a greater focus on indigenous innovation. Both foreign and Chinese companies contribute to growth in these two components of the industrial system within a policy framework which seeks to promote greater value-added through indigenous innovation. The evidence to date, however, suggests that Chinese companies have only achieved a modest level of success to date in displacing the ongoing dominant position of foreign companies particularly in China's high-technology sectors. Some progress has been made, however, in the private sector's share of economic activity in contrast to the declining share of state owned enterprises (SOEs).

Introduction

Despite its impressive growth rate since its opening to the world economy nearly 40 years ago, China's economy is still transitioning toward some hybrid form of market or mixed ownership economy. Among the major developments that have marked this transition was China's accession to the WTO in December 2001, which led to deep structural changes that are at the core of its transformation toward a modern market-based economy.

As a latecomer to technology development, China faces major challenges in catching up with more developed regions which tend to dominate the trajectory of technology development. China emerged as a major location for international investment by MNCs and has competed for international investment and developed specific specializations particularly in production and assembly. In 2006, China pledged the end of the five-year schedule of market opening measures as the price of admission to the WTO and began a significant industrial policy reorientation toward 'indigenous innovation'. China's adjustment to the global downturn in the 2008 international financial crisis was helped by a state stimulus package of $586 billion. While the stimulus package helped the economy do better than expected in the short-term, it was inevitable that China's economy would shift to a lower gear in the mid-and long-term because its development model had outlived its usefulness. The crucial challenge, therefore, is transitioning this development model.

During this transition, a major shift in state policy has sought to re-focus the thrust of the economy from a low-cost manufacturing model based on export processing to a more sustainable model associated with higher value-added activity. Breznitz and Murphree (2011) note that while China may be weak in novel-product innovation, it excels in incremental innovation by adapting existing technologies to the local market. With China's ongoing dependence on foreign technology and its weak indigenous innovation, some wonder whether a transition economy in the context of globalization can be successful in adopting an indigenous innovation strategy, and whether its domestic market can be sufficient to support such an inward looking strategy (Liu and Cheng, 2011). Meanwhile, China needs to shift from a saving and investing to a consuming society, with domestic consumers replacing those in other countries as the financial crisis abates.

Among some of the interrelated features associated with China's recent economic transformation is the dominant role of FDI, particularly in export processing and in high-tech sectors, the rapid ageing and decline in the labor force associated with China's very low fertility rate, partly influenced by its one-child policy, and the huge environmental challenges resulting from the rapid pace of economic growth. Innovation-driven development is one important option which would help China tackle these challenges. However, China's innovation capability is weak when facing the international competition in the age of globalization. On the other hand, Jiang et al. (2016) suggest that Chinese firms participating in a global production network can make an important contribution to indigenous innovation through learning by doing. Global competition can also promote the innovative competence of Chinese enterprises in the absence of policy protection.

The main thrust of this chapter will focus on the implications of China's ongoing high level of dependence on foreign sources of technology, as reflected in the significant role of foreign investors in China's high-technology exports, despite the determination of China's policymakers to reduce this dependence by promoting indigenous innovation. In the context of this policy concern, the chapter will examine the extent to which Chinese companies have progressed, particularly in relation to their involvement in China's high-technology trade. Some reference will also be made to the growing competition within China's domestic economy between Chinese and foreign companies. With China's evolving role within the GVCs of leading technology corporations, an overall upgrading of China's industrial profile has been under way.

Methodology and data

As mentioned in the theoretical section, while much of the analysis to date on China's evolving economic development has focused on trade theory, making use of trade statistics to examine the relationship between trade patterns and economic development; such an analysis within an era of increasingly globalized economic activity has limitations (Karabell, 2009; Sturgeon and Gereffi, 2009).

The global value chain is increasingly used by researchers and policymakers as an effective conceptual framework in which to analyze the implications of fragmented production for particular regions and countries. This can help to avoid the exaggerated evaluation of gains to a particular economy by an uncritical examination of trade data, which is particularly relevant in the case of China, whose key role in many value chains is a somewhat subordinate one as a low-cost assembly location of components imported from other countries. Xing and Detert (2010) note that conventional trade statistics are not consistent with trade where global production networks and production fragmentation determine cross-country flows of parts, components and final production. Using the 'direct value-added exports' indicator, which evaluates the added value to particular countries of their exports, Horn et al. (2010) found that China's export sector contributed 19 to 33 percent of total GDP growth between 2002 and 2008, which was only half of the export contribution indicated by traditional total export measures. Thus, this chapter pays particular attention to the quality of traded goods and the share of indigenous content reflecting the local value-added.

In seeking to determine the extent to which Chinese companies have evolved technologically during China's recent period of rapid economic growth, the approach taken in this chapter is to exploit both trade data and company interviews, which provide the opportunity to consider the evolving role of different company types in trade and also in the domestic market. The need to consider both the trade activity and the domestic economy relates to how economic activity has evolved during recent decades with a greater focus on export-led growth initially and the more recent involvement of both foreign and Chinese companies in the domestic economy.

The success of Chinese companies in the domestic market is 'the synchronisation of China's export upgrading and domestic market growth, rather than export alone' (Zhou, 2008, 2354). An unusual feature of China's development has been the rare combination of a very large domestic market with a high level of FDI that is focused on this domestic market (Brandt and Thun, 2010). The tendency in many studies of China's economic development to date has been to adopt an either/or approach: to either focus on trade or on the domestic economy, rather than on interactions between both; or to focus on either foreign or Chinese companies while not paying attention to the many interactions between them. Recent reality in China is more complex, with a range of interactions between different sectors of the economy and between different types of companies.

Two limitations apply to Chinese data relating to foreign investment. Although China was the primary global exporter of high-tech products in 2012, most of these exports were derived from FIEs rather than Chinese firms (Xing, 2011). The second issue is that perhaps up to 50 percent of FIEs investment relates to 'round tripping' investment by Chinese companies seeking benefits awarded to foreign investors in China or seeking an overseas stock market listing, which is not reflected in official statistics (Sharman, 2012; Vlcek, 2010; Xiao, 2004).

Although it is essential to distinguish firm ownership as clearly as possible in order to evaluate the success or otherwise of the new indigenous innovation policy, the complexity of clarifying investment relationships between firms within a globalized economy has become very challenging. The two main shareholders of the highly successful Chinese e-commerce firm, Alibaba, for example, are Softbank with 31.8 percent and Yahoo with 15.3 percent of shares in 2015. Ever since the Chinese company, Geely bought Volvo from the Ford Motor Company in 2010, Volvo is officially defined as a foreign company under Swedish law and is treated as a foreign company in China. Because of the significant complications of deciphering the ownership structure of a large number of firms, use will be made of data relating to the top 200 exporting companies and in greater detail to the top 20 exporting companies for 2001 and 2012. These data provide insights into the changing profile of China's exports generally, and particularly those from the high-tech sector, while also giving some insight into the issue of 'round tripping'. This annually published listing of China's top exporting firms allows us to distinguish between different company types in terms of ownership, sector and volume of exports.

In order to delve further into the relationship between foreign companies and the Chinese state within the context of the relatively new indigenous innovation policy, around 100 hours of interviewing was completed with the senior management of foreign multinationals in Shanghai during a number of visits between 2009 and 2017. In a few cases, the same companies were interviewed more than once, which provided insights into developments and views over time. While a wide range of sectors were involved in keeping with the multinational company profile in Shanghai, the main focus of the case studies used in this chapter is on U.S. and European technology companies, who play a dominant role as innovators in technology sectors. In some cases the companies were involved in a range of sectors, including ICT, energy, medical equipment and transport equipment. Most of the companies are major global corporations and many have R&D centers in China.

China's subordinate role in GVCs

China's economic take-off since the late 1970s owes much to its integration in global trade networks and global value chains (OECD, 2012, 54). China's involvement in GVCs reflects its increasing dependence on imported raw materials, parts and components, and services to meet the export demand for a wide range of final capital and consumer goods. Regarding its role in GVCs, the primary impression is that China only contributes and captures low value within the GVC. Since a large part of GVC value-added in developing countries is generated by affiliates of MNCs, the contribution to local GDP can be limited because of low 'value capture'. Manufacturing of the iPhone 4 provides a stark example of such low value capture: after importing key components from various countries including the U.S., Germany, Japan and Korea, China added only $6.54 of the $194.04 factory gate price of the product it exported (De Backer, 2011).

This is the case in a country like China, which has attracted significant offshore production FDI but acts mainly in a low position within global value chains as an assembler of increasingly sophisticated products. While China's participation in GVCs has played a significant role in developing its huge processing sector in recent decades, the low value-added accruing to China, together with issues such as technology dissemination, skill-building and overall industrial upgrading, have been major factors in driving China's more recent development in industrial policy toward indigenous innovation.

Attracting FDI to China

In the early stages of China's integration into the world economy after the reform and opening-up policy, it had little choice but to rely heavily on attracting FDI because China's economic growth needed investment and technology. China became hugely successful in attracting FDI, becoming one of the most significant locations for such investment, with much of it coming from neighboring countries in East Asia offshoring more basic tasks to China as they moved further up the value chain. Neighboring Asian economies, including Japan, South Korea, Hong Kong and Taiwan exploited the low-cost advantages of China to which they offshored assembly functions. All of these neighboring Asian countries have become major sources of foreign investment in China, developing strong value chain linkages with the mainland.

The integration of Taiwan's electronics sector with the Chinese mainland has been particularly impressive, with Taiwanese companies playing a key role in China's electronics sector (Saxenian, 2007). Computer manufacturing is dominated by Taiwanese companies and suppliers who control this part of the supply chain from Mainland China (Hart-Landsberg, 2011). In a detailed analysis of patents in China, Boeing and Sandner (2011) found that two-thirds of a sample of intermediate value class patents were accounted for by foreign firms, but with 78 percent coming from Taiwanese firms like the huge Taiwanese contract manufacturer Foxconn, with access to a global R&D and production network in Europe, North America and Asia.

Initially much of the investment came to develop the export processing sector in what was a low-cost location with a plentiful labor supply. Because its opening-up coincided with the increased internationalization of supply chains, China rapidly became interconnected with assembly activity in Asia and grew at an impressive rate. This was facilitated by the offshoring of production by large multinational companies seeking lower cost locations, together with Chinese state policy promoting export processing by generous tax breaks. Associated with this role has been its significant dependence on foreign technology sources and on foreign markets, as multinational corporations offshored their mainly low value-added assembly activities to China while retaining the higher value-added functions in more developed regions.

Over time, however, the factors underlying China's comparative advantage for FDI have evolved, with a much greater focus by many more recent investments on the domestic market. While still important, FDI is no longer an increasing contributor to China's industrial output, fixed investment and tax revenues (OECD, 2012, 54). State policy toward FDI has also evolved, and since 2006, China has become much more selective about the type of FDI it seeks to attract, partly in response to the relatively disappointing results of the earlier policy of providing market access in exchange for technology transfer (Davies, 2012). Rather than being an important source of employment creation, foreign capital was expected to bring advanced technology and expertise to China (Economist Intelligence Unit, 2012).

With the decline in the labor force, the rapid ageing of the population associated with very low fertility and the rising cost of labor, some economists have pointed to China's passing the Lewis Curve, resulting in a decline in surplus rural labor which was so plentiful in earlier decades (Cai, 2010; Eberstadt, 2012). The global downturn in recent years did not affect China as severely as other regions during the earlier stages (2008–2011), partly because of the huge state stimulus package. After 2011, because of excess production capability generated by the stimulus package, with the continuous appreciation of the Chinese RMB and the recession in export markets, China's export-led growth model faced considerable challenges.

According to the World Investment Report 2016 (UNCTAD, 2016), Hong Kong (China) and Mainland China ranked second and third as host economies for FDI inflows in 2015, just after the U.S. Developing Asia, with FDI inflows reaching $541 billion in 2015 – a 16 percent increase – remained the largest FDI recipient region in the world. The growth was primarily driven by increased FDI in East Asian economies. FDI rose by 25 percent to $322 billion in 2015, reflecting large equity investments related to a corporate restructuring in Hong Kong and dynamic FDI flows to China's services sector. MNCs have provided China with FDI over many decades to support manufacturing joint ventures, and consequently exports from China quickly emerged as an important competitive threat to Western manufacturers.

All of these developments, however, have been characterized by strategic attempts to locate key intellectual property (IP) activities in their home countries. When Japanese companies, who were among the first to offshore to China in the 1990s, began establishing R&D centers there, they sought to retain their most advanced technologies locked away from Chinese competitors (Segal, 2011). More recently significant FDI linkages have been forged with the U.S. and Europe, with increasing integration of both trade and global production networks between these regions. While this pattern of development associated with global integration follows similar trends in other regions, it appears that China presents particular challenges to the protection of intellectual property by global corporations, and with its more recent determined policy push for indigenous innovation, it presents a more threatening environment to lead technology corporations despite its relative openness to date toward FDI.

Besides FDI inflows, China is increasingly becoming a large investor. Against the general downward trend in FDI outflows from developing and transition economies, China was a notable exception: its outward FDI remained high, rising from $123 billion to $128 billion in 2015, as a result of which it held its position as the third largest investor in the world (UNCTAD, 2016). The research evidence demonstrated that China's pattern of FDI outflow is largely consistent with the Investment Development Path (IDP) hypothesis, and there is no apparent need to cite China's institutions and unique path to economic reform as having a direct influence on FDI outflows (Liu et al., 2005). Certainly, reforms have contributed to economic development itself, such as the growth of GDP per capita, investments in human capital, exports and inward FDI. These are all influences on FDI outflows, and institutions, location, networks and so on, and thus will have an indirect impact on OFDI through per capita GDP. Although Chinese FDI outflow now represents a massive new business threat to Western firms, only 5.9 percent of it has been in the manufacturing sector (Ministry of Commerce et al., 2015).

Value-added in exports to the word

China's exports have seen a rapid growth since the reform and open-door policy. In the late 1990s, export processing was particularly encouraged, but in 2000, the quota for mandatory exports to which wholly-owned foreign enterprises were subject was removed as part of the preparations for WTO entry (Economist Intelligence Unit, 2012). Obviously, WTO entry is an important divide for China's international trade, particularly exports. An examination of export performance before and after the entry into the WTO reveals an average growth rate of about 16 percent before the WTO, and an average growth rate around 30 percent after the WTO until the 2008 international financial crisis. However, the quality of these exports is a more important question both for innovation and value-added.

The empirical research indicates that Chinese manufacturing exports were concentrated in the low quality products, and the share of high quality products was relatively low (Table 3.1). Low quality product exports were the primary driving force of rapid export growth since the reform and opening-up policy.

Table 3.1 Exports of Chinese manufactured products by quality (percent)

Year	Before the accession to WTO			After the accession to WTO		
	1995	1998	2001	2002	2006	2010
High quality	3.7	4.5	33.6	36.2	14	5.8
Middle quality	9	11.5	16.1	11.2	32.1	31.7
Low quality	87.4	84	50.3	52.6	53.9	62.6

Source: Li et al., (2014)

Note: Export products are divided into three types: high quality product, middle quality and low quality. If the unit value of a product is lower than three-quarters of the world average level, the product can be regarded as a low quality product; if it is higher than five-quarters, the product can be regarded as a high quality product; if it ranges between high and low, the product can be regarded as a middle quality product.

Over time, and before accession to WTO, the quality of Chinese export products experienced considerable improvement. In particular, the share of high quality products increased from 3.7 percent in 1995 to 33.6 percent in 2001. Meanwhile the share of low quality products decreased from 87.04 percent to 50.3 percent, and the share of middle quality products also increased. However, this positive development momentum changed after entry into the WTO. There was a complete reversal in the trends. The share of high quality products dropped sharply, and the share of low quality rose, which suggests that China may have dropped into the 'quality trap'. After WTO accession, China's rapid growth of exports is related to a large number of new exporting enterprises, some of which manufactured low quality products and had lower export competitiveness. The general fall in export quality resulted from the fact that they entered into international markets with low price products.

It is significant to highlight the indigenous value-added (IVA) share of exports. According to estimations comparing rows [1] and [4], we can see that although the direct IVA share for Chinese owned enterprises (COEs) is very close to that for Foreign Invested Enterprises (FIEs) (20.92 versus 18.12), the COEs' total IVA share is larger (75.07 versus 47.13) (Table 3.2). Within each ownership type, the difference between ordinary and processing exports in total IVA share is larger than the difference in direct IVA share. As expected, ordinary exports have a higher indigenous content share compared with processing exports, regardless of the ownership type. COEs have slightly higher total IVA share than FIEs for

Table 3.2 Indigenous and foreign value-added share of China's exports in 2007 (percent)

Total merchandise	Direct IVA	Total IVA	Total FVA
[1] Total exports by COEs	20.92	75.07	24.92
[2] Processing exports by COEs	15.58	35.46	64.52
[3] Ordinary exports by COEs	22.14	84.11	15.89
[4] Total exports by FIEs	18.12	47.13	52.86
[5] Processing exports by FIEs	16.64	37.3	62.7
[6] Ordinary exports by FIEs	23	79.53	20.46
[7] Total gross exports	19.33	59.17	40.82

Source: Ma et al. (2015)

Note: Ma et al.'s (2015) estimation results for the share of indigenous value-added (IVA) and foreign value-added (FVA) in China's processing and ordinary exports by Chinese-owned enterprises (COEs) and foreign-invested enterprises (FIEs) in 2007. The direct IVA is the direct value-added incurred in each sector as income to primary inputs, whereas the total IVA and FVA account for the iterated usage of inputs from other sectors.

ordinary exports, whereas they have slightly lower total IVA share than FIEs for processing exports. The total IVA share of COEs within the same trade mode is very close to that of FIEs. For example, if we compare rows [2] and [5] with processing exporters, the total IVA share for COEs is 35.4, whereas that for FIEs is 37.3. Overall, about 59.2 percent of China's exports are indigenous or have Chinese content, whereas 40.8 percent have foreign content. In 2007, the gross value of China's exports was $1.22 trillion, and thus the gross indigenous content in export was $720 billion.

IVA differs substantially across ownership in certain sectors (Table 3.2). The composition of gross exports and gross domestic content in exports is by firm type. Almost half of the indigenous content is attributed to COEs' ordinary exports, and 4.8 percent of indigenous content is attributed to their processing exports. Thus, COEs contribute only about 55 percent of gross indigenous content in exports with the rest coming from FIEs. While ordinary FIE exports account for about 17.8 percent processing FIEs contribute nearly 27.5 percent.

From 1995 to 2011, Chinese IVA has increased from 66.6 percent to 67.9 percent (Table 3.3). Within this small increase, Chinese IVA sent to a consumer economy decreased from 56.9 percent to 51.3 percent, and IVA sent to third

Table 3.3 The value-added (VA) components of gross exports (percent)

Items	China		US		Japan		Germany		UK	
	1995	2011	1995	2011	1995	2011	1995	2011	1995	2011
IVA sent to consumer economy	56.9	51.3	68.4	59.4	70.4	52.2	63.9	49.4	62.4	52.0
IVA sent to third economies	9.5	15.6	19.4	24.9	23.8	32.8	20.7	24.1	19	24.7
IVA re-imported in the economy	0.2	1.0	0.8	0.7	0.2	0.4	0.6	1	0.3	0.4
Foreign VA content of exports	33.3	32.1	11.4	15	5.6	14.6	14.8	25.5	18.2	22.9

Note: *Indigenous value-added sent to consumer economy* corresponds to the domestic value-added embodied either in final or intermediate goods or services that is directly consumed by the importing economy. *Indigenous value-added sent to third economies* represents the domestic value-added contained in intermediates (goods or services) exported to a first economy that re-exports them to a third economy as embodied in other goods or services. *Indigenous value-added re-imported in the economy* outlines the domestic value-added of exported intermediates, or inputs, that is sent back to the economy of origin as embodied in other intermediates and used to produce exports. *Foreign value-added content of exports* is also referred to as vertical specialization. This indicator corresponds to the value-added of inputs that were imported in order to produce intermediate or final goods/services to be exported.

Source: Trade in value-added and global value chains: statistical profiles www.wto.org/english/res_e/statis_e/miwi_e/countryprofiles_e.htm

economies increased from 9.5 percent to 15.6 percent. This indicates that China increased value-added to intermediate products and reduced value-added to final products. The foreign VA share of exports decreased from 33.3 percent to 32.1 percent. In nearly 20 years, the Chinese IVA share just increased a little: 1.3 percent. Comparatively speaking, the Chinese IVA share 67.9 percent is lower than other countries in 2011, with the U.S. at 85 percent, Japan at 85.4 percent, Germany at 74.5 percent and Japan at 77.1 percent. Due to the globalization of production, the IVA share of all four countries decreased while the foreign VA share increased, with Germany and Japan's IVA share decreasing the most. It is clear, therefore, that China still needs to increase its IVA content of exports.

Value-added in ICT exports

Table 3.4 provides a breakdown of indigenous content from subsectors of ICT in 2007. It is worth noting that the IVA share for most ICT-related sectors are lower than that of total merchandise, with only two other sectors being a little higher. The IVA share of total merchandise is 59.2 percent that is higher than four major industrial sectors. Of these, Electronic component's IVA share is only 31.4 percent. The IVA share for processing exports is much lower than that for ordinary exports in these sectors, and most of China's exports from ICT-related sectors are processing exports rather than ordinary exports. In fact, the processing exports by COEs and FIEs in China result from the assembly of imported

Table 3.4 Decomposition of indigenous value-added by sectors in 2007 (percent)

Selected industry	CP	FP	CN	FN	Total
Electronic component	36.8	21.9	72.8	76.7	31.4
Cultural and office equipment	37.7	27.6	75.2	75.5	33.1
Telecommunication equipment	33.3	33.2	74.7	66.8	39.6
Electronic computer	19.7	42.4	66.2	70.9	42.5
Other electric machinery and equipment	37.8	36.9	79.6	76.9	61.5
Other electronic and communication equipment	61.8	60.8	81.2	72.4	64.4
Total merchandise	35.5	37.3	84.1	79.5	59.2

Source: Ma et al. (2015)

Note: This table gives the decomposition of domestic content by manufacturing sectors. CP means processing exports by COEs; FP means processing exports by FIEs; CN means ordinary exports and domestic sales by COEs (CN); and FN means ordinary exports and domestic sales by FIEs.

parts and components. For example, small and middle-sized Japanese enterprises (SMEs) as suppliers of large electronics companies often moved their assembly plants to China in order to respond to pressures to reduce costs (OECD, 2012, 79). These SMEs export key components to their Chinese plants and re-import the finished products.

Indeed, computer and electronics is the largest export industry in China, but its IVA share is the lowest, at only 45 percent, which is also lower than Japan's 82.8 percent (see Table 3.5). Compared with other major countries, China's IVA share in wholesale and retail trade is higher than that of the U.S. and the UK. By 2008, FIEs in China accounted for 85 percent of processing trade, while they also accounted for 29 percent of ordinary trade, suggesting that in addition to

Table 3.5 Top export industries: domestic and foreign VA content exports in top five economies (2011)

Top five economies		Top three export industries	Percent share in industry total gross exports			Percent share in economy total gross exports	
			IVA	Foreign VA	Total	IVA	Foreign VA
China	1.	Computer and electronic	45.0	55.0	100.0	10.7	13.1
	2.	Wholesale and retail trade	95.9	4.1	100.0	12.6	0.5
	3.	Textiles	73.5	26.5	100.0	7.5	2.7
The US	1.	Wholesale and retail trade	95.3	4.7	100.0	9.1	0.4
	2.	Chemical products	82.0	18.0	100.0	7.1	1.6
	3.	Transport and storage	89.5	10.5	100.0	3.9	0.8
Japan	1.	Wholesale and retail trade	93.8	6.2	100.0	16.3	1.1
	2.	Computer and electronic	82.8	17.2	100.0	12.4	2.6
	3.	Motor vehicles	86.1	13.9	100.0	11.5	1.9
Germany	1.	Motor vehicles	68.6	31.4	100.0	9.9	4.5
	2.	Machinery and equipment	73.3	26.7	100.0	8.4	3.1
	3.	Chemical products	70.4	29.6	100.0	6.9	2.9
UK	1.	Other business services	88.5	11.5	100.0	12.0	1.6
	2.	Financial intermediation	90.7	9.3	100.0	11.1	1.1
	3.	Wholesale and retail trade	87.6	12.4	100.0	8.5	1.2

Source: Trade in value-added and global value chains: statistical profiles www.wto.org/english/res_e/statis_e/miwi_e/countryprofiles_e.htm

their involvement in the assembly of imported inputs, they were also involved in local procurement and other interactions with Chinese industries (OECD, 2012). Thus, while processing trade was mostly due to FIEs, the smaller part due to Chinese companies was shifting from simple contract assembly to 'full-package' manufacturing involving full control of all stages from material procurement to product design. The OECD report also notes in the case of Japanese companies that supply inputs to large electronic companies often relocate their assembly plants to China in order to reduce costs (OECD, 2012, 79).

The outcome for China, however, was little different than that of other world regions in which the operations of global corporations go to significant lengths to retain their intellectual property within the confines of the corporation's boundaries. While China has had some measure of success to date in acquiring technology from foreign companies, whether the policy they have pursed so far has been the most effective one remains open to question. In fact some Chinese scholars have been wondering whether market forces in a globalizing world will allow a transitional economy such as China to succeed with its indigenous innovation policy (Liu and Cheng, 2011). All states seek to achieve the highest level of benefit from the FDI sector, and with such a rapid rate of growth in one of the world's largest markets, few states have been in such a powerful bargaining position as China to exert considerable pressure on foreign investors to share their technological know-how.

There is little doubt that the Chinese state has long grown impatient with the relatively low level of benefits arising from its subordinate network position and has been actively seeking to transform its development model toward a greater exploitation of knowledge-related activities. China's achievements to date in investing in the necessary infrastructure to bring about such a transformation has been impressive, but the necessary major shift in the center of gravity of higher value-added activity to China, while ostensibly under way, is likely to take a number of decades to bring to completion. In 2009 at the unveiling of key indigenous innovation regulations, Premier Wen stated that 'only by using the power of science and technology will China, this massive ark, be able to produce the immeasurable ability to allow nobody to stop our advance forward' (quoted in McGregor, 2010, 6).

While it is likely that geopolitical considerations among Western powers may seek to constrain to some extent China's technological progress, for the most part such an ascendency is likely to be associated with the strategies of major global technology corporations, as they seek to gain control over an increasing market share in different world regions. In 2007, a Chinese official responsible for technology policy referred to the challenges facing China as follows:

> The majority of the market is controlled by foreign companies, most core technology relies on imports, the situation is extremely grave as we are further pressured by developed countries who use blockades and technology controls – if we are not able to solve these problems we will forever be under the control of others.

> (quoted in McGregor, 2010, 17)

The frequently expressed dissatisfaction of Chinese leaders with China's role as a low-cost manufacturer of low-cost products in markets with low margins partly explains its nationalist agenda in science and technology, but a side effect of the political drive behind technology development policy is the huge challenge involved in building the necessary institutions and culture of innovation (Segal, 2011).

Foreign Vs Chinese companies' contribution to China

This section examines trends during the post WTO accession period relating to the contribution of foreign (including JVs in some cases) and Chinese companies (including SOEs and private sector companies) to the Chinese economy and to trade. Following the classification of COEs and FIEs, companies operating in China can be usefully divided between SOEs, which play a dominant, though declining, role in key sectors of strategic interest to the state, FIEs – operating either as part of JVs or Wholly-Owned Foreign Firms (WOFEs) – and those Chinese companies that make up the private sector. Some would suggest that during the early opening-up period, when China hoped to gain access to badly needed technology from foreign firms in exchange for market access, foreign companies were in an advantaged position in the economy, being provided with tax holidays and other incentives. One of the features of the post WTO period, however, was the strong preference among foreign companies to move from JVs to WOFEs.

SOEs have long played an important role from the days of the centrally planned economy, but that role has been significantly reduced in recent times, as China has sought to make these companies more productive. However, they continue to have a monopolistic position in sectors such as defense and security, energy and telecommunications, from which private firms generally, both foreign and Chinese, are excluded. It has been suggested that private sector companies constituted the sector most discriminated against by the state, and a recent World Bank report argues for policy initiatives to release more fully the innovative potential of this important sector (World Bank and Development Research Center of the State Council, China, 2012). While policymakers are planning to develop a more mixed ownership economy with SOEs retaining monopolies in only critical sectors, the pace of reform has been quite slow.

All exporters of high-tech products

China's role within GVCs is becoming more sophisticated, but what is less clear is the extent to which Chinese-owned companies are beginning to substitute foreign companies in this upgrading. In relation to China's trade data, which provide some evidence of upgrading, it is useful to distinguish between ordinary and processing trade (OECD, 2012). Around two-thirds of the former, which dramatically increased to $721 billion by 2010, is accounted for by indigenous Chinese firms, and involves high domestic value-added activity in mainly labor-intensive sectors. With its share of world trade in parts and components increasing by 9.2 percent between 1995 and 2007, China is gradually becoming

Table 3.6 Exports of high-tech products by firm ownership 2002–2013 (percent)

Types	2002	2003	2004	2005	2006	2007	2008	2009	2010	2011	2012	2013
WOFEs	55.4	61.9	65	67.4	68.6	68.2	67.6	67.5	66.5	67	60.7	54.7
JVs	23.9	21.4	20.6	18.9	17.6	17	16.3	15.7	15.7	14.5	16.8	17.4
SOEs	15.1	10.4	8.5	7.4	6.9	7.3	7.4	6.9	6.9	5.8	5.7	5.6
Others	5.7	6.3	5.9	6.2	6.8	7.6	8.7	9.9	10.9	11.7	16.9	22.2

Source: MOST. China High-tech Industry Data Book (2003–2013), www.sts.org.cn/sjkl/gjscy/index.htm.

a key supplier. Although around 85 percent of processing trade, which totaled $211 billion in 2007, is accounted for by foreign firms, the role of Chinese firms in this trade has been shifting from simple assembly to 'full package' manufacturing with the emergence of an Original Equipment Manufacturing (OEM) sector, which is dominated by major Taiwanese companies.

Despite being one of the world's largest economies, China's dependency on imported intermediate inputs at 27.4 percent of total inputs reflects its ongoing subordinate position in global value chains, while compared to other large manufacturing exporters, China retains less value-added in ICT sectors such as office, accounting and computer manufacturing. In examining the ownership structure of high-tech exports, the pattern is quite clear (Table 3.6). Although the share of FIE (WOFEs and JVs) exports decreased from 79.3 percent in 2002 to 72.1 percent in 2013, FIEs dominated the exports of China's high-tech products since 2002. This is the main reason for low IVS in the ICT-related sector. At the same time, the share of SOE exports sharply dropped to 5.6 percent in 2013 and the share of others particularly the private sector increased to 22.2 percent from 5.7 percent in 2002, indicating the rapid growth of the private sector in high-tech.

Top 200 exporters of all products

The three main ownership categories of China's top 200 importing firms in Figures 3.1 show that the share of FIEs' number rose to 52 percent with the share of private-owned enterprises (POEs)'s number rising to 16 percent in 2012, but the share of SOEs' number falling from 41 percent to 32 percent. More than half of the top 200 importing companies have been FIEs, reaching a peak of 130 in 2005 and trending downwards slightly since then. SOEs accounted for 82 in 2012 and fell to 60 by 2010. Private companies have constituted the smallest group accounting for only 10 in 2001, but rising to 25 by 2010.

The three main ownership categories of China's top 200 exporting firms in Figures 3.2 show that the share of FIEs' number rose to 66 percent, with the share of POEs' number rising to 14.5 percent in 2012, but the share of SOEs' number falling from 45.5 percent to 19.5 percent. The number of FIEs has

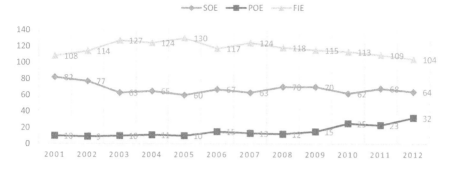

Figure 3.1 Number of company types among top 200 importers

Source: A list of Top 200 Chinese Trade Firms in 2012, China Customs Magazine, General Administration of Customs of China

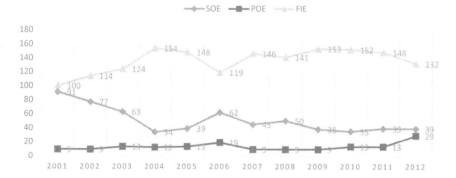

Figure 3.2 Number of company types among top 200 exporters

Source: A list of Top 200 Chinese Trade Firms in 2012, China Customs Magazine, General Administration of Customs of China

grown from 100 in 2001 to 148 in 2005 and ending up at 152 after some fluctuations. SOEs numbered 91 in 2001 but have fallen back considerably to 35 in 2010. The smallest category is made up of private companies, numbering only 9 in 2001 and growing only to 13 by 2010.

In terms of the share of the value of exports accounted for by different firm types, there was very little change in relation to the two main categories of firms, but interestingly the share for POEs increased from three percent to 10.1 percent reflecting the early stages of an emergence of China's private sector. With fewer SOEs listed among the top 200 exporters in 2012, and with only a two percent drop in their share of exports since 2001, the process of scaling up the average size of SOEs is obvious.

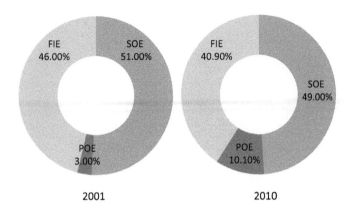

Figure 3.3 The export shares of the top 200 exporters by ownership

Top 20 exporters of all products

The top 20 exporting companies in China for 2001 and 2012 reveal important structural changes in the profile of exporting companies in addition to providing some detailed background in changes in ownership categories (Table 3.7 and Table 3.8). In 2001, the composition was three FIEs, four local SOEs, 12 central SOEs and one JV. By 2012, the profile had changed considerably with 16 FIEs, one local SOE, one central SOE, one JV and one POE, reflecting the growing significance of FIEs among top exporters in China and the beginning of a private company appearance. There were also important changes in the geographical background of parent companies. In 2001, there were two U.S. enterprises, one from Taiwan, a JV with a Finnish company, and four local SOEs from Shanghai. By 2012, there were 13 companies from Taiwan, three from Korea, a JV with a Finnish company and one local SOE from Suzhou. Compared to a much more diverse range of sectors in 2001, including food, energy and textiles, the profile of the top 20 exporting companies in 2012 was predominantly in ICT and electronics manufacturing, reflecting the shift to China of the assembly of high-technology goods, particularly by Taiwanese companies. In keeping with China's phenomenal economic growth during this decade and with the role of exports in that growth, the total value of the top 20 exporting companies increased from $25.9 billion in 2001 to $179.9 billion in 2012, with the average value being $1.3 billion in 2001 and $8.9 billion in 2012.

The dominant role of Taiwanese companies in China's electronics and ICT sectors is revealed in Table 3.7. Foxconn was the most significant exporting company and in addition to its six subsidiaries among the top 20 exporting companies in 2012, it had an additional five subsidiaries among the top 200 exporters which in total accounted for $79.3 billion or 17.3 percent of the total value of exports

Table 3.7 Top 20 Exporting Firms based in China in 2001

Rank	Name	The controlling shareholder	Parent location	Ownership	Industry	Techno-logy level	Exports ($ million)
1	Orient International Holding Co., Ltd.	Shanghai SASAC	Shanghai	Local SOE	Foreign trade	Low	2138.8
2	Hongfujin Precision Industrial (Shenzhen) Co., Ltd.	Foxconn Technology Group	Taiwan	FIE	ICT	High	2031.78
3	Shanghai SVA (Group) Co., Ltd.	Shanghai SASAC	Shanghai	Local SOE	Electronics	High	1747.97
4	China Coal Import & Export Group Co., Ltd.	Central SASAC	China	Central SOE	Energy	Low	1688.09
5	China Potevio Information Industry Group	Central SASAC	China	Central SOE	ICT	High	1637.75
6	China National Chemicals Import & Export Corporation	Central SASAC	China	Central SOE	Multi-sectoral	Low and High	1634.51
7	Motorola (China) Electronics Co., Ltd.	Motorola, Inc.	U.S.	FIE	ICT	High	1613
8	China Shipbuilding Trading Co., Ltd.	China State Shipbuilding Corporation (Central SASAC)	China	Central SOE	Foreign trade	Low	1376.33
9	Shanghai Textile Holding (group) Company	Shanghai SASAC	Shanghai	Local SOE	Textile	Low	1321.31
10	China Petrochemical International Co., Ltd.	China Petroleum & Chemical Corporation (Central SASAC)	China	Central SOE	Foreign trade	Low	1232.5
11	China National Petroleum Corporation	Central SASAC	China	Central SOE	Energy	Low and High	1183.49
12	China Machinery and Equipment (group) Company	Central SASAC	China	Central SOE	Machinery	Middle	1126.51

(Continued)

Table 3.7 (Continued)

Rank	Name	The controlling shareholder	Parent location	Ownership	Industry	Techno-logy level	Exports ($ million)
13	International Information Products (Shenzhen) Co., Ltd.	IBM (percent) and China Great Wall Computer Group Company (percent)	the U.S.	FIE	ICT	High	1028.82
14	China Electronics Import and Export Corporation	China Electronics Corporation(under Central SASAC)	China	Central SOE	Foreign trade	Low	965.76
15	China International Marine Containers (Group) Ltd. (CIMC)	China Ocean Shipping (Group) Company and China Merchants Holdings (under China SASAC)	China	Central SOE	Modern transportation	Low	958
16	China National Offshore Oil Corporation	Central SASAC	China	Central SOE	Energy	Low and High	893.03
17	Shanghai Light Industry Holding Company (Group)	Shanghai SASAC	Shanghai	Local SOE	Multi-sectoral	Low	867.34
18	China National Cereals, Oils & Foodstuffs Import & Export Company	Central SASAC	China	Central SOE	Foods	Low	850.13
19	Shenhua Group Co., Ltd.	Central SASAC	China	Central SOE	Energy	Low and High	833.56
20	Dongguan Nokia Mobile Phones Corporation	Nokia (China) Investment Co., Ltd and Dongguan Nanxin Industry Development Co., Ltd.	Finland	FIE and SOE	ICT	High	832.55

Source: A list of Top 200 Chinese Trade Firms in 2012, China Customs Magazine, General Administration of Customs of China. Additional information collected by authors.

Note: SASAC: State-Owned Asset Supervision & Administration Committee

Table 3.8 Top 20 exporting firms based in China in 2012

Rank	Name	The controlling shareholder	Parent location	Ownership	Industry	Technology level	Exports (million $)
1	Futaihua Industrial (Shenzhen) Co., Ltd	Foxconn Technology Group	Taiwan	FIE	ICT	High	25222
2	Tech-Com (Shanghai) Computer Co., Ltd.	Quanta Computer Corporation	Taiwan	FIE	ICT	High	23950
3	Hongfujin Precision Electronics (Zhengzhou) Co., Ltd	Foxconn Technology Group	Taiwan	FIE	ICT	High	15735
4	Pegatron (Shanghai) Co., Ltd.	Pegatron Corporation	Taiwan	FIE	Electronics	High	15143
5	Hongfujin Precision Electronics (Chengdu) Co., Ltd	Foxconn Technology Group	Taiwan	FIE	ICT	High	11994
6	Huizhou Samsung Electronics Co., Ltd.	Samsung Electronics Co., Ltd.	Korea	FIE	ICT	High	9422
7	Huawei Technologies Co., Ltd,	Huawei Investment Holdings Limited	China	POE	ICT	High	8555
8	Hongfujin Precision Electronics (Yantai) Co., Ltd	Foxconn Technology Group	Taiwan	FIE	ICT	High	6999
9	Pegatron (Suzhou) Co., Ltd.	Pegatron Corporation	Taiwan	FIE	Electronics	High	6664
10	Tech-Front(Chongqing) Computer Co., Ltd.	Quanta Computer Corporation	Taiwan	FIE	ICT	High	6518
11	Suzhou Delta International Logistics Co., Ltd.	Suzhou Logistics Center Co., Ltd. (Suzhou Industrial Park Administration Committee)	Suzhou	Local SOE	Logistics	Low	6200
12	Hongfujin Precision Industrial (Shenzhen) Co., Ltd	Foxconn Technology Group	Taiwan	FIE	ICT	High	6042
13	Nokia Solutions and Networks Co., Ltd	Nokia Corporation	Finland	FIE	ICT	High	5356
14	ZTE Corporation	ZTE Holding Company (35.5 percent)	China	SOE	ICT	High	5166

(Continued)

Table 3.8 (Continued)

Rank	Name	The controlling shareholder	Parent location	Ownership	Industry	Technology level	Exports (million $)
15	Suzhou Samsung Electronics Computer Co., Ltd.	Samsung Electronics CO., Ltd.	Korea	FIE	ICT	High	5055
16	Dongguan Samsung Eyeshot Co., Ltd.	Samsung Display Co., Ltd.	Korea	FIE	ICT	High	4632
17	Compal Information Technology (Kunshan) Co., Ltd.	Compal Electronics Inc.	Taiwan	FIE	ICT	High	4479
18	Compal Electronics Technology (Kunshan) Co., Ltd.	Compal Electronics Inc.	Taiwan	FIE	ICT	High	4454
19	Tianjin Samsung Communication Technology Co., Ltd.	Samsung Electronics Co., Ltd. and Tianjin Middle Ring Electron Information Group Co., Ltd.	Korea	FIE and SOE	ICT	High	4240
20	Hongfujin Precision Electronics (Chongqing) Co., Ltd	Foxconn Technology Group	Taiwan	FIE	ICT	High	4152

Source: A list of Top 200 Chinese Trade Firms in 2012, China Customs Magazine, General Administration of Customs of China. Additional information collected by authors.

Note: SASAC: State-Owned Asset Supervision & Administration Committee

Table 3.9 Foxconn subsidiaries among China's top 200 exporting companies 2012

Rank	Subsidiary	Exports ($ billion)
1	Futaihua Industrial (Shanghai)	25.2
3	Hongfujin Precision Electronics(Zhengzhou)	15.7
5	Hongfujin Precision Electronics(Chengdu)	11.9
8	Hongfujin Precision Electronics(Yantai)	6.9
12	Hongfujin Precision Industrial (Shenzhen)	6.0
20	Hongfujin Precision Electronics (Chongqin)	4.1
33	Hongfujin Precision Industrial (Wuhan)	2.9
64	Hongfutai Precision Electronics(Yantai)	1.8
69	Foxconn Precision Electronics(Taiyuan)	1.6
79	Fuhuajie Industrial (Shenzhen)	1.5
105	Futaijing Precision Electronics(Beijing)	1.2
	Total	79.37

Source: A list of Top 200 Firms of Chinese Trade in 2012, China Customs Magazine

of all 200 top exporters (Table 3.9). The presence of major Chinese companies like Huawei and ZTE among the top high-tech exporters is also noteworthy of the emerging challenge from local companies.

With China's membership of the WTO, this period from 2001 to 2012 has been one of considerable change not only for China but for the global economy generally. While China introduced economic reform alongside its opening-up process, the pace of economic reform has lagged considerably behind the opening-up of its economy. In order to transform its model of economic growth, China needs to upgrade its industrial structure. With SOEs continuing to constitute important components of the economy, their overall industrial profile is focused on traditional sectors such as resources, energy, food, transportation and machinery, and only a few companies such as Datang are involved in high-tech sectors. It is not surprising, therefore, that new industrial sectors in China, such as the internet and information and communications technologies, have emerged mainly from the private sector or through foreign investment. Most of the private companies are quite small compared to SOEs. China's opening-up was associated with significant shifts in global value chains, and while the ICT sector continues to dominate, new sectors such as biotechnology are emerging. Initially, global OEMs in ICT were major contributors to economic growth in Taiwan and Korea, but in order to reduce costs, much of this activity was relocated to the

Chinese mainland, integrating China into global value chains. As a consequence, processing trade is the main contributor to Chinese foreign trade, involving the upgrading of products in China by technology FIEs.

While Taiwan and Korea created a series of excellent firms, such as Samsung, LG, Foxconn and ASUS, through learning by doing in the OEM process, Chinese OEM firms became major manufacturers of electrical household appliances. Additional time is necessary in learning by doing for Chinese companies to become a major force in ICT production, although some small firms are already involved in the production networks which are dominated by Taiwanese and Korean firms.

China's effort to improve its own added value

Two faces of China's mixed industrial system

Indeed, China's economic system is a mixture of FDI-based and indigenous industries, giving two distinct faces to China's industrial system. On the one hand, since the economic reform in 1978, China has implemented a package of institutional changes to attract FDI, expecting the beneficial spillover effects of FDI to facilitate the technological progress of domestic firms. Originally, China's open policy toward FDI was restricted to four special economic zones (SEZs) transformed into open economic areas and located in four coastal cities. During the 1980s, various derivatives of SEZs spread over most of the country and progressively emerged as open areas to FDI. But if the geographic openness increased, the sectoral openness to FDI remains strongly guided by the *Foreign Investment Industrial Guidance Catalogue*, which specifies the types of foreign investors that should be encouraged, restricted or prohibited, depending on their respective sectors of activity. The specified sectors are changing all the time, with the most recent being the 2015 version of the catalogue (NDRC, 2015; Tang and Hussler, 2011). On the other hand, China has launched a series of reform measures for supporting the industrial system, such as national S&T programs, developing universities and public research institutions, establishing the national patent office, creating technology markets, building science and technology industrial parks, launching productivity promotion centers and so on.

It could be argued that China's economic progress has benefited significantly from the attraction of major technology corporations, but it must also be acknowledged that the volume of FDI going to China also reflects the fragmenting of production and value chains in a more globalized era, resulting in the greater integration of major Chinese regions into these networks (Sturgeon, 2003). The ongoing tendency, however, to analyze these developments both within policy and academic circles using the narrow framework of trade theory may create an obstacle toward developing more innovative policies to improve China's competitiveness within global value chains.

Following the trade data analysis above, the development of China's high-tech industries clearly shows two faces (Table 3.10). One is that of the FIEs, including

Table 3.10 China's high-tech industries by ownership (RMB billions)

Year		2001	2002	2003	2004	2005	2006	2007	2008	2009	2010	2013
Total	Value	309.5	376.9	503.4	634.1	812.8	1005.6	1162.1	5708.7	6043.0	7470.9	11604.9
FIEs	Value	115.8	206.0	289.5	398.9	532.4	646.6	728.6	4010.6	3971.3	4863.7	6592.9
	Percent	37.4	54.7	57.5	62.9	65.5	64.3	62.7	70.3	65.7	65.1	56.8
SOEs	Value	47.2	123.4	145.5	135.6	142.2	127.0	150.3	648.7	675.2	786.6	1214.9
	Percent	15.3	32.7	28.9	21.4	17.5	12.6	12.9	11.4	11.2	10.5	10.5
Others	Value	146.5	47.5	68.4	99.6	138.2	232.0	283.2	1049.4	1396.5	1820.6	3797.0
	Percent	47.3	12.6	13.6	15.7	17.0	23.1	24.4	18.4	23.1	24.4	32.7

Source: MOST. China High-tech Industry Data Book (2003–2013), www.sts.org.cn/sjkl/gjscy/index.htm.

Notes: The development indicators of Chinese high-tech industries changed in Chinese statistics, and the indicators are value-added between 2001 and 2007, gross industrial output value between 2008 and 2010, and revenue from principal business since 2013. SOE refers to state owned and state-controlled firm.

WOFEs and JVs which accounts for 56.8 percent of total development outcomes and the other is comprised of SOEs and others (indigenous content), which accounts for 43.2 percent. In this sense, China is not only a mixed system of foreign and indigenous, but it is also an important location within GVCs. While China's primary influence is within its own borders, the complex integration of both foreign and Chinese companies in China into global networks requires a policy approach which can improve China's competitiveness within these networks rather than one which seeks to contain innovation within China (Yeung, 2009; Mememdovic, 2008).

The challenge of industrial upgrading

While some scholars are quite positive about the approach adopted by China and the level of upgrading of the industrial profile, others are critical of the overly directive approach of the state in the market, suggesting that 'techno-nationalism' has slowed the evolution toward greater technological sophistication (Li et al., 2012; OECD, 2012). Rather than constructing protectionist, inward-looking policies, it is argued that emerging countries like China need to learn to deal effectively with the permeable borders of knowledge-creation and innovation, as technology development now encompasses the output of many workers in different global locations (Salter, 2009; Segal, 2011).

The geography of the global production network of the semiconductor industry, for example, illustrates some of the major challenges faced by China in relation to developing high-technology industry. Despite the fact that the center of gravity of semiconductor demand has shifted to China, following China's role as a major global manufacturing hub, and with the presence of many of the world's major semiconductor companies with operations in China, the fact is that much of the activity is at the lower end of the value chain. Although China set itself some very high targets in relation to self-sufficiency in integrated circuits in 2006, Ernst (2011) questioned how these could be attained in what is one of the most globalized industries. Meanwhile, China has made only modest progress in developing semiconductors despite major policy initiatives accompanied by significant state funding, while Taiwan, which had a much earlier start and more effective industrial policy, has come to play a major role in the semiconductor sector. More generally, Taiwanese companies have shifted much of their electronics manufacturing to Mainland China to benefit from a low-cost location as well as from a rapidly growing market. The huge disparity between the global production and consumption of semiconductors, as reflected by China's relatively lower role in this significant production network, reflects some of the major challenges which China must yet face in seeking to become an important player in high-technology sectors.

China's attempts to catch up in the semiconductor industry, while being relatively optimistic, also clarifies the main areas of weakness (Ernst, 2016). Despite accounting for one-third of global demand, Chinese semiconductor companies produce less than 13 percent of that demand. Semiconductors account for around 50 percent of Chinese exports, with the ICT sector making up around one-third of Chinese exports. While a few Chinese companies have made good progress, most companies lag behind global leaders that are prepared to invest in China to gain short-term market access and to facilitate China's integration into the semiconductor global value chain.

A recent report on semiconductors to the U.S. President notes that Chinese industrial policies pose a real threat to semiconductor innovation and U.S. security (Executive Office of the President, 2017). It specifies those areas in which China is lagging behind the U.S. and Taiwan in this sector, such as the manufacturing of advanced-logic chips. Also, its many foundry companies are one-and-a-half generations behind in volume production and all advanced memory chip companies in China are foreign-owned. Its 400 or so fabless semiconductor companies are also technologically lagging and focus mainly on low-end and mid-range parts of the market, making tailored products for the China market.

While there is little doubt that China's economic structure is undergoing an underlying change from the assembly and processing of low-technology goods to high-technology products, and while some level of know-how has been transferred to Chinese companies through foreign investment, some critical technologies have not yet been mastered (Li et al., 2012). Using a world electronics dataset, Van Assche and Gangnes (2010) suggest that there is little evidence of upgrading in China's electronics sectors. In a study which focused on the exporting role of foreign manufacturing multinationals in China which excluded developments in the domestic market, Moran (2011) notes that foreign manufacturing investors have been responsible for 96 percent of all Advanced Technology Products (ADP) since 2002, and that Chinese exporters are not even 'keeping up' let alone 'catching up' with foreign companies in China. In arguing that Chinese companies have received few spill overs from multinationals, Moran (2011, 3) also suggests that:

> the accumulated evidence simply does not show FDI to be a powerful source for indigenous-controlled industrial transformation. In the case of exports, the production of increasingly sophisticated goods destined for international markets from China has been remarkably well constrained and contained within the plants owned and controlled by foreign MNCs and their international suppliers. China has remained a low value-added assembler of more sophisticated inputs imported from abroad – a 'workbench' economy largely bereft of the magnified benefits and externalities from FDI enjoyed by other developing countries.

Since tariffs and quotas are no longer available as tools to protect its market in the wake of its accession to the WTO, McGregor (2010) argues that China is making use of its rapidly growing market and powerful regulatory regime to reduce its reliance on foreign technology and payment of associated license fees. Among the measures being used to achieve these objectives are domestic technology standards, which can block or delay penetration of the local market by foreign technology as well as the production of a catalogue of products eligible for access to the public procurement market. Although similar measures such as local content requirements, joint ventures and forced technology transfers have been used by other Asian countries, it has been suggested that China's approach is more aggressive, with new complex regulations being constantly modified to keep companies off balance, and with China being criticized specifically for using access to its domestic market to leverage the transfer of technology for use in the high-speed rail sector (Hout and Ghemawat, 2010; Anderlini and Dickie, 2010; McGregor, 2010).

The experience of other Asian countries provide some lessons for China's future, but the challenges of achieving significant industrial upgrading during a more globalized era may prove quite daunting, particularly when Chinese policy is so focused on its own domestic economy. In relation to the potential for industrial upgrading, Henderson and Nadvi (2011) suggest upgrading might involve indigenous firms that were formerly subordinate within a global production network could over time become more innovative and thus have the capacity to contribute to higher value-added activities.

The push for indigenous innovation

China's determination to reduce reliance on foreign technology and to gain greater control over intellectual property explains the push from 2006 onwards toward indigenous innovation. This policy, however, creates certain tensions between, on the one hand the need to develop Chinese technology, and on the other ensuring that China continues to benefit from its growing integration into global innovation networks, by acknowledging the key role the country plays in the global production networks and global value chains of lead technology corporations (Yeung, 2009). In an evaluation of this new policy, Liu and Cheng (2011) call for a more open innovation policy to help Chinese companies reach the necessary level of innovation to compete internationally, and wonder whether the large domestic market in China which helps local companies prosper more easily may also slow down the urgency for them to become more innovative. Others have suggested that China's market allows Chinese companies to scale copycat products without crossing national borders (McGregor, 2010).

During the drafting of China's most recent 15-year "Medium- to Long-Term Plan for the Development of Science and Technology (2006–2020)" (MLP), China's technical community argued that the country could no longer expect to receive core technologies from international sources and policy should focus on indigenous innovation (Serger and Breidne, 2007). Although many economists have argued that at its current level of development, there was greater potential for China to benefit from spillovers created by foreign MNCs in China, others have found limited benefits from such spillovers and suggest that innovation from both indigenous and foreign sources was complementary and necessary (Boeing and Sandner, 2011; Xu and Sheng, 2012; Fu and Gong, 2011). It is clear that state planners hope to end China's overdependence on foreign corporations for industrial and technological capacities (Hong, 2017, 6).

The distinction can be made between the political objective of the Chinese state to achieve technological autonomy and the pragmatic approach of many Chinese companies who, rather than cutting themselves off from global markets, have considerable cooperation with companies in Japan, Korea and Taiwan (Segal, 2011). An important aspect of the new indigenous innovation policy involves developing the capacity among Chinese companies to absorb foreign technology and to optimize its exploitation for the local market. Some of China's leading firms such as Huawei have called for a more open innovation policy which would allow them more easily to cooperate with foreign firms (Liu and Cheng, 2011).

Initially policymakers expected, perhaps somewhat naïvely, that Chinese companies would benefit greatly from a policy which sought technology transfer in exchange for market access and which was underpinned by a requirement on foreign companies to be part of a joint venture with a local company. China's ambition to become a technology leader is made difficult by being a latecomer to areas of high-technology such as semiconductors and software architecture that are dominated by global corporations from outside China. Not only are Chinese companies kept in subordinate positions in global value chains by dominant global corporations, but Froud et al. (2014) argue that large contract manufacturers like Taiwan's Foxconn are also in a subordinate position relative to these companies.

Since China's accession to the WTO in 2001, many foreign companies have shifted toward WOFEs, in order to have more control over their operations and to protect their IP, but China continues to pressure foreign companies to share IP. It is argued that China's push for indigenous innovation is partly influenced by political factors and a tendency toward techno-nationalism, but other considerations including poor levels of absorption and assimilation of imported technology have also been important (Whalley and Zhou, 2007). A distinction should be made between a relatively small number of highly successful, innovative Chinese companies in high-technology sectors and many SOEs which are still undergoing transformation from the earlier command economy (Boeing and Sandner, 2011). While Chinese leaders and policymakers realize the urgency of moving China's development model more toward knowledge exploitation, they appear to be still struggling to find the most effective way forward. Although always strongly influenced by political considerations, China shows evidence of adopting a pragmatic approach, which is often based around hard bargaining with foreign investors (Ernst, 2011).

Doing business in the era of China's indigenous innovation

With China's relatively recent shift in focus toward a greater emphasis on promoting indigenous innovation, it might be expected that MNCs operating in China would have some concerns about the implications of this evolving policy for their activities. Based on our interviews and analysis, it would not be too surprising to find that some tensions exist between the objectives of MNCs, who seek to use factors of production in China to continue their relatively dominant position in value chains, and the objectives of the Chinese state which seeks to benefit from the presence of these companies through technology transfer and which seeks to promote ownership and control of intellectual property and technological innovation over time.

Perhaps the most fascinating aspect arising from our company interviews was the nuanced perspectives of managers toward the challenges faced by their companies to increasing their market share in this new policy environment, but also the surprising level of empathy expressed by many of them in relation to China's own objectives. The interview material with these foreign companies allows us to go a little deeper into the processes behind some of the trends already outlined.

'A revolutionary new paradigm'

During the 1980s, technology was transferred by large technology multinationals to their joint ventures in China at a very high cost to China in the form of royalties and license fees. From the mid-1990s, many of these companies began to offshore some manufacturing to this low-cost location, and in more recent years, they have made some investments in R&D activity in China. But the global model of R&D and innovation which multinationals have traditionally developed seeks to contain intellectual property within the boundaries of their organizations without providing any advantages to potential competitor companies. The reaction of interviewees to China's evolving policy environment was, however, quite nuanced, reflecting considerable understanding of the objectives involved, even when this made competing in the local market more difficult.

Some interviewees described the new policy environment in China in more dramatic terms. The manager of a medium-sized U.S. technology multinational said that China had come up with

> a brutally new way – a new paradigm for doing things, telling everyone, this is the way we are doing it and everything has to change. This is a revolutionary new paradigm, which involves evolutionary change, causing things to be done better in a gradual way. Everybody must jump on board and follow this approach and we will get a big market that way.
>
> (2011 interview)

This view was echoed by a manager from a large U.S. technology company, experiencing growing competition from local companies who said: 'Yeah, I think that right now the Chinese government is reasserting itself and saying either my way or the highway'.

The same manager expressed an understanding of the Chinese approach by saying:

> If I was the Chinese government, I would do the same thing, because I would also want to make sure that I am not paying royalties to multinationals. So

I would want to create my own standards. But I think you might shoot yourself in the foot because the standards might only be applicable for the China market.

At the same time he was somewhat critical of the Chinese government's insistence on indigenous innovation for firms who sought to sell into the Chinese procurement market. He regarded the requirement to build your IP in China as 'welcome copiers' and 'so, I don't think that any multinational would actually do it' (2011 interview). Thus, while local managers appreciated what China was trying to achieve, they did not necessarily agree with the approach being taken such as focusing on domestic technology standards, which not only would create additional challenges for their own operations, but could also, in the view of some, inhibit local companies from being globally competitive.

'Understand'

A similar level of empathy was expressed by another manager in the same large U.S. technology company. Being a son of Chinese immigrants to the U.S., where he began his career working for this company, he later moved to the home of his ancestors. He explained that

> over time, I began to understand the problem that China is dealing with is on a wholly different magnitude, a wholly different scale than any Western country has ever encountered, and we don't know what is the right way of working with 1.3 billion people . . . we have to give people the benefit of the doubt, that the government are trying to do the right thing here. Yes, everybody is trying to get the market, but if you are in somebody else's house you need to go by their rules, and you figure out ways of helping the government by your own moral standpoint . . . helping them to become more successful and helping the people at the same time . . . I mean China does not want to be just the resources and labor of the world . . . the economy has to move up the value chain . . . that's part of the drive for innovation, IP, etc., . . . the question is really how to do it? . . . the policies are for directional guidance.

He went on to be quite critical of the approach taken by many foreign multinationals toward doing business in China:

> in my personal opinion, most of the multinational decision makers have not lived here . . . they don't understand the history and the background of the country because it is difficult to relate 50 years of growing up in the West and apply that to China, which has a very different set of values and assumptions, and this explains sometimes what used to work elsewhere does not work here. Well, it is a different world with a very different value system.
>
> (2011 interview)

While China still needed the contribution of multinationals, this dependence had declined more recently, and it was understandable that China should seek to move urgently up the value chain. Previously, multinationals were privileged with tax and other incentives, but now there was a more level playing field, with multinationals under more pressure to negotiate and bargain with policymakers to gain market access. Thus, while there were obvious sources of tension in the relationship between China and foreign companies, it was clear to many interviewees that China was in an unprecedented and powerful position in this relationship because of its market size, and it was necessary to work out some form of acceptable sharing of benefits over time through negotiation and compromise.

There was general agreement that multinationals could not change China in a fundamental way and must operate within the new rules, and that their challenge was to seek to identify how the market was evolving and to outpace local competition through higher levels of innovation. It was acknowledged that considerable dissatisfaction had been expressed by multinationals about perceived special treatment given to SOEs, and that while the market was 'open in theory', the products of multinationals, which might be of higher quality, could be excluded from the market because of the higher costs compared with local competitors. While there was agreement that with the continuing significant role of the state in the economy, that China was not a 'market economy', yet they felt that there was no going back to the previous era after accession to the WTO, whose rules provided some comfort for foreign investors. Obviously China is not unique in the role that SOEs play in particular sectors of the economy that are deemed critical in terms of security and defense, but the extent of state involvement in China continues to be quite significant, and despite announcing plans to develop a more mixed ownership economy over time, the pace of change has been quite slow. Multinational companies were experiencing particular difficulties in areas such as public procurement, where the state had greater control over market access.

'Chinese innovation was emerging'

The Chinese-born manager of a major global technology company established one of the earlier joint ventures in China. The company had restructured its operations more recently to allow for an easier sharing of technology and intellectual property between its Chinese operation and its headquarters, provided one of the strongest defenses of China's policy to develop its own domestic technology standards in areas like 3G for mobile technology. Notwithstanding his own acute awareness of growing competition from local companies, and thus the increasing pressure to maintain market share in China, he argues that China's development of the Time Division Synchronous Code Division Multiple Access Standard (TD-SCDMA) was successful and provided experience for both Chinese engineers and telecommunications companies, which could in turn be used for developing the 4th generation wireless technology, and allow China to play a bigger role than heretofore in the development of global standards. Nevertheless, Chinese scholars such as Liu and Cheng (2011) express some skepticism about the relative success of TD-SCDMA, arguing that even major SOEs like China Mobile were reluctant to commit themselves fully to the project, while Breznitz and Murphree (2011) present a more negative evaluation of this experiment as an example of continuing interference from the Chinese state in the market.

This interviewee, however, argues that TD-SCDMA is not a local standard, as some Indian operators were also interested in using it, seeing it as more suitable to their needs. He argues that because of China's size, it was necessary to design a different standard to suit local conditions, and that part of the reasoning behind it related to its successful deployment in China initially and afterwards internationally. He also mentioned foreign military involvement in telecommunications development which created political issues for China (2011 interview). In this particular instance, it was fascinating to observe those tensions between China's objectives and those of foreign companies reflected in the views of this Chinese-born manager, who, on the one hand sought to ensure that the company he worked for had the ability to compete and outperform local companies, while acknowledging that his country had every right to pursue its own technological ambitions.

The tensions between the two sets of players are summarized rather succinctly by the manager of a global telecommunications company who claimed that while their revenues were growing in China as the market itself expanded, they were losing market share to local competitors. He acknowledge that there were many perspectives on these issues, but that

> his own view was that while Chinese innovation was emerging, it was mainly focused on the local market: Chinese innovation for the global market, that remains to be seen . . . I think it has a long way to go . . . I think that the global MNCs will still be leading technology innovation for global markets, but I don't think that they will have much traction in China . . . Because of the nature of the legal system, no MNC CEO would put his reputation on the line for China . . . For the China products they will try to build them in China, so they will say that the IP is lost . . . so what! . . . MNCs could be fairly confident that Chinese companies won't be able to use this technology to sell into the West because of superior IP protection, but a Chinese company could take the technology and sell it in Nigeria and you cannot do anything about it.
>
> (interview 2011)

While it is difficult to say how representative any case study company is in terms of scope, these comments do illustrate the type of pragmatic approach that companies adopt in an environment that is known to have weak intellectual property protection, and in which local companies in particular sectors are becoming more competitive.

'Interdependence' between China and the outside world

The Chinese-born intellectual property manager of a major European technology company with very significant involvement in the Chinese market argued that it was understandable that the Chinese would try to set up a system which does not allow the market to be flooded completely with foreign products (2011 interview). While this company, like other foreign technology companies, had control and ownership over key technologies that were of strategic interest to China, both in the energy and transport sectors, it was necessary for the company to develop a *modus vivendi* with the Chinese authorities if they were to benefit significantly from major contracts, not only within China, but also with local companies abroad. Within this evolving relationship of collaboration, Nolan's (2012) argument, that within the current matrix of interdependence and the continuing dominant role of major Western corporations, that China needs the outside world more than the world needs China, makes much sense.

Also, a Chinese-born manager of a very large U.S. technology company, who had completed her postgraduate studies in the U.S. and also began her career in that company in the U.S., pointed to the experience in the U.S. where local companies had been prevented by the state from purchasing equipment from Huawei, one of China's successful telecommunications companies, because of supposed national security reasons. She went on to argue that it was reasonable that the Chinese state should also have such concerns about the possibility of software programs gathering intelligence, and thus providing it with understandable reasons for not purchasing the software and hardware of foreign companies. She went on to express a strong empathy for China's new policy of indigenous innovation (2011 interview). In addition to the likely nationalistic influences, which affect many people in different countries, who are proud of their nation's emergence after a long period with low levels of development, these views were also partly influenced by the tensions of management seeking to be successful in a country where the business environment often reflected different cultural values than the objectives set by their company headquarters, often with little appreciation of local nuances.

A Chinese-born manager of another major U.S. technology company explained that the company's view was that

> there must be give-and-take in the relationship with China. It's about negotiation . . . if we are not prepared to give anything, we will have to compete with other multinationals from Japan, Europe and Korea as well as a large number of smaller Chinese companies.
>
> (2010 interview)

This willingness to collaborate with China's government in order to both help the country develop its own industries, while at the same time seeking to help their own corporation to be successful in the Chinese market reflected pragmatism based on experience and familiarity with local conditions. Many of these companies we interviewed continue to dominate innovation in the particular sectors in which they operate in China, and are therefore part of the Western technology hegemony that China wishes to challenge with its policies in order to reduce its dependence on foreign technology. However, in some cases China is proving to be a much more difficult market for foreign companies than in the earlier period of opening-up, and their future expansion in and successful penetration of China's very attractive market will depend on a pragmatic approach toward sharing intellectual property (*The Economist*, 25 January, 2014).

References

Anderlini, J. and Dickie, M., 2010, 'China: A future on track', *Financial Times*, 23.

Boeing, P. and Sandner, P., 2011, 'The innovative performance of China's national innovation system', Available at www.frankfurtschool.de/clicnetclm/fileDownload.do?goid=000000275822AB4. Accessed 06/24/2017.

Brandt, L. and Thun, E., 2010, 'The fight for the middle: Upgrading, competition, and industrial development in China', *World Development*, 38(11), 1555–1574.

Breznitz, D. and Murphree, M., 2011, *Run of the Red Queen*, New Haven, Yale University Press.

Cai, F., 2010, 'Demographic transition, demographic dividend, and Lewis turning point in China', *China Economic Journal*, 3(2), 107–119.

Davies, K., 2012, 'Inward investment in China and its policy context', Available at www.vcc.columbia.edu/files/vale/documents/Profiles_China_IFDI_24_Oct_2012_-_FINAL.pdf. Accessed 06/24/2017.

De Backer, K., 2011, 'Global value chains: Preliminary evidence and policy issues', The Committee on Industry, Innovation and Entrepreneurship (*CIIE*) Meeting 31 March–1 April. Available at www.oecd.org/sti/ind/47945400.pdf. Accessed 06/24/2017.

Eberstadt, N., 2012, 'Looking towards 2030: A new world coming into focus', *Economic Affairs*, 32(1), 17–25.

The Economist, 2014, 'China loses its allure', January 25, 2014.

Economist Intelligence Unit, 2012, 'Serve the people – the new landscape of foreign investment in China', Available at www.eiu.com/public/topical_report.aspx?campaignid=chinafdi2012. Accessed 06/24/2017.

Ernst, D., 2011, 'Indigenous innovation and globalization: The challenge of China's standardization strategy', UC Institute on Global Conflict and Cooperation and the East-West Center. Available at www.eastwestcenter.org/publications/indigenous-innovation-and-globalization-challenge-chinas-standardization-strategy. Accessed 06/24/2017.

Ernst, D., 2016, 'China's bold strategy for semiconductors – zero-sum game or catalyst for cooperation?' *East-West Center Working Papers*, 9.

Executive Office of the President, 2017, 'Report to the President: Ensuring long-term U.S. leadership in semiconductors', President's Council of Advisors on Science and Technology.

Froud, J., Sukhdev, J., Leaver, A. and Williams, K., 2014, 'Financialization across the Pacific: Manufacturing cost ratios, supply chains and power', *Critical Perspectives on Accounting*, 25(1), 46–57.

Fu, X. and Gong, Y., 2011, 'Indigenous and foreign innovation efforts and drivers of technological upgrading: Evidence from China', *World Development*, 39(7), 1213–1225.

Hart-Landsberg, M., 2011, 'The Chinese reform experience: A critical assessment', *Review of Radical Political Economics*, 43(1), 56–76.

Henderson, J. and Nadvi, K., 2011, 'Greater China, the challenges of global production networks and the dynamics of transformation', *Global Networks*, 11(3), 285–297.

Hong, Y., 2017, *Networking China – The Digital Transformation of the Chinese Economy*, Champaign, IL, University of Illinois Press.

Horn, J., Singer, V. and Woetzel, J., 2010, 'A truer picture of China's export machine', Available at www.mckinsey.com/insights/globalization/a_truer_picture_of_chinas_export_machine. Accessed 06/24/2017.

Hout, T.M. and Ghemawat, P., 2010, 'China Vs the world – whose technology is it?' *Harvard Business Review*, 88(12), 94–103.

Jiang, M.S., Branzei, O. and Xia, J., 2016, 'DIY: How internationalization shifts the locus of indigenous innovation for Chinese firms', *Journal of World Business*, 51(5), 662–674.

Karabell, Z., 2009, *Superfusion: How China and America Became One Economy and Why the World's Prosperity Depends on It*, New York, Simon and Schuster.

Li, K., Jiang, W. and Song, L., 2014, The mystery of changes in the quality of China's exports: A micro-level explanation based on market entry. *Social Science in China*, 3, 80–103 (In Chinese).

Li, L., Dunford, M. and Yeung, G., 2012, 'International trade and industrial dynamics: Geographical and structural dimensions of Chinese and Sino-EU merchandise trade', *Applied Geography*, 32, 130–142.

Liu, X., Buck, T. and Shu, C., 2005, 'Chinese economic development, the next stage: Outward FDI?', *International Business Review*, 14(1), 97–115.

Liu, X. and Cheng, P., 2011, 'Is China's indigenous innovation strategy compatible with globalisation? Available at www.eastwestcenter.org/sites/default/files/private/ps061.pdf. Accessed 06/24/2017.

Ma, H., Wang, Z. and Zhu, K., 2015, 'Domestic content in China's exports and its distribution by firm ownership', *Journal of Comparative Economics*, 43(1), 3–18.

McGregor, J., 2010, 'China's drive for "indigenous innovation"', Global Regulatory Cooperation Project and US Chamber of Commerce. Available at www.uschamber.com/sites/default/files/reports/100728chinareport_0.pdf. Accessed 06/24/2017.

Mememdovic, O., 2008, 'Part 1: Editorial, International Journal of Technological Learning', *Innovation and Development*, 1(3), 227–236.

Ministry of Commerce, 2015, *Statistical Bulletin of China's Outward Foreign Direct Investment*, Beijing, China Statistics Press.

Moran, T.H., 2011, 'Foreign manufacturing multinationals and the transformation of the Chinese economy: New measurements, new perspectives', Working Paper 11–11, Washington, DC, Peterson Institute for International Economics.

National Development and Reform Commission, 2015, 'Foreign investment industrial guidance catalog (2015 revise)', Available at www.sdpc.gov.cn/zcfb/zcfbl/201503/W020150402620481787669.pdf. Accessed 06/24/2017.

Nolan, P., 2012, 'Is China buying the world?' *Challenge*, 55(2), 108–118.

OECD, 2012, 'China in focus: Lesson and challenges', Available at www.oecd.org/china/50011051.pdf. Accessed 06/24/2017.

Salter, B., 2009, 'State strategies and geopolitics of the global knowledge economy: China, India and the case of regenerative medicine', *Geopolitics*, 14, 47–78.

Saxenian, A., 2007, *The New Argonauts*, Cambridge, MA, Harvard University Press.

Segal, A., 2011, *Advantage: How American Innovation Can Overcome the Asian Challenge*, New York, W. W Norton & Company.

Serger, S. and Breidne, M., 2007, 'China's fifteen-year plan for science and technology: And assessment', *Asia Policy*, 4, 135–164.

Sharman, J.C., 2012, 'Chinese capital flows and offshore financial centers', *Pacific Review*, 25, 317–337.

Sturgeon, T.J., 2003, 'What really goes on in Silicon Valley? Spatial clustering and dispersal in modular production networks', *Journal of Economic Geography*, 3, 199–225.

Sturgeon, T.J. and Gereffi, G., 2009, 'Measuring success in the global economy: International trade, industrial upgrading, and business function outsourcing in global value chains', *Transnational Corporations*, 18(2), 1–35.

Tang, M. and Hussler, C., 2011, 'Betting on indigenous innovation or relying on FDI: The Chinese strategy for catching-up', *Technology in Society*, 33(1), 23–35.

UNCTAD, 2016, 'United Nations Conference on Trade and Development', World Investment Report 2016, United Nations, United Nations Publication.

Van Assche, A. and Gangnes, B., 2010, 'Electronics production upgrading: Is China exceptional?' *Applied Economics Letters*, 17, 477–482.

Vlcek, W., 2010, 'Byways and highways of direct investment: China and the offshore world', *Journal of Current Chinese Affairs*, 39(4), 111–142.

Whalley, J. and Zhou, W., 2007, 'Technology upgrading and China's growth strategy to 2020', Available at www.cigionline.org/publications/2007/3/technology-upgrading-and-chinas-growth-strategy-2020. Accessed 06/24/2017.

World Bank, Development Research Center of the State Council, the People's Republic of China, 2012, *China 2030: Building a Modern, Harmonious, and Creative High-Income Society*, Washington, DC, World Bank. Available at http://documents.worldbank.org/curated/en/781101468239669951/China-2030-building-a-modern-harmonious-and-creative-society. Accessed 06/24/2017.

Xiao, G., 2004, 'People's republic of China's round-tripping FDI: Scale, causes and implications', Available at www.adbi.org/files/2004.06.dp7.foreign.direct.investment.people.rep.china.implications.pdf. Accessed 06/24/2017.

Xing, Y., 2011, 'China's exports in information and communication technology and its impact on Asian countries', *Economic Change Restructuring*, 44, 135–147.

Xing, Y. and Detert, N., 2010, 'How the iPhone widens the United States trade deficit with the People's Republic of China, Asian Development Bank Institute', Available at www.adbi.org/files/2010.12.14.wp257.iphone.widens.us.trade.deficit.prc.pdf. Accessed 06/24/2017.

Xu, X. and Sheng, Y., 2012, 'Productivity spillovers from foreign direct investment: Firm-level evidence from China', *World Development*, 40(1), 62–74.

Yeung, H.W-C., 2009, 'Regional development and the competitive dynamics of global production networks: An East Asian perspective', *Regional Studies*, 43(3), 325–351.

Zhou, Y., 2008, 'Synchronising export orientation with import substitution: Creating competitive indigenous high-tech companies in China', *World Development*, 36(11), 2353–2370.

4 China's increasing participation in the ICT GVC

A meso view

China's increasing participation in the ICT GVC is related to modularization of product architecture, globalization of production, and outsourcing and offshoring of manufacturing. This chapter maps the involvement of China-based companies in the ICT GVC through synthesizing evidence from international trade data. Companies within the ICT GVC are divided into three types: Own Brand Manufacturers (OBMs), component companies and Electronic Manufacturing Services (EMS). The firm-level trade data provide us with an overall picture of the structure and relationships of the three types of companies by nationality, while also identifying the key players. The result shows that, and while several Chinese companies particularly internet companies are rising rapidly, China continues to linger in the low value-added segments of the ICT GVC because of its ongoing dependence on foreign technology and its associated IP.

Introduction

The modularization of product architecture and globalization of production have given rise to an increasing process of manufacturing outsourcing. Before outsourcing and offshoring of manufacturing to China was feasible, the whole range of functions remained vertically integrated within large corporations. Over time, however, what had been complex tasks based on tacit knowledge became more codifiable and digitizable, and therefore more amenable to outsourcing (Sturgeon, 2003). As these functions became more standardized it was possible to contract companies in ever more competitive locations to take on substitute roles for part of the overall process of production. The GVC of the ICT sector has undergone considerable evolution in recent decades, with China's participation in this chain growing in significance (Cooke, 2013a). Although the most innovative aspects associated with shaping the trajectory of creation-related activities continue to be dominated by Western technology corporations, the center of gravity of most of the manufacturing and assembly work of the key products and devices has shifted to Asia, with China playing an increasingly important role in production (Schimmer et al., 2010; APEC Policy Support Unit, 2013).

Much of the manufacturing and assembly work of the Taiwanese companies was relocated to Mainland China for cost reasons, with PC manufacturing in the Pearl River Delta (PRD) and laptop manufacturing concentrated in the Yellow River Delta (YRD). Major clusters of Taiwanese supplier companies had followed their key clients to the mainland, establishing significant ICT clusters in cities like Dongguan (Yang, 2007). Much of the activity was related to the lower levels of the value chain, with hundreds of companies specializing in supplying computer peripherals, such as keyboards, drivers, and monitors. These clusters were composed of various tiers of suppliers with Foxconn, the major contract manufacturer as Tier 2, various Taiwanese companies suppliers to EMS as Tier 3, including companies producing keyboards and motherboards, resisters and inductors (Yang, 2007).These clusters epitomized the earlier stages of the ICT GVC's evolution, or what Cooke (2013b) refers to as the historic GPN, dominated by Western companies like Dell and HP.

Indeed China has evolved to become one of the most significant centers for ICT production worldwide. Much of the activity located there continues to be related to manufacturing and assembly, with the greater proportion of the key components being developed outside China and being imported as intermediate products before being re-exported as finished products or increasingly sold in the domestic market (Guillaume et al., 2011). Over time, however, as the technology itself evolved toward a greater reliance on mobile devices, and particularly smartphones and tablets, the geography of production underwent change, with shifts to interior cities like Chongqing and Chengdu, with lower labor costs and greater proximity to the labor supply, and also significant incentives from the provincial governments of these cities to develop new clusters of production.

In tracing the evolution of the ICT GVC, it is necessary to examine various elements, including the rapid pace of change in the technology itself, in the complex interconnected network of many companies involved, and in the spatial evolution of the value chain with the ongoing search for greater levels of competitiveness. All of these elements need to be explored in order to explain changes in the global value chain, and the increasing role played by major companies and locations in China in these developments. In terms of governance and control of the GVC, Gereffi (2014) suggested that this was related to the complexity of knowledge being transferred from lead companies to networks of suppliers. For example, although a company like Apple has an increasing impact on the dynamism of China's high-tech exports, in terms of international trade statistics it remains quite invisible, even though its managers are involved in monitoring production in its supplier factories and suppliers in some cases use equipment purchased by Apple (Chan et al., 2013; Clelland, 2014).

While, this is not to suggest that there are not considerable levels of innovation in China, but much of it is incremental in nature and is related to the functions in which most ICT companies in China are specializing, such as assembly (Breznitz and Murphree, 2011; Brandt and Thun, 2011). Because of this reality, while the Chinese economy has benefited from having much of the world's high-tech manufacturing located in it, the added value accruing to China through manufacturing sophisticated products such as the iPhone for companies like Apple is only a small proportion of that which accrues to companies who own and control the core IP, and therefore have considerable power in dictating the rules governing the GVC and the supplier companies (Xing and Detert, 2010). It is this key issue of China being increasingly central to the ICT GVC globally, while continuing to play a relatively subordinate role within it that this chapter seeks to elaborate.

As China's economy itself undergoes considerable changes with a significant reduction in labor supply, rising labor costs, the unsustainable nature of further growth in investment in export processing and the pressure of natural resource consumption and environmental pollution, policymakers are attempting to transition China's role through promoting indigenous innovation by using domestic technical standards, and seeking intellectual property in exchange for access to the public procurement market (Grimes and Du, 2013; Xia, 2012 a, b). While China is no longer willing to continue playing a subordinate role in the ICT GVC, it faces a major dilemma in balancing its need to exploit its growing participation in globalized high-tech activity, and at the same time boosting its ownership of intellectual property. Referring to China's lack of fundamental competitiveness in high-tech value-added production, Chen and De Lombaerde (2013) claim that there is no consensus within Chinese political circles on how China could move up the value chain. China's main bargaining chip in making demands on foreign investors remains its rapidly growing market in a world where growth in other regions is disappointing.

To date, however, despite the fact that increasingly sophisticated ICT production is being located in China – although for the most part controlled by non-Chinese companies – China has made only modest progress in key areas such as the software architecture of operating systems or in semiconductor chip design, two core areas which continue to determine the trajectory of the industry (Lin et al., 2011). The ongoing fascinating strategy of mainly Western technology corporations, together with companies from Japan, South Korea and Taiwan who continue to dominate the upper reaches of the value chain or smiling curve, to use a different analogy, and who seek to exploit the competitive features of locations in China, without losing control of the key elements of the GVC through IP leakage, is one of the key questions explored in this chapter.

This exploration seeks to determine the extent to which Taiwanese companies, initially, and more recently Chinese companies, have succeeded in taking on more complex tasks in the ICT GVC. One of the interesting questions that arises in relation to this is whether so much of the fundamental activity (even if it is at the lower levels of the GVC) which has now been located in China makes these locations considerably indispensable to the GVC for a long period to come, and whether the gradual process of substitution and upgrading that has characterized the evolution of the ICT GVC in China could have major implications for the control of these activities in the future. Is there a tipping point at which a location like China becomes indispensable to major global corporations if they are to remain competitive? Or can these global corporations continue to keep China in a subordinate role in the ICT GVC, similar to what some have described as the 'modularity trap', which could make advancing up the value chain very challenging?

Methodology and data

With globalization, increased fragmentation of production has resulted in 80 percent of global trade occurring within global value chains, which are typically coordinated by MNCs, with the cross-border trade of inputs and outputs taking place within their networks of affiliates, contractual partners and arm's length suppliers (UNCTAD, 2013). Despite this reality, however, trade data have been extensively used to examine the relationship between trade patterns and economic development, and researchers continue to be restricted in many cases to exploiting trade data, which can provide rich insights into the functioning of global value chains. Because the growing extent of outsourcing and offshoring can in many cases mask the significant role played by major technology corporations in exercising considerable power within these chains, the limitations at the macro-level in an increasingly globalized era have been highlighted (Karabell, 2009; Sturgeon and Gereffi, 2009). Account must also be taken of the limitations of gross export shares in indicating the true extent of involvement in a particular GVC. Although China's role within GVCs is becoming more sophisticated, what is less clear is the extent to which Chinese-owned companies are beginning to substitute for foreign companies in this upgrading (OECD, 2012; Xia, 2012 a, b, c).

This study employs trade data at the firm-level to investigate China's increasing participation in the ICT GVC, and also to provide insights into the changing profile of activities carried out in that part of the ICT GVC located in China. In seeking to determine the extent to which China's increasing participation in the ICT GVC during its recent period of rapid economic growth has benefited Chinese companies, the approach taken in this chapter is to exploit trade data specific to key ICT companies operating in China which provide the opportunity to consider the evolving role of China-based OBMs, component and EMS companies in the ICT GVC. The classification of trading companies into OBMs, component and EMS companies, which builds on the work of Bonaglia and Goldstein (2007) and Yang (2014a), allows us to quantify the contribution of each grouping in the ICT GVC, and explain how the contribution of different types of companies has evolved from 2001 to 2012. In compiling a database of a large number of companies in the ICT GVC, this simple three-fold classification system frequently encounters dilemmas as the boundaries between the three groupings of companies, particularly between OBMs and EMS companies, have become increasingly blurred over time as the ICT sector evolved and company business models responded to change. Some companies, such as Samsung, are involved in a range of activities, being a major brand name as well as being a significant supplier of components to competitor companies like Apple.

Since most of China's trade in high-tech products is derived from foreign firms first, these data reflect how China has increasingly attracted a major concentration of global technology companies, deepening China's integration into the ICT GVC because of its comparative advantage, particularly in relation to production and assembly. Second, the data also reveals how China has become a major global manufacturing center ('the world's factory') for ICT. In addition to elucidating the functioning of China's role in the ICT GVC, the trade data provide a more realistic insight into the contribution of the ICT sector to China's trade balance. Finally, by providing us with detailed imports and exports of specific firms over time, the firm-level data help to avoid the pitfalls associated with 'round tripping' investment to locations such as Hong Kong. With the huge growth in outsourcing by major technology companies in recent years, much of their production in China remains invisible in the trade data, masked by the trading activity of EMS.

Our primary datasets are derived from the China Customs trade database published (in Chinese) as a list of China's Top Exporting Firms and also a list of China's Top Trading Firms (Imports and Exports) for the years 2001 to 2004 by *China Customs Magazine*. From 2005 to 2012, two separate lists of the Top Exporting Firms and the Top Importing Firms were published. Because of this change in how the data were published, we derived the volume of imports for each firm from 2001 data on overall trade. Then, we abstracted all ICT firms from the listings, showing their imports and exports in billions of U.S. dollars for 2001, 2005 and 2012. Quite a number of firms on these lists had more than one subsidiary operating in China, and in a few cases had up to a dozen subsidiaries. For example, 12 subsidiaries of Foxconn and eight subsidiaries of Samsung appeared on the lists. In all these cases we amalgamated the total imports and exports of all subsidiaries into one entity, 'Foxconn' or 'Samsung', creating new lists of ICT companies which included all their imports and exports from all their subsidiaries on the list of top trading companies. Finally, we separated all ICT companies into three groupings of OBMs, component companies and EMSs according to their predominant production activities, adding the nationality of each company with the help of company and other relevant websites.

We selected 2001, 2005 and 2012 as three key years to be examined in detail. With China's entry into the WTO in 2001, this can be seen as a key starting point for China's integration into the ICT GVC. In 2006, China published its *Medium- and Long-Term Plan for the Development of Science and Technology* (MLP), in which 'indigenous innovation' became the new innovation strategy, replacing the previous policy of imitation and copying. Our dataset from 2001 to 2012 allows us to evaluate to some extent the effects, if any, of this new policy on the ICT sector. The aggregate data on the ICT sector in China are derived from a variety of statistical sources published in Chinese by the Ministry of Commerce, Bureau of Industry, Security, Import and Export Control for 2005 and 2012, and by the Division of Development and Planning of the Ministry of Science and Technology for 2001. Data were also derived from the China *High-tech Industry Data Book 2013*.

In addition to the primary focus in this chapter on firm-level trade data, our interpretation of trends revealed by these data is also influenced by interviews with the management of foreign multinational technology companies in Shanghai between 2009 and 2017, which also contributes to Chapter 3. Interviews were conducted with key management personnel, with each lasting at least one hour, and covering a range of issues associated with the recent evolution of their activities in China and their adaptation to the changing policy environment.

Particular attention was also given to the growing competition from Chinese technology companies in the domestic market.

The composition of China-based ICT companies

Although China has become one of the world's largest exporters of high-tech products, as mentioned in Chapter 3, the aggregate data for 2012 indicate that 77.5 percent of high-tech exports come from FIEs, of which 60.7 percent were from wholly-owned foreign firms (WOFEs) and 16.8 percent from joint ventures (JVs) (China High-tech Industry Data Book, 2013). ICT is the biggest sector of high-tech industry, and this section investigates the national/regional origin of China-based ICT companies by three company types.

The profile composition of China-based ICT companies

Having amalgamated all ICT subsidiaries in the Top 200 lists of international trade (ICTin200), there were 55 importers and 53 exporters in 2001, 62 importers and 77 exporters in 2005 and 30 importers and 56 exporters in 2012, reflecting important changes during this period (Table 4.1). Accordingly, the import value of ICTin200 increased to $104.742 billion in 2005 from $29.225 billion in 2001, increasing nearly 2.6 times in the first five years, and increased to $148.675 billion in 2012, increasing only 42 percent relative to what it was in 2005. The growth rate in the export value of ICTin200 was more than that of import value. The export value of ICTin200 increased almost fivefold from

Table 4.1 Imports and exports of China-based ICT firm by types ($ billion)

Types	Imports			Exports		
	2001	*2005*	*2012*	*2001*	*2005*	*2012*
ICTin200 (Number)	55	62	30	53	77	56
ICTin200 (Value)	29.225	104.742	148.675	25.950	153.590	317.259
All in China	46.861	161.134	360.88	41.788	201.663	520.77
ICTin200 /All in China (%)	62.365	65.003	41.198	62.099	76.162	60.921
Component	4.926	23.731	22.551	3.758	22.891	29.745
EMS	6.255	45.869	74.805	5.678	63.027	195.628
OBM	18.044	35.142	51.319	16.514	67.672	91.886

Sources: China Customs Magazine, 2001, 2005 and 2012; Division of Development and Planning, Ministry of Science and Technology (2001); Ministry of Commerce, Bureau of Industry, Security, Import and Export Control (2005); Ministry of Commerce, Bureau of Industry, Security, Import and Export Control (2012); China High-tech Industry Data Book (2013).

'All in China': total value of international trade in computer and communication technology and electronic technology products in China.

$25.9 billion in 2001 to $153.5 billion in 2005, and then more than doubled again to $317.2 billion by 2012.

Apart from imports in 2012 (41.2 percent) the trade of ICTin200 accounted for more than 60 percent of national trade in ICT products, with the highest share reaching 76.1 percent of exports in 2005. Much of China's ICT trade was concentrated in a few companies, reflecting the development of the ICT sector in China. ICTin200 imports increased from 62.4 percent in 2001 to 65.0 percent in 2005, while exports increased from 62.1 to 76.2 percent. During the same period China's ICT trade shifted from deficit to surplus with ICT exports becoming more centralized in fewer companies. From 2005 onwards the trend moved in the opposite direction, with ICTin200's share of total imports falling from 65.0 to 41.2 percent, and its share of exports from 76.1 to 60.9 percent, indicating greater decentralization in the ICT sector and a reduction in the role of the ICTin200 listed companies. Since most companies in our sample were big FIEs, it is possible that Chinese small and medium-sized enterprises (SMEs) began to play a growing role in ICT trade, perhaps aided by the recent push for indigenous innovation.

As the design of ICT products such as the PC, mobile handset and tablet became more modular, each product consisted of multiple modules with a product architecture that specifies which modules are part of the system and their specific functions (Brandt and Thun, 2011). Modularity facilitated outsourcing of manufacturing and design, while the geography of the GVC underwent considerable change through offshoring. The composition of ICTin200 imports and exports shifted from being OBM-dominated in 2001 to an increasing dominance of EMS companies by 2012, which provides evidence of modularization (Figure 4.1). The share of OBM company imports declined from 61.7 percent in 2001 to 34.5 percent in 2012, with a more modest decline in the share of component companies, and with the EMS companies' share of imports increasing from 21.4 to 50.3 percent. A similar evolution occurred in relation to exports,

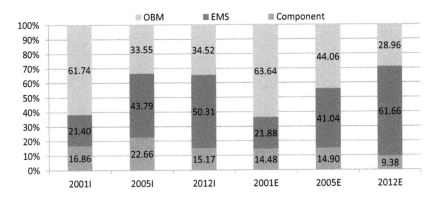

Figure 4.1 The composition changing of China-based ICT company by company type (percent)

Source: See Table 4.1

and this provides evidence of the ICT GVC evolution in China with growing outsourcing by OBMs to EMS, and with the production of major ICT companies in China being hidden in the exports of EMS companies.

Within the modular system of ICT production, core companies dominated the GVC while more peripheral component companies obtained limited profits (APEC Policy Support Unit, 2013). In the PC sector, the Wintel (Windows+Intel) model reflected the global dominance of Intel in microprocessors and Microsoft in operating systems. The more recent development of the smartphone, which is increasingly encroaching on the older model of desktop computing, has given rise to the Quadroid (Qualcomm+ Android) model, with Qualcomm dominating the production of microprocessors for smartphones and Google playing a leading role in the development of the Android open-source operating system. It is interesting to note that while Intel and Microsoft exercise considerable control in the ICT GVC, both companies have been struggling with the more recent shift to mobile devices, providing opportunities for other companies to become significant suppliers. Alongside this major shift in the ICT sector, Apple developed a separate closed iOS operating system for its iPhone and iPad products. It is worth noting that Apple's closed system for its PC products, however, was not as popular as that for its more recent mobile products. The possible reason is that the iOS operating system for its mobile products is more user-friendly than that for its PC products.

Although there have been significant differences between ICT sectors and also between major corporations in each sector, the overall thrust in recent years has been for OBMs to outsource much of the manufacturing and design to the EMS sector to achieve lower costs in the assembly process and also to reduce the costs of component supply chain logistics. A major consequence of these developments has been to push much of the global ICT manufacturing toward Asia and more recently most of the assembly activity to China, to benefit both from lower costs and a rapidly growing market for ICT products. Within a short few years, China has become the pre-eminent assembly location for the ICT GVC. Initially much of the outsourcing and offshoring by Western ICT companies went to Taiwan, but very rapidly much of this activity has been relocated to Mainland China by Taiwanese companies who continue to dominate the sector (Yang, 2014a; Kawakami and Sturgeon, 2011).

Modular production has facilitated multinational companies in establishing factories in China in order to take advantage of low costs, good infrastructure and highly developed supply networks necessary for manufacturing operations. The data indicate a fall in the number of joint ventures (JVs) from 29 in 2001 to 12 in 2012, which reflects the greater freedom of foreign companies in China since WTO membership. It is notable that no JVs were found among Taiwanese companies and that seven of the twelve remaining JVs in 2012 belonged to Samsung. Entry by foreign companies into the domestic market, however, has been restricted to forming a JV with a state-owned company, with the policy objective of Chinese companies acquiring technological knowledge through these JVs (Brandt and Thun, 2011). Thus in our data, the company's nationality indicates the origin of the investment, with 'multination' referring to companies with more than one foreign investor.

The country/economy of origin of China-based ICT companies

It is useful to examine the origins of major ICT companies that have outsourced their manufacturing to China. In this section, the country/economy of origin of three company types is investigated respectively. OBMs from a larger number of countries were involved in China's ICT trade in 2001 than in subsequent years, as companies from certain countries disappeared from the list of top traders (Table 4.2). Imports by brand companies expanded to $51.3 billion during this period compared with $91.8 billion in exports. The rate of increase in exports was more impressive from 2001 to 2005 compared with the later period, which presumably was affected by the global economic crisis. In 2001, exports by OBMs at $16.5 billion were less than imports at $18.0 billion, but by 2012, exports of $91.8 billion were much more significant than imports of $51.3 billion, reflecting the huge growth of assembly activity in China's ICT GVC during this period. Korean OBMs were outstanding in being responsible for both imports and exports, with the key company being Samsung and its subsidiaries.

It should be noted that Samsung is not only a major OBM, but has integrated brand, component supplier and manufacturing functions into one entity, with around one-third of its revenue coming from supplying key components such as microprocessors to competitor companies like Apple (APEC Policy Support Unit, 2013). In contrast to Samsung's in-house model, Apple outsources almost all of its production, while Motorola outsources 45 percent and Nokia 32 percent (Lee and Gereffi, 2013). While $35.97 billion of imports from Korean OBMs in 2012 accounted for 70.8 percent of the total of top importing ICT companies, Korean OBM exports in the same year of $34.7 billion, which was the largest

Table 4.2 Total imports and exports of China-based OBM companies by country/ economy of origin ($ billion)

Country	Imports			Exports		
	2001	*2005*	*2012*	*2001*	*2005*	*2012*
The U.S.	3.737	3.666		3.930	11.227	9.881
Japan	2.883	4.563	4.447	4.370	10.042	9.983
Canada	0.486					
Finland	2.036	1.642		2.085	3.503	5.356
Germany	1.131	0.634		0.500	0.817	
Netherlands	0.938	0.530		0.549	1.584	
Sweden	0.520			0.568		
Switzerland	0.145			0.280	0.399	
Korea	2.625	11.559	35.973	2.436	15.252	34.661
Taiwan	0.848	7.610	1.093	1.284	11.105	2.126
Multination	0.386	2.813	2.629	0.226	8.375	5.289
Mainland	2.309	2.125	7.177	0.285	5.368	24.590
Total	18.044	35.142	51.319	16.514	67.672	91.886

Sources: See Table 4.1

value of any nationality, accounted for a much smaller 39.0 percent. Growth in the contribution of mainland OBMs, both in terms of imports of $7.1 billion (14 percent) and exports of $24.6 billion (26.8 percent) in 2012 was impressive. Both the U.S. and Japanese brands continued to be relatively important to 2012, but this was before the demise of brands like Motorola more recently.

Total imports of $22.6 billion by ICTin200 component companies in 2012 were less than that of $23.7 billion in 2005, suggesting a growth in the sourcing of components from suppliers located in China (Table 4.1). By 2005, imports of $9.4 billion by Taiwanese component companies had already outstripped those of U.S. companies at $6.7 billion, and a similar ratio characterized 2012 when imports from Taiwanese Component companies of $11.1 billion were greater than the U.S. figure of $8.8 billion (Table 4.3). By 2005, Taiwanese companies were already playing a major role in the PC/laptop GVC, and it is clear that this role has continued to expand over time.

By 2012, imports by European and Japanese component companies, which previously had played a relatively small role, had disappeared. The two key economies of origin of component-exporting companies were again the U.S. and Taiwan, with $11.6 billion of U.S. company exports showing considerable growth from 2005 compared with Taiwan's more modest growth to $9.2 billion. While the contribution from mainland Chinese companies was very small, Hong Kong company exports of $4.2 billion were considerable. Research to date suggests that key core components of ICT products like computers and smartphones are being sourced, for the most part, from outside Mainland China, although recent reports tentatively argue that activity within China could soon influence up to 50 percent of hardware design globally (Orr and Thomas, 2014; APEC Policy Support Unit, 2013). Table 4.3 shows that exports by component companies located in China of $29.7 billion in 2012 have grown impressively, being much greater than imports of $22.6 billion. Yet, while an increasing proportion of

Table 4.3 Imports and exports of China-based component companies by country/economy of origin ($ billion)

Country	Imports			Exports		
	2001	*2005*	*2012*	*2001*	*2005*	*2012*
The U.S.	2.193	6.732	8.794	1.945	8.184	11.592
Japan	0.557	1.148		0.286	1.132	1.861
Europe	0.150			0.167		0.905
Taiwan	0.154	9.357	11.097	0.155	7.149	9.242
Hong Kong	1.290	1.129	1.350	0.753	2.784	4.155
Multination	0.582	4.588		0.452	2.766	
Korean			1.31			1.99
Mainland		0.777			0.876	
Total	4.926	23.731	22.551	3.758	22.891	29.745

Sources: See Table 4.1

Table 4.4 Imports and exports of China-based EMS/ODM companies by country of origin ($ billion)

Country	Imports			Exports		
	2001	2005	2012	2001	2005	2012
The U.S.	1.718	4.951	5.396	0.725	5.275	6.711
Canada		0.599			0.447	
Taiwan	2.832	36.66	64.4	4.051	54.68	181.611
Finland	0.282					
Hong Kong	0.141	0.499	3.477		0.476	3.853
Singapore		0.687	1.532		0.466	1.251
Korea						1.060
Multination	0.162			0.204		
Mainland	1.120	2.473		0.698	1.683	1.142
Total	6.255	45.869	74.805	5.678	63.027	195.628

Source: See Table 4.1

components is being assembled in China or may undergo some processes such as testing, only a small proportion of core components, such as microprocessors, are designed in China (PWC, 2014).

According to these data (Table 4.4), EMS activity in China took off significantly between 2001 and 2005, although Taiwanese companies and their supplier networks had already been relocating to Mainland China some years before that (Yang, 2007). Exports from EMS companies in China expanded hugely from $63 billion in 2005 to $195.6 billion in 2012, while the growth in imports by EMS companies from $45.9 billion to $74.8 billion during the same period was much lower.

While it is likely that some local Chinese companies have been supplying more basic components to an increasing extent in more recent years, many supplier companies followed their major clients particularly from Taiwan, but also from other countries when they relocated to China. Although the added value of assembly work by the EMS sector in China typically adds only around 3 percent of the total product price, the volume of assembly work, which has grown very significantly in China, particularly since 2005, makes a significant economic contribution. While China has become the major global assembly center for ICT products, much of the EMS sector is dominated by Taiwanese firms, with Foxconn playing a dominant role in the sector. While Foxconn is the assembler for a number of major technology corporations, around 40 to 50 percent of its revenue comes from Apple. It should be noted that while much of Apple's production in China is assembled by Foxconn, and Apple plays a major role in shaping the ICT GVC in China, this production is treated in these trade data as being derived from Foxconn. The contributions of U.S. and Hong Kong EMS companies are relatively modest and have not grown to any great extent.

In a recent extensive *New York Times* report, Barboza (2016) provides important insights into how the local government in Zhengzhou, where around half of the world's iPhones are made, have facilitated the Foxconn and Apple operations with a special customs zone. Previously, most MNC products made in China had to be shipped out of the country and brought back to be taxed as imports. In the Zhengzhou customs zone Foxconn can sell the products to Apple, who in turn can sell them to their subsidiaries. Rather than having to physically ship goods across any border, these transactions are carried out electronically, thus eliminating the need to pay duties or taxes on imported components.

The overall picture, therefore, from 2001 to 2012, is that some foreign companies have disappeared down the rankings of China's major ICT importers and exporters either because of outsourcing more functions to EMS companies, or because of mergers and acquisition (M&A), or because of failure to compete. By 2012, through a process of consolidation, the country of origin of the key contributors has been reduced in number, with the U.S. and Taiwan being important in components, Korea and the Mainland in OBMs, and Taiwan dominating the EMS/ODMs sector. Before relocating much of its assembly work to the mainland, Taiwan had already established itself as an important center for fabless chip manufacturing.

Key ICT companies in China by types

Having outlined the evolution of the three main groupings of companies by their country/economy of origin, attention will now be given to identifying the contributions of key companies within those groupings. The focus will be on the top 25 importing and exporting companies, which also include additional subsidiaries listed among the top 200 companies. The top 25 ICT companies account for approximately 50 percent of the total volume of China's ICT trade for these years. Tables 4.5, 4.6 and 4.7 present the companies included in top 25 ICT companies list in groupings of OBMs, component companies and EMS companies, showing their imports and exports for 2001, 2005 and 2012. All companies of any type that appears in any of the three years within the top 25 ICT companies list are included in these tables respectively, but they may not appear in each year.

The many examples of connections between OBMs, component companies and EMSs through client relationships, joint ventures and mergers and acquisitions over time create some difficulties in allocating companies to the most suitable category. Bonaglia and Goldstein (2007) track the transition of companies in developing countries from Original Equipment Manufacturers (OEMs) selling their own products with a foreign firm's brand affixed, to Original Design Manufacturers (ODMs), but note that a much smaller number have further progressed into Original Brand Manufacturers (OBMs).

Own brand manufacturers

Table 4.5 illustrates the varying fortunes of the major OBMs among the top 25 ICT companies operating in China between 2001 and 2012. With its focus on the trading activity of these companies, these data do not reveal the extent to which China's domestic economy has become a more significant aspect of their

Table 4.5 Imports and Exports of OBM companies among the top 25 ICT companies by year ($ billion)

Country	Company	Imports			Exports		
		2001	2005	2012	2001	2005	2012
The U.S.	Dell	0.14	0.77		0.22	2.43	1.89
	IBM	0.8			1.3	3.72	3.42
	Motorola	2.63	2.9		1.92	7.76	2.65
Taiwan	ASUS	0.4	4.8		0.41	6.21	
	BenQ	0.32	0.79		0.36	2.36	
	Micro-Star		1.6			1.61	1.06
Sweden	Ericsson	0.52	1.19		0.57	2.3	
The Netherlands	Philips	0.94	0.53		0.55	1.58	
Multination	Sony-Ericsson			2.63			4.07
Mainland	China Electronics				0.14		2.5
	Huawei	0.61	1.06	4.37		2.05	12.13
	Lenovo	1.09				1.36	2.71
	Unicom	0.43					
	ZTE	0.23	0.54	2.81		0.78	5.17
Korea	LG	1.02	1.77	8.24	0.98	3.56	5.8
	Samsung	1.42	9.79	27.73	1.25	11.69	28.86
Japan	Canon	0.39	0.98	2.18	0.78	2.44	3.36
	Epson	1.23	1.06		1.34	1.54	1.29
	Sanyo	0.25			0.32		
	Sharp	0.11	1.25	2.26	0.26	1.94	2.34
	Sony	0.34	0.61		0.36	0.98	
	Uniden	0.23			0.31	0.5	
Germany	Siemens	1.13	0.63		0.5	0.82	
Finland	Nokia	2.04	1.64		2.08	3.5	5.36
Canada	Nortel Networks	0.49					
Total		16.76	31.91	50.22	13.65	59.13	82.61

Sources: See Table 4.1

business activity in more recent years. Also hidden is the significant production of major technology companies such as Apple and HP because of their increased use of outsourcing, with much of their exporting being masked by that of EMS companies.

While Samsung, with its almost fully in-house production model is a very significant OBM with exports of $28.8 billion and imports of $27.7 billion in 2012, around one-third of its revenue is generated by its role as a major component supplier. This is reflected in the exports from four of Samsung's subsidiaries in China: $9.4 billion from its Huizhou manufacturer of the Galaxy mobile phone; $5.0 billion of laptops from its operation in Suzhou; $4.6 billion worth of display panels from an operation in Tianjin; and $4.5 billion of mobile phones from a separate operation in Tianjin.

Although of a smaller order, LG is also a significant Korean OBM exporter and also a supplier of components. With the Koreans, Chinese OBMs have also risen to the top of the list of major exporters with Huawei, a major global telecom equipment company in second place, exporting $12.1 billion in 2012 and ZTE exporting $5.17 billion. China Electronics (Zhongguo Dianzi), a SOE, is a more modest performer with $2.5 billion exports in 2012. Nokia is the only remaining European company with $5.36 billion exports, before being later sold to Microsoft. Motorola has also experienced a similar demise with part of the company being acquired by Google initially and more recently by Lenovo. It is remarkable to see the decline over time of U.S., European and Japanese OBMs, while Korean and Chinese OBMs replace them.

Some of this decline in their role as major exporters from China may be explained by the increased use of outsourcing. But the fading of major ICT brands is also the result of intense competition, with companies like Philips and Siemens offloading less profitable consumer production and in some cases benefiting from licensing their technology to local companies. PC production has evolved in recent years as an area of very tight profit margins, with its modularity facilitating greater outsourcing. While being one of the more modest exporters on the list, Lenovo with $2.7 billion exports in 2012 has outpaced Dell's $1.8 billion. Although Apple and Samsung have emerged as major global winners, particularly in smartphones, Chinese brands such as Xiaomi and Oppo have recently emerged as significant challengers within the local market.

Component companies

While China's success in creating globally successful brands in the ICT sector is impressive, particularly in competition with long-established Western technology companies, a very significant element in controlling the technological trajectory of the ICT GVC is the role played by major component companies, which also account for a significant proportion of the added value of ICT products. Many component companies such as Intel in semiconductors and Seagate in hard disk drives (HDDs) have long dominated the technological development of ICT products and continue to be designed and developed outside China, but their assembly and testing is increasingly outsourced to companies in China.

Overall the value of trade among the top 25 ICT component companies is quite modest, with imports at $22.5 billion being larger than exports at $16.1 billion in 2012, which reflects the growing importance of China as a major ICT assembly location (Table 4.6). Seagate, which together with Western Digital (not mentioned in these lists), form a duopoly in the production of hard disk drives globally, was the largest exporter ($3.4 billion) in 2012 and also a significant importer ($1.08 billion), and outsources production of HDDs to Kaifa or Shenzhen Kaifa Keji, which features on the list of EMS companies.

Intel, which is only listed as importing $3.6 billion in 2012 is the world's largest semiconductor company and came first in China, capturing 13.8 percent of the market. Since 2001, Intel has focused on its core competency of chip manufacturing while outsourcing Intel-branded motherboards to EMSs like Foxconn.

Table 4.6 Imports and exports of component companies among the top 25 ICT companies by year ($ billion)

Country	Company	Imports			Exports		
		2001	2005	2012	2001	2005	2012
The U.S.	Intel	0.42	2.40	3.59	0.40	2.49	
	Micron			2.24			2.22
	SanDisk			1.89			3.44
	Seagate	1.38	1.56	1.08	1.38	1.95	2.95
Taiwan	AU Optronics		3.45	4.01		1.83	
	Datung		2.30				
	TPK			1.69			
	Innolux		1.94	5.40		1.97	3.77
Multination	Hailiang storage	0.46			0.45		
	LG-Philips		3.35			1.22	
Japan	Mitsumi	0.44		1.31			
Korea	SK Hynix			1.35			
	Jingda Electronic						
Hong Kong	TPV Electronics	0.86	1.13		0.75	2.78	3.27
Total		3.56	16.13	22.55	2.99	15.43	15.65

Source: See Table 4.1

In a recent interview, one of Intel's vice-presidents noted that Intel's strategy for China's supply chain was to target the local market, and that products made in China might not be suitable for other countries (Chen and Tsai, 2014). Samsung's production, which is not visible in this list, comes second in China with 7.6 percent of the market for chips, and SK Hynix capturing 4.0 percent of the market. SK Hynix had imports of $1.3 billion in 2012 and was a major supplier of Dynamic Random Access Memory (DRAM) chips and flash memory to Apple, ASUS, IBM, HP and Dell. Micron, which was the largest U.S. maker of memory chips for PCs, imported $2.2 billion.

Indeed, while 56 percent of global consumption of semiconductors took place in China, China's own semiconductor industry only accounted for about 12 percent of worldwide production, and companies like Intel, Samsung and SK Hynix played a significant role in that production (PWC, 2014). PWC also notes, however, the possibility of one or two Chinese companies being among the top 30 suppliers to the market, but it points out that 28 percent of semiconductors used in China were purchased outside the country because of supply chain concerns of some customers such as controlling key inventory items and protecting intellectual property. The reliance of China's semiconductor industry on the U.S. industry is partly related to the complexity of chip design and manufacturing and the high level materials science required (Orr and Thomas, 2014). But with the center of gravity of electronics goods manufacturing shifting to China, both Intel's Fab 68 plant in Dalian and Samsung's advanced wafer fab plant in Xi'an are examples of significant inward investments in this sector. Fab 68 in Dalian has been making older generations of Intel chips because U.S. export restrictions bar Intel from producing its leading-edge technology in China. In 2015, Intel announced a plan which will spend up to $5.5 billion to convert a microprocessor factory in Dalian to make a new class of memory chip. The U.S. company Qualcomm, with 2.6 percent of the Chinese market for semiconductors, and a dominant supplier of smartphone applications processors, is not mentioned in the data because of outsourcing arrangements with EMS companies.

In addition to hard disk drives and flash memory, the other important sector reflected in the trade of component companies is the display or thin-film-transistor-crystal display (TFT-LCD) panel sector. While Samsung is a major supplier of processors to companies like Apple, it is also the world leader in TFT-LCD display, and together with LG and Taiwanese companies AU Optronics and Innolux account for 83 percent of the global output of this sector (Yang et al., 2012), indicating that the center of gravity of this sector is firmly in Asia. Innolux, listed in Table 4.6 as a component companies, is a world leading supplier of TFT-LCD panels for computers and mobile devices. AU Optronics, with exports of $2.9 billion and imports of $4.0 billion in 2012, was the result of a merger of Acer Display and Unipac Optoelectronics in 2001. In 2006, it acquired Quanta Display, and its combined share of the global market was 17 percent. In 2010, it invested in a new plant in Kunshan (Jiangsu Provinces) in China, having received approval from Taiwan on condition that the technology at home was more advanced. TPK, with imports of $1.69 billion in 2012, is a leading Taiwanese supplier of touch technology solutions for computers and mobile devices, reflecting the more recent shift in computing technology. The Hong Kong-based company, TPV Electronics, with exports of $3.27 billion in 2012, is one of the world's largest manufacturers of computer monitors. LG Philips, which is listed in Table 4.6 as a component company, is a joint venture between LG and Philips and focuses on LCD panels for laptops and TVs. LG's extensive localization of production in China has contributed to its success internationally, becoming one of the most popular washing machine brands in the U.S. in 2007, and the world's second largest LCD TV manufacturer in 2007.

EMS companies

One of the most significant developments in China's increased involvement in the ICT GVC during this period has been the enormous growth of outsourcing and offshoring by major technology companies and the subsequent growth in the EMS sector, dominated by Taiwanese companies, and particularly Foxconn.

While 22 EMS companies featured among the top 25 ICT companies during this period, only 10 were major exporters by 2012, with Foxconn exporting $80.35 billion (Table 4.7). Among its top five exporting plants were the following: $25.2 billion worth of mobile phone parts from Shenzhen (Guangdong Province); $15.7 billion of smartphones from Zhengzhou (Henan Province); $11.9 billion worth of laptops and tablets from Chengdu (Sichuan Province); $6.9 billion of computers, laptops, DVDs and components from Yantai (Shandong Province); and $6.0 billion of computer, communication and electronic products from Shenzhen (Guangdong Province). This reflects both the range of activity of Foxconn and its recent shifts to interior locations to achieve greater competitiveness in a sector with very tight profit margins.

With $37.0 billion exports in 2012, Quanta is the world's largest contract PC manufacturer, with HP and Dell being major clients and most of its production in China. Wistron Info, which was a spinoff from Acer, designs and manufactures desktop PCs, servers, LCD TVs and handheld devices for HP, Acer and Dell and exported $11.9 billion of production in 2012. With the center of gravity of ICT assembly having moved to Mainland China, the trade data in Table 4.7 indicate that Taiwanese companies had a major advantage over EMS companies from elsewhere. It would also appear to be the case that much of the exports of these EMSs mask the production of their major clients. In Foxconn's case, it is estimated that 40–50 percent of its revenue is generated by Apple. Pegatron, which was spun off from ASUS in 2010 and exported $22.7 billion in 2012, is also a major competitor with Foxconn for Apple contracts. Having relocated some of its operations to the interior of China in recent years, Foxconn appears to have lost out to some extent to Pegatron, which would raise questions about the suggestion that Apple's power within the ICT GVC has been diminished (Yang, 2014b). Inventec, with exports of $9.7 billion in 2012, manufactures on behalf of HP, Toshiba, Acer and Fujitsu Siemens. Although Taiwanese companies are responsible for the production and final assembly of much of the EMS market,

Table 4.7 Imports and Exports of EMS/ODM companies among the top 25 ICT companies by year ($ billion)

Country	Company	Imports			Exports		
		2001	2005	2012	2001	2005	2012
The U.S.	ChipPAC	0.50			0.36		
	Flextronics	0.46	2.70	2.16	0.19	3.02	2.82
	Jabil Circuit		0.61	1.70		0.68	2.95
	Solectron	0.52	0.64			0.53	
Taiwan	Compal	0.23	2.51		0.31	6.62	
	Elitegroup	0.30	1.42		0.48	1.54	
	First International Computer	0.25			0.31		
	Foxconn	1.63	16.00	47.41	2.03	17.44	80.35
	Inventec		5.00			7.29	9.71
	Kinpo Electronic	1.19					16.20
	Lite-On IT		1.31			1.94	
	MiTAC	0.67	1.01		0.76	2.63	
	Pegatron			5.53			22.77
	Quanta		6.53	6.03	0.16	11.92	37.03
	Universal Scientific		0.59	1.45		0.45	
	Wistron InfoComm		1.87	1.72		3.04	11.92
Singapore	STATS ChipPAC		0.69	1.53		0.47	1.25
Mainland	Shenzhen Kaifa	0.39	0.79		0.44	0.74	1.14
	SMIC	0.55	0.90			0.95	
Hong Kong	Goldland Electronics			1.82			2.04
	Singular Gold			1.65			1.81
Total		6.69	42.57	71	5.04	59.26	189.99

Sources: See Table 4.1

Notes: In 2004, STATS merged with ChipPAC to form STATS ChipPAC; Shanghai Lucent merged with Jabil Circuit in 2002 and with Nokia in 2016. Ambit Microsystems has been a subsidiary of Foxconn Electronics (trade name: Hon Hai Precision Industry) since March 2004 when they merged.

it should be noted that most semiconductor chips continue to be manufactured by companies like Flextronics and ChipPAC rather than Foxconn and Quanta.

Motorola, Samsung and Huawei in China

Indeed, focusing on some specific ICT companies is useful to gain insights into China's role in the ICT GVC. Thus, Motorola, Samsung and Huawei are selected as case studies in this section for several reasons. First, from the perspective of ownership, Motorola and Samsung are foreign invested firms, and Huawei is a Chinese indigenous firm, which could reflect the shifting of China's participation in ICT GVC through foreign and indigenous content. Second, from the perspective of development, Motorola represents other firms that have declined, like Nokia and Alcatel, while Samsung represents firms that are in fashion, and Huawei represents firms that are catching up, like ZTE and Xiaomi. Third, from the perspective of products, Motorola, Samsung and Huawei all provide mobile devices; Motorola and Huawei manufacture communications equipment; Motorola and Samsung manufacture semiconductors, although Samsung also manufactures office equipment, components like displays and other products.

Motorola

Motorola Inc. was an American multinational telecommunications company based in Schaumburg, Illinois, U.S. which began business in 1928. In 1987, Motorola opened a representative office in Beijing and entered the Chinese market. In 1992, Motorola (China) Electronics Ltd. of sole American ownership was established in Tianjin Economic and Technological Development Area, where today the company runs one of the world's major manufacturing facilities for communications equipment.

Motorola's development in China has involved four major strategies. The first was focused on investing in technology transfer and increased intensity in research and development. The second was management localization, which involved nurturing local management personnel. The third was supporting domestic products, which involved training providers in China and localizing the production of supporting products. The fourth was the implementation of joint ventures and cooperation projects. Each of these four strategies sought to convince the Chinese state of the company's long-term commitment to the market (Wang, 2010).

In 2006, Motorola China had three wholly-owned companies, one holding company, five joint venture firms and 25 branch companies located in China. Of these, Motorola (China) Electronics and Hangzhou Motorola Mobile Communication Device were two main exporters. Until 2008, Motorola's investment in China totaled about $3.5 billion, being one of the largest foreign-invested enterprises in China. In order to improve their relations with the Chinese state, Motorola, like other FIEs, were willing to facilitate China's efforts to improve its technological position by investing in R&D, developing new value-added software and undertaking training initiatives. Over time and after numerous interactions, these activities and resource exchanges between Motorola and key network constituents were accepted as 'approved features of current and future interactions and relationships' (Low and Johnston, 2008, 874). Motorola seems to have successfully secured and managed their network legitimacy.

Despite these efforts, the company lost around $4.3 billion from 2007 to 2009 and was divided into two independent public companies, Motorola Mobility and Motorola Solutions, in 2011. In order to prepare Motorola's spinoffs, Motorola

Table 4.8 Imports and exports of Motorola companies among the top 200 traders ($ billion)

No.	Time	Subsidiaries	2001E	2005I	2005E	2012I	2012E	Products
1	1992	Motorola (China) Electronics	1.613	2.358	6.451			Cell phone, wireless communication equipment, semiconductor
2	1996	Hangzhou Motorola mobile communication device	0.310	0.537	1.311			CDMA, GSM mobile, communication device
3	2010	Motorola mobile technology (China)					2.653	Communication device and network equipment
		Total	1.923	2.895	7.762		2.653	

Source: See Table 4.1

Notes: As mentioned in Methodology and data, China Customs (in Chinese) published a list of China's Top Exporting Firms and a list of China's Top Trading Firms (Imports and Exports) in 2001 list. Although we could derive the import data for each firm in the 2001 list according to total trade and export, it is hard to know the import information of each firm's subsidiaries in China. Thus, row 1 in 2001 has a value of zero.

China set up a new company – Motorola Mobile Technology (China) – which focused on mobile devices and broadband services, while Motorola (China) Electronics continued to work on business mobile solutions and network systems. According to the trade data in Table 4.8, China continues to be a manufacturing base of mobile devices for Motorola providing products for the global market, but the mobile solutions and network systems business is focused on China's market. Seven months after Motorola Mobility was spun off as an independent company, Google acquired it for $12.5 billion. After this acquisition in 2013, Motorola's phone business retreated from Mainland China.

On January 29, 2014, Google announced that Lenovo planned to acquire Motorola Mobility's smartphone business for approximately $2.91 billion. Google retained ownership of the vast majority of Motorola Mobility's patent portfolio, including active patent applications and invention disclosures. As part of its ongoing relationship with Google, Lenovo received a license for this rich portfolio of patents and other company intellectual property. Additionally Lenovo received over 2,000 patent assets, as well as the Motorola Mobility brand and trademark portfolio. On October 30, 2014, Lenovo finalized its purchase of Motorola Mobility from Google.

More recently, Motorola announced it will re-enter the Chinese smartphone market, which is one of the biggest in the world. It should be remembered that at one time Motorola had a 40 percent share of China's smartphone market.

Lenovo's acquisition of Motorola, however, is not just about devices. Lenovo's strategy is to use Motorola to kickstart its smartphone entry into the U.S. market, while Motorola will use Lenovo's influence overseas to tap into markets it has failed to penetrate to date (Ion, 2015). The rise and fall of the Motorola brand both within China and globally, and its more recent evolution into an alliance with one of China's successful companies, provides an interesting case study of how the fortunes of foreign companies in China can wax and wane.

Samsung electronics

Samsung Electronics is the flagship division of the Samsung Group, the largest group in South Korea, accounting for 70 percent of the group's revenue in 2011. It is the world's second largest information technology company by revenue, after Apple. Samsung Electronics has assembly plants and sales networks in 80 countries and employs around 370,000 people. As of June 30, 2016, Samsung Electronics' consolidated subsidiaries totaled 160 (Samsung Electronics' Business Report Q2 2016). The *Global Value Chain Analysis on Samsung Electronics* (The Commercial Section of the Canadian Embassy in the Republic of Korea, 2012) traces each step of the mobile product division's value chain, while analyzing the R&D system in depth.[1] Samsung's increased internationalization is reflected in a higher proportion of manufacturing, sales and gradually an increasing volume of R&D taking place outside of Korea.

Increasingly production of mobile phones is being located in Vietnam as opposed to China. However China, which has about 30 Samsung subsidiaries, is expected to be the major component manufacturing location in the future (see Table 4.9). Of these, 15 subsidiaries were listed among the top 200 traders in China. Huizhou Samsung Electronics which produces the GALAXY mobile phone, the most popular mobile product on the market, is Samsung's most important exporter, while Tianjin Samsung Communication Technology also provides other mobile devices.

In 2011, the main assembly locations for Samsung mobile phones were Korea, China and Vietnam, while its three components logistics centers for Asia were Tianjin, Shanghai and Hong Kong. In addition, Suzhou Samsung Electronics and Computer was its main exporter of laptops, and Dongguan Samsung Display the main exporter of important display components for electronics devices (see Table 4.10).

To date Samsung's product divisions developed the final products usually in Korea, but in the future production is more likely to be located in China.

R&D is the main focus of seven of Samsung's 30 subsidiaries in China, which accounts for 23.3 percent of total subsidiaries, but none of these, from Samsung's perspective, is a major subsidiary. Samsung's global R&D network spans six Samsung centers in Korea, and 18 more across the U.S., UK, Russia, Israel, India, Japan and China – not to mention their organizations in Universities across the globe (see Table 4.11).

Table 4.9 The list of consolidated subsidiaries in China

No.	Name of Subsidiaries	Date of Establishment	Major business	Dec 31, 2015 Assets	% ownership	Classified as major subsidiary (Y/N)
1	Samsung Display Dongguan Co., Ltd.	2001.11	Display panel production	1,276,263	Over 50%	Y
2	Samsung Display Tian Jin Co., Ltd.	2004.06	Display panel production	958,820	Over 50%	Y
3	Samsung Electronics Hong Kong Co., Ltd.	1988.09	Sale of electronic goods	948,800	Over 50%	Y
4	Suzhou Samsung Electronics Co., Ltd.	1995.04	Production of home appliances	637,485	Over 50%	Y
5	Samsung Suzhou Electronics Export Co., Ltd.	1995.04	Production of home appliances	385,732	Over 50%	Y
6	Samsung (CHINA) Investment Co., Ltd.	1996.03	Sale of electronic goods	12,748,395	Over 50%	Y
7	Samsung Mobile R&D Center, China-Guangzhou	2010.01	R&D	52,046	Over 50%	N
8	Samsung Tianjin Mobile Development Center	2010.08	R&D	24,628	Over 50%	N
9	Samsung R&D Institute China-Shenzhen	2013.03	R&D	12,014	Over 50%	N
10	Samsung R&D Institute China-Xian	2013.07	R&D	12,349	Over 50%	N
11	Samsung Electronics Suzhou Semiconductor Co., Ltd.	1994.12	Semiconductor processing	836,562	Over 50%	Y
12	SEMES (XIAN) Co., Ltd.	2013.07	Semiconductor equipment	1,001	Over 50%	N
13	Samsung Electronics (Shandong) Digital Printing Co., Ltd.	1993.03	Production of printers	853,982	Over 50%	Y
14	Samsung Electronics Huizhou Co., Ltd.	1992.12	Production of electronic goods	6,192,974	Over 50%	Y
15	Tianjin Samsung Electronics Co., Ltd.	1993.04	Production of TV and monitors	858,675	Over 50%	Y
16	Beijing Samsung Telecom R&D Center	2000.09	R&D	65,595	Over 50%	N

(Continued)

Table 4.9 (Continued)

No.	Name of Subsidiaries	Date of Establishment	Major business	Dec 31, 2015 Assets	% ownership	Classified as major subsidiary (Y/N)
17	Tianjin Samsung Telecom Technology Co., Ltd.	2001.03	Production of telecom products	2,075,123	Over 50%	Y
18	Shanghai Samsung Semiconductor Co., Ltd.	2001.10	Sale of semiconductor and display panels	3,792,437	Over 50%	Y
19	Samsung Electronics Suzhou Computer Co., Ltd.	2002.09	Production of electronic goods	886,593	Over 50%	Y
20	Samsung Suzhou Module Co., Ltd	2002.09	Display panel processing	684,646	Over 50%	Y
21	Samsung Suzhou LCD Co., Ltd	2011.07	Display panel production	2,784,122	Over 50%	Y
22	Shenzhen Samsung Electronics Telecommunication Co., Ltd.	2002.02	Sale of telecom products	118,697	Over 50%	Y
23	Samsung Electronics Shanghai Telecommunication Co., Ltd.	2001.11	Sale of telecom and network products	6,151	Over 50%	N
24	Samsung Semiconductor (China) R&D Co., Ltd.	2003.04	R&D	24,818	Over 50%	N
25	Samsung Electronics China R&D Center	2004.05	R&D	35,644	Over 50%	N
26	Samsung (China) Semiconductor Co., Ltd.	2012.09	Semiconductor production	9,742,388	Over 50%	Y
27	Samsung Semiconductor Xian	2016.04	Sale of semiconductor and display panels	0	Over 50%	N
28	Samsung Electronics (Beijing) Service Company Ltd.	2005.01	Services	160,151	Over 50%	Y
29	Tianjin Samsung LED Co., Ltd.	2009.05	LED production	349,963	Over 50%	Y
30	Tianjin Samsung Opto-Electronics Co., Ltd.	1994.02	Camera/camcorder production	125,762	Over 50%	Y

Source: Samsung Electronics Business Report Q2 2016

Table 4.10 Imports and exports of Samsung companies among the top 200 traders ($ billion)

No.	Set up	Subsidiaries	2001E	2005I	2005E	2012I	2012E	Products
1	1992	Huizhou Samsung Electronics	0.299		0.791	8.597	9.422	Mobile phone GALAXY
2	1993	Tianjin Samsung Electronics			0.535	1.483	1.366	Video play, DVD
3	1993	Samsung Electronics (Shandong) Digital Printer					1.194	Office equipment (print, fax etc.)
4	1993	Shandong Samsung Communication Equipment		0.397	0.784			Office equipment (print, fax etc.)
5	1993	Tianjin Samsung Electrical Machine	0.315					Electronic and electrical components
6	1994	Samsung Electronics (Suzhou) Semiconductor		4.318	3.538	3.895		semiconductor
7	1995	Suzhou Samsung Electronics	0.155					white household appliance
8	1996	Shenzhen Samsung Display			0.701			Display
9	1997	Dongguan Samsung Display		0.470	0.658	3.623	4.632	Display
10	1998	Tianjin Samsung Electronics Display	0.233		0.629			Display
11	2001	Tianjin Samsung Communication Technology		1.847	1.178	4.522	4.240	mobile phone
12	2002	Suzhou Samsung Electronics Display	0.247	1.404	1.468	2.246	1.016	Display
13	2002	Suzhou Samsung Electronics and Computer		0.667	0.885	1.332	5.055	laptop
14	2002	Shenzhen Samsung Kejian Mobile Telecommunication Technology		0.683	0.525			Samsung CDMA mobile phone
15	2004	Tianjin Samsung Mobile Display				2.036	1.932	Mobile Display
		Total	1.248	9.786	11.692	27.734	28.857	

Source: See Table 4.1

Notes: See Table 4.8

Table 4.11 Samsung global R&D network

No.	Center name	R&D area	Location
1	Samsung Information Systems America, Inc. (SISA)	Strategic parts and components, core technologies	U.S.
2	Dallas Telecom Laboratory (DTL)	Technologies and products for next-generation telecommunications systems	U.S.
3	Samsung Electronics Research Institute (SERI)	Mobile phones and digital TV software	EU
4	Moscow Samsung Research Center (SRC)	Optics, software algorithms and other new technologies	Russia
5	Samsung R&D Institute India – Bangalore (SRIB)	System software for digital products, protocols for wired/wireless networks and handsets	India
6	Samsung Telecom Research Israel (STRI)	Hebrew software for mobile phones	Israel
7	Beijing Samsung Telecommunication (BST)	Mobile telecommunications standardization and commercialization for China	China
8	Samsung Semiconductor China R&D (SSCR)	Semiconductor packages and solutions	China
9	Samsung Electronics (China) R&D Center (SCRC)	Software, digital TVs and MP3 players for China	China
10	Samsung Yokohama Research Institute	Core next-generation parts and components, digital technologies	Japan
11	Samsung Poland R&D Center (SPRC)	STB SW Platform Dev., EU STB/DTV commercialization	EU
12	Samsung R&D Institute India – Delhi (SRID)	S/W Platform and Application Design, Graphic design	India

Source: Samsung Electronics Website, Research and Development

Three of the seven R&D subsidiaries – Beijing Samsung Telecommunication (BST), Samsung Semiconductor China R&D (SSCR) and Samsung Electronics (China) R&D Center (SCRC) – are listed on Samsung's global R&D network, which indicates that other subsidiaries with an R&D function merely support manufacturing and sales. These networks analyze the latest technology trends to specify which technologies might offer the greatest benefits. While Samsung's focus on China for sourcing components is currently appropriate, in the future Vietnam could also become a competing location. China, therefore, faces considerable challenges in retaining the interest of global corporations like Samsung.

Huawei

Huawei is an important Chinese manufacturer in the telecoms equipment industry as mentioned above. In fact, as China's primary manufacturer of telecoms equipment, and indeed as a major global player in this sector, the company constitutes a significant portion of the history of the industry in China. The four domestic firms, Huawei, ZTE, Datang and Great Dragon Technology, are central to the development of the ICT industry in China. Chinese people use the term 'Great China' to describe those four companies because by combining in reverse order the first character from the names of these companies (Ju-Great Dragon, Da-Datang, Zhong-ZTE, Hua-Huawei), the phrase 'Great China' is created in Chinese (Fan, 2006). This phrase reflects China's pride in these domestic companies that have risen rapidly and competed confidently with the giant MNCs, with Huawei achieving the greatest level of success through leadership, intensive R&D and internationalization.

Huawei's founder and sole leader since its inception, Ren Zhenfei, was convinced that the country's 'exchange market for technology' policy was mistaken and would result in a loss of the domestic market to MNCs. Not only were Chinese companies unable to obtain foreign technologies to the extent that was expected, but they faced many other disadvantages compared with global corporations (Fan, 2006). Thus, at the outset, Ren established clear goals

> to develop the national industry, not to set up joint ventures with foreign companies, to closely follow global cutting-edge technology, to insist on self-development, to gain domestic market share, and to explore the international market and compete against international rivals.
>
> (Xiao, 2002, 127)

Through these goals, Ren aimed to build Huawei into a world-class and technologically advanced telecoms equipment manufacturer.

Table 4.12 Imports and exports of Huawei companies among the top 200 traders ($ billion)

No.	Set up	Subsidiaries	2001E	2005I	2005E	2012I	2012E	Products
1	1987	Huawei Technologies	1.062	2.052	1.717	8.555		networking and telecommunications equipment and services
2	1993	Huawei Device				2.649	3.574	smartphones, tablet computers and other communication device
		Total	1.062	2.052		4.366	12.129	

Source: See Table 4.1

Notes: See Table 4.8

Huawei ignored the lucrative stock and real estate businesses in the early 1990s and 'was stubborn enough to put all his eggs in one basket', investing heavily in R&D. Huawei has over 70,000 product and solution R&D employees, comprising more than 45 percent of its total workforce worldwide. In addition to China, 16 R&D centers were established in Germany, Sweden, the U.S., France, Italy, Russia and India with the goal of taking the lead in research, innovation and implementation of future networks.

In 2014, Huawei invested RMB 40.8 billion ($6.6 billion) in R&D, which was 14.2 percent of revenue compared with 12 percent for Microsoft, 10.4 percent for Amazon and 14.9 percent for Google (Truong, 2015). In 2016, Huawei invested RMB 76.391 billion, which was 14.6 percent of revenue bringing Huawei's cumulative spend on R&D to more than RMB 300 billion (Huawei's Research & Development, 2016). This high internal R&D investment is a direct result of its founder's determination to improve the company's innovation capability. In-house R&D has turned out to be the most important factor for domestic firms to improve their innovation capability.

Internationalization plays an important role in the catch-up race of emerging countries' MNCs. Internationalization for Huawei, as for many other MNCs from emerging economies, has been a key means for achieving strategic learning, capability building and company growth (Sun, 2009). The first step toward internationalization in Huawei's case was providing customized design for a 'number portability service' for Hutchison Telecoms of Hong Kong in 1996. It took Huawei only three months to complete this contract compared with European competitor quotations of at least six months, and the price was only half of that of competitors (Li and Cui, 2004). Indeed, Huawei has adopted various entry modes for different international markets, including JVs in Russia, export entry mode in South America, Asia and Africa, and contractual entry modes in North America, Western Europe and other regions (Wu and Zhao, 2007).

Meanwhile, other factors such as external alliances have contributed to Huawei's improvement in innovation capability. The company has actively undertaken joint R&D laboratories with foreign companies, such as Texas Instruments (TI), Motorola, International Business Machines Corporation (IBM), Intel, Ageare, ALTERA, SUN, Microsoft and NEC, focusing on various telecom technologies. In addition, the active role of the government, clustering of R&D functions, an industry trend moving toward configuration technology, and sub-sector linkages have all contributed to Huawei's successful development, which shows that the government can play a positive role in guiding and helping domestic firms to accumulate innovation capabilities.

FIE perspectives on China's participating in ICT GVC

Many of the foreign technology companies interviewed in Shanghai between 2009 and 2017 were very focused on penetrating the Chinese domestic market and had some interesting observations in relation to the intense competition from local Chinese companies. Many interviewees were impressed with the significant strides made by Huawei, leaving the former world leader Ericsson in second place in the global market, despite being almost excluded from the U.S. market, possibly for political reasons. The manager of a significant foreign competitor said he would respect companies like Huawei and ZTE for being aggressive and flexible, that they were unlike publicly quoted companies, and because of considerable support from the Chinese government they could adopt a more flexible approach toward structuring deals, and they were prepared to make a loss for up to two years by providing equipment to clients.

Together with other interviewed managers, he agreed that Huawei, while not being a technology leader, in the sense of coming up with radically new products, had achieved significant business success and that it showed it was possible to sustain market dominance without being a technology leader. Among the reasons he gave for their ability to increase their market share was their focus on customer requirements, and their practice of co-designing products with their customers. He also noted that once they decided that a particular option was the correct one, they had significant resources to invest in it, and that while being a technology follower, they had an impressive ability to adapt ideas from Western companies and apply them more effectively to the Chinese market. He explained that while it might take Ericsson up to five years to produce an upgrade, Huawei's approach was to split upgrades into smaller sections and to edge their way forward in the market gradually. Other interviewees acknowledged that Chinese companies had mastered the technology very well, and in some cases they won contracts because of providing more and better features, including better customer service (Interview 2015).

A manager of a mid-sized U.S. semiconductor company explained that his company in China worked with Chinese companies like Huawei, Haier and also with U.S. companies like Dell. They also worked with Taiwanese EMS companies, engaging with them in Taiwan, and then through their own engineers collaborating with their engineers in their plants in locations like Shenzhen. In relation to the semiconductor sector in China, he noted that none of the very sophisticated work, like developing the next (semiconductor) node to make it smaller, was carried out in China. He explained that the most advanced technology nodes were not yet in China and that much of the activity carried out by Intel, for example, was back end manufacturing. He pointed out that it was not possible to have recently graduated engineers working on next generation processors since that work required people who had been learning from a master for 10–20 years. However, with the important role played by managers from Taiwan, Chinese companies could leapfrog the need to develop local engineers from scratch and could be expected to move toward higher levels of innovation within 10–15 years (Interview 2011). Other interviewees noted that the Chinese market presented particular challenges for foreign multinational companies, whose products were often too highly priced and were facing considerable competition from local companies who were seeking to move up the value chain.

While acknowledging the ongoing regulated nature of the Chinese market, such as the requirement for foreign investors who wish to set up internet services in China to form a joint venture with a local company, the manager of a major U.S. software company showed considerable understanding of the approach adopted by the Chinese government. Noting that the existence of a fully free market would make it very difficult for local companies to compete with major global internet companies, he foresaw that regulation would evolve over time, converging to a situation of almost equal opportunity for both foreign and local companies. Apart from regulatory barriers, this interviewee also felt that the approach taken by the headquarters of some multinational companies was sometimes based on a remote understanding of the market, which also contributed to the slow progress of their companies in China (Interview 2011). Such views, based on considerable experience of running foreign operations in China, provide useful contextual background in helping to understand the patterns already analyzed in the previous sections, suggesting that there is a wide range of factors at work explaining both the rise of Chinese brands despite the overall slow progress in radical technological innovation.

Thus while China has creatively adopted existing ICT technologies, it has had very modest success with indigenous innovation. As Hong (2017, 79) has suggested, 'the global competition of building a ubiquitous, mobile, broadband network to enable next-generation innovation, business and consumption further amplifies China's technological deficits in the critical internet-related digital areas'.

Is BAT the future of China's ICT sector?

With the continuing shifts in the ICT GVC in an era of mobile devices, cloud computing and expanding ecommerce, it seems that the potential for Chinese companies to create more intense competition for established global corporations is considerable. Whether they can gain greater market penetration globally without the necessary progress in vital areas of intellectual property remains to be seen.

In addition to being one of the largest internet companies in the world, Alibaba is also the world's largest retailer, having surpassed Walmart in April 2016. Having forced eBay out of China's domestic market, the group's websites accounted for 60 percent of all parcels delivered in China and 80 percent of online sales by September 2014 (The New York Times, Nov 11, 2014). In 2014, Alibaba's IPO, the biggest public offering in history, showed that Chinese tech firms have a distinct advantage as they become more global. The reaction to Alibaba's rise, however, has been quite different in China and in the U.S. While many Chinese consider Alibaba, which is based in Hangzhou, to be a role model in innovation and entrepreneurship, they also wonder why it did not IPO in China. In the U.S., on the other hand, many regard Alibaba, China's largest e-commerce company, as one of the most valuable U.S.-traded tech companies, almost on par with Facebook and older tech giants like IBM. By adopting foreign technologies to the needs of developing markets, the company now serves 80 million customers in 250 countries (Abrami et al., 2014). As Alibaba is poised to expand its presence in international markets, so also are the other two major 'BAT' companies, Baidu, which is China's 'Google', and Tencent, which is China's major social networking company. In 2014, the BAT companies were listed among the world's top 10 internet companies. Moreover, JD.com, Xiaomi, NetEase and others have also shown their international competitiveness in China's market. On March 5, 2015, the Chinese premier, Li Keqiang, launched the 'Internet Plus' plan in the *Report on the Work of the Government*. 'The plan', the official organ stated, 'aims to integrate mobile Internet, cloud computing, big data and the Internet of Things with modern manufacturing, to encourage the healthy development of e-commerce, industrial networks, and Internet banking, and to help Internet companies increase international presence'.(Li, 2015).[2]

Obviously, the Internet is not just a technology or business tool, but also an important part of a national strategy for future competitiveness. Despite the rhetoric, however, Beijing's strict control of internet content is likely to constrain the potential of such initiatives. It should also be noted that the success of Chinese internet companies in China must be evaluated in the context of what is one of the most controlled sectors in the economy, with little evidence of success to date by non-Chinese companies.

Value creation

As mentioned above, more attention needs to be given to the capability to create added value, which is reflected in company profit levels. In Alibaba's case, 80 percent of its revenue comes from online commerce in China, with only 9 percent from outside markets and 2 percent from cloud computing and internet infrastructure (Alibaba Annual Report, 2015). Alibaba primarily derives revenue from online marketing services where sellers pay marketing fees to acquire user traffic, commissions based on Gross Merchandise Volume (GMV) for transactions settled through Alipay and membership fees. In 2015, pay-for-performance (P4P), marketing services and display marketing services accounted for 48 percent of total revenue, while commissions and fees from membership and value-added services accounted for 30 percent and 8 percent, respectively. In other words, Alibaba earns rent from internet throughput and platform position, which is similar to a commercial real estate company.

In 2015, Tencent's revenue increased by 30 percent to an impressive RMB 102.9 billion. Revenue from Value-Added Services (VAS business), including its online gaming business, digital content subscription services, QQ Membership subscription services and virtual item sales increased by 27 percent to RMB 80.7 billion, and accounted for 78.4 percent of the total. Revenue from online advertising business increased by 110 percent to RMB 17.5 billion, accounting for 17 percent of the total (Tencent Annual Report, 2015). In other words, Tencent earns rent from content, services, virtual production and advertising based on its two instant messaging platforms, QQ and Wechat, which is similar to an entertainment company. Because the Chinese Firewall, which controls the Internet, has blocked Google services such as Google search, Gmail, YouTube, maps, etc., the Android ecosystem in China is chaotic and is being replaced by WeChat that provides a wide range of mobile services (Thun and Sturgeon, 2017). They go on to point out that Tencent's WeChat is a private company that has benefited from state policy to block foreign competitors, but it has succeeded in China's highly competitive market.

In 2015, Baidu generated 83.7 percent of its revenue from the provision of search services, 10.5 percent from transaction services and 7.87 percent from iQiyi, an online video platform (Baidu Annual Report, 2015). Search services are keyword-based marketing services targeted at and triggered by internet users' search queries, which contribute the largest proportion of Baidu's total revenues among three operating segments. Transaction services mainly include Qunar, Baidu Nuomi and Baidu Takeout Delivery (Waimai). iQiyi is an online video platform with a content library that includes copyright movies, television series, cartoons, variety shows and other programs. iQiyi derives most of its revenue from online advertising services. In other words, Baidu earns rent from internet throughput and advertising, which is similar to an advertising company. While Baidu functions as China's 'Google', Google's service itself remains quite unstable in China since relocating its servers to Hong Kong in 2010 because of its unwillingness to comply with government requests to filter its search results. Other major Western internet companies that are blocked from China's market include YouTube, Facebook and Twitter.

In the final analysis, BAT companies have a high dependency on internet throughput and market size which is central to the network effort of internet economics. In fact, valuable content is its core advantage and its content lies in the middle segments between internet throughput and users. In 2014, China's Baidu, Alibaba and Tencent all moved into content creation. Big web companies in China are uniquely positioned to take advantage of providing content when you consider that 60 percent of Chinese consumers watch TV and movies on their cell phones or tablets (Coonan, 2014).

Ownership

An important part of China's policy shift toward indigenous innovation in 2006 was about strengthening local firms and their innovation outcomes. The focus was on Chinese companies as opposed to all companies operating in China. Yet, while most BAT company operations are conducted in Mainland China and most of their revenue is sourced from China, Alibaba, Baidu and Tencent are all registered in the Cayman Islands, and BAT's main shareholders are foreigners. In other words, rather than being Chinese companies, they are companies that operate in China and provide evidence that companies that are willing to comply with China's strict internet regulations can succeed in the country.

Alibaba has two beneficial owners with greater than 5 percent of total ordinary shares. One is the Japanese software corporation SoftBank, which accounts for 31.8 percent, and the other is Yahoo, accounting for 15.3 percent in 2015. SoftBank Corp. is a public company listed on the Tokyo Stock Exchange and Yahoo! Inc. is a public company listed on the NASDAQ Global Select Market.

In addition, Jack Yun MA controls 7.6 percent of shares and Joseph C. TSAI 3.1 percent. In order to control the company, Jack Ma created the Alibaba Partnership which currently has 30 members. Unlike dual-class ownership structures that employ a high-vote class of shares to concentrate control among a few founders, the partnership approach is designed to embody the vision of a large group of management partners. The most important point is that the Alibaba Partnership has the exclusive right to nominate and appoint up to a simple majority of the members of their board of directors, which is nominated by a shareholder meeting or by the main shareholders generally.

Baidu's major shareholders include Robin Yanhong Li with 16.1 percent, and Baillie Gifford & Co (a Scottish partnership) with 7.2 percent. To our knowledge, approximately 79.0 percent of the total outstanding ordinary shares were held by four shareholders in the United States, including approximately 78.2 percent held by The Bank of New York Mellon, the depositary of Baidu's American depositary shares program (ADS).

Tencent's major shareholders are MIH TC with 33.51 percent, Advance Data Services Limited with 9.1 percent and JPMorgan Chase & Co. with 6.24 percent. MIH TC is controlled by Naspers Limited through its wholly-owned intermediary companies, MIH (Mauritius) Limited, MIH Ming He Holdings Limited and MIH Holdings Proprietary Limited. Naspers is a broad-based multinational internet and media group, offering services in more than 130 countries.[3] Advance Data Services Limited is wholly-owned by Ma Huateng, the founder of Tencent. The ownership profile of these companies provide an interesting illustration of how free market economics within the international arena works hand in hand with a restrictive regulatory environment in China's hybrid economy. On the other hand, China is becoming more open to foreign investment in the internet sector, while becoming more restrictive in controlling internet content within China.

In addition, the variable interest entity (VIE) structure, an elaborate legal arrangement, designed 14 years ago to help Chinese tech and financial companies that hold restricted government-issued domestic licenses to raise money overseas should be mentioned. The Alibaba Group is set up as a traditional VIE, which is a structure invented in the 1990s to allow foreign investors to have limited ownership in Chinese companies. VIE structures allow offshore-listed companies to consolidate domestic Chinese firms in their financial statements by creating the appearance of ownership. Of the more than 200 Chinese companies listed on the New York Stock Exchange and the NASDAQ, 95 use a VIE structure and have audited financial filings for 2013. They include China's biggest internet companies, such as Baidu and JD.com. It is unclear, however, how enforceable the rights of VIEs are in Chinese courts, as they have not been tested to date.

Monopoly

According to their market share, the BAT companies are the big three in China's internet market. Baidu holds 72 percent of the search market, with little opposition from Google, whose services are restricted in China. Alibaba Holdings, the e-commerce behemoth, holds more than 50 percent of the e-commerce market and Alibaba's Taobao.com, an online retail site, currently has more than 370 million users. Tencent is China's largest instant messaging provider, occupying 76 percent of market share.

Despite leading in their respective domains, Tencent and Baidu are aggressively expanding their business portfolios, and they are seeking to enter the e-commerce field. Alibaba is also seeking to enter the social network and entertainment sectors, while Baidu is reported to be expanding into the social space. In China, almost all internet companies are related to BAT, or have been acquired or invested in by BAT. Clearly, an internet oligopoly has formed among Chinese internet enterprises, with BAT taking up to 70 percent of the total market value of all listed internet companies in China (Qiang, 2011).

The three internet giants hold stable monopolized positions in the sectors of search engines, instant messaging and e-commerce, respectively, which poses challenges to the interests of internet users, the prosperity of the industry and government supervision. More importantly, such a concentration of ownership and control is not conducive to the innovative development of China's internet sector. The Chinese government should formulate rules to prevent large corporations from abusing their dominant position, as this would provide for a more positive development of China's internet market. Because of political considerations associated with national security, it is unlikely that the market will be opened to direct competition from Western internet companies.

Notes

1 The Commercial Section of the Canadian Embassy in the Republic of Korea commissioned this report to the Korea Associates Business Consultancy Ltd. (www.kabcltd.com) www.albertacanada.com/korea/images/GlobalValueChainAnalysis-SamsungElectronics.pdf.
2 Li, K.,2015 *Report on the Work of the Government.* www.gov.cn/guowuyuan/2015-03/16/content_2835101.htm
3 Its principal operations are in ecommerce (i.e. classifieds, online retail, marketplaces, online comparison shopping, payments and online services), video entertainment and print. With a market capitalization of over $66 billion it is the largest company in Africa and the 7th largest internet company in the world.

References

Abrami, R.M., Kirby, W.C. and McFarlan, F.W., 2014, 'Why China can't innovate and what's it's doing about it', Harvard Business Review, 3, 107–111.

Alibaba Group, 2015, 'Alibaba annual report 2015', Available at www.alibabagroup.com/en/ir/presentations/pre150507.pdf. Accessed 07/18/2017.

APEC Policy Support Unit, 2013, 'Global supply chain operation in the APEC region: Case study of the electrical and electronics industry', Available at http://publications.apec.org/publication detail.php?pub_id=14311. Accessed 07/18/2017.

Baidu, 2015, 'Baidu annual report 2015', Available at http://media.corporate-ir.net/media_files/IROL/18/188488/reports/Baidu%202015%2020-F.PDF. Accessed 07/18/2017.

Barboza, D., 2016, 'How China built "iPhone city" with billions in perks for Apple's partner', Available at www.nytimes.com/2016/12/29/technology/apple-iphone-china-foxconn.html?smid=tw-share. Accessed 07/18/2017.

Bonaglia, F. and Goldstein, A., 2007, 'Strengthening productive capacities in emerging economies through internationalisation: Evidence from the appliance industry', Available at www.oecd.org/dev/39147683.pdf. Accessed 07/18/2017.

Brandt, L. and Thun, E., 2011, 'Going mobile in China: Shifting value chains and upgrading in the mobile telecom sector', *International Journal of Learning, Innovation and Development*, 4(1–3), 148–180.

Breznitz, D. and Murphree, M., 2011, *Run of the Red Queen*, New Haven, Yale University Press.

Chan, J., Pun, N. and Selden, M., 2013, 'The politics of global production: Apple, Foxconn and China's new working class', *The Asia-Pacific Journal*, 28(2), 100–125.

Chen, L. and De Lombaerde, P., 2013, 'China moves up the value chain: What can be learned from the Asian NICs?' *International Area Studies Review*, 16(4), 407–430.

Chen, M. and Tsai, J., 2014, 'Taiwan IT supply chain has considerable global influence, says Intel VP', Available at http://world.einnews.com/article/209662551/as8-yWBUJLjycjT7. Accessed 07/18/2017.

China Customs Magazine, 2001, 2005 and 2012 (In Chinese), The list of Top 200 firms in foreign trade. Available at www.ccmag.cn/NewsAction.jspa. Accessed 07/18/2017.

Clelland, D., 2014, 'The core of the Apple: Dark value and degrees of monopoly in global commodity chains', *Journal of World-Systems Research*, 20(1), 82–111.

Cooke, P., 2013a, 'Global production networks and global innovation networks: Stability versus growth', *European Planning Studies*, 21(7), 1081–1094.

Cooke, P., 2013b, 'The ICT-led model of economic evolution in global innovation networks: ICT and eco-innovation as qualitative comparison', In P. Cooke, G. Searle, K. and O'Connor, ed. *The Economic Geography of the IT Industry in the Asia Pacific Region*, Oxon, UK, Routledge.

Coonan, C., 2014. China's Baidu, Alibaba, Tencent Move Into Content Creation. Available at www.hollywoodreporter.com/news/chinas-baidu-alibaba-tencent-move-759808. Accessed 07/18/2017.

The Commercial Section of the Canadian Embassy in the Republic of Korea (2012). Global Value Chain Analysis on Samsung Electronics. Available at www.alberta-canada.com/korea/images/GlobalValueChainAnalysisSamsungElectronics.pdf. Accessed 07/18/2017.

Division of Development and Planning, Ministry of Science and Technology (2001). Statistical results of China's trade in high-tech products in 2001. Available at www.scsti.org.cn/oldweb/report2/11.doc.Accessed 07/18/2017.

Fan, P., 2006, 'Catching up through developing innovation capability: Evidence from China's telecom-equipment industry', *Technovation*, 26(3), 359–368.

Gereffi, G., 2014, 'Global value chains in a post-Washington Consensus world', *Review of International Political Economy*, 21(1), 9–37.

Grimes, S. and Du, D., 2013, 'Foreign and indigenous innovation in China: Some evidence from Shanghai', *European Planning Studies*, 21(9), 1357–1373.

Guillaume, G., Lemoine, F. and Unal, D., 2011, 'China's foreign trade in perspective of a more balanced economic growth', Available at www.cepii.fr/PDF_PUB/wp/2011/wp2011-03.pdf. Accessed 07/18/2017.

Hong, Y., 2017, *Networking China – The Digital Transformation of the Chinese Economy*, Champaign, IL, University of Illinois Press.

Huawei, 2016, 'Huawei's annual report 2016', Available at www.huawei.com/-/media/CORPORATE/PDF/annual-report/AnnualReport2016_cn.pdf?la=zh. Accessed 07/18/2017.

Ion, F., 2015, 'Motorola will re-enter the Chinese market with a new smartphone, the Moto X Pro', Available at www.pcworld.com/article/2865804/motorola-will-re-enter-the-chinese-market-with-a-new-smartphone-the-moto-x-pro.html. Accessed 07/18/2017.

Karabell, Z., 2009, *Superfusion – How China and America Became One Economy and Why the World's Prosperity Depends on It*, New York, Simon & Schuster.

Kawakami, M. and Sturgeon, J.T., 2011, *The Dynamics of Local Learning in Global Value Chains: Experiences From East Asia*, Houndmills, Palgrave Macmillan.

Lee, J. and Gereffi, G., 2013, 'The co-evolution of concentration in mobile phone global value chains and its impact on social upgrading in developing countries', Available at www.capturingthegains.org/publications/workingpapers/wp_201325.htm. Accessed 07/18/2017.

Li, C. and Cui, H., 2004, 'The report of Huawei internationalization', *IT Time Weekly*, 18, 24–38.

Li, K., 2015, Report on the Work of the Government. Available at www.gov.cn/guowuyuan/2015-03/16/content_2835101.htm.

Lin, G., Wang, C., Zhou, Y., Sun, Y. and Wei, Y., 2011, 'Placing technological innovation in globalising China: Production linkage knowledge exchange and innovative performance of the ICT industry in a developing economy', *Urban Studies*, 48(14), 2999–3018.

Low, B. and Johnston, W., 2008, 'Securing and managing an organization's network legitimacy: The case of Motorola China', *Industrial Marketing Management*, 37(7), 873–879.

Ministry of Commerce, Bureau of Industry, Security, Import and Export Control, 2005, 'Statistics of China's Trade in High-tech Products in 2005', Available at http://cys.mofcom.gov.cn/article/m/cv/aa/200601/20060101434187.shtml. Accessed 07/18/2017.

Ministry of Commerce, Bureau of Industry, Security, Import and Export Control, 2012, 'Statistics of China's trade in high-tech products in 2012', Available at http://cys.mofcom.gov.cn/article/m/cv/aa/201302/20130200019690.shtml. Accessed 07/18/2017.

Ministry of Science and Technology of the People's Republic of China, 2013, 'China high-tech industry data book 2013', Available at www.sts.org.cn/sjkl/gjscy/data2013/data13.pdf. Accessed 07/18/2017.

Mozur, P. and Wang, S. (2014) For online retailers like Alibaba, Singles' Day in China is a bonanza, *The New York Times*, Nov 11, 2014.

OECD, 2012, *China in Focus: Lesson and Challenges*, Paris, OECD.

Orr, G. and Thomas, C., 2014, 'Semiconductors in China: Brave new world or same old story?' Available at www.mckinsey.com/insights/high_tech_telecoms_internet/semiconductors_in_china_brave new_world_or_same_old_story. Accessed 07/18/2017.

PWC, 2014, 'China's impact on the semiconductor industry: 2014 update', Available at www.pwccn.com/home/eng/tech_china_impact_on_semiconductor_ind.html. Accessed 07/18/2017.

Qiang, X., 2011. Baidu, Tencent, Alibaba forming oligopoly on Chinese Internet. Available at www.chinadaily.com.cn/bizchina/2011-02/18/content_12042514. htm. Accessed 07/18/2017.

Samsung Electronics, 2016, 'Samsung electronics' business report Q2 2016', Available at www.samsung.com/us/aboutsamsung/ir/ireventpresentations/earningsrelease/downloads/2012/20160728_conference_eng.pdf. Accessed 07/18/2017.

Schimmer, M., Mueller-Stewens, G. and Sponland, P., 2010, 'The battle between Apple, Microsoft and Google: Strategic lessons from a converging internet industry 2000–2010', Available at www.ifb.unisg.ch/~/media/internet/content/dateien/instituteundcenters/ifb/lehre/lehrbuecher%20und%20fallstudien/case%20studies/the%20battle_310-245-1s_inspection%20copy_c_en.pdf. Accessed 07/18/2017.

Sturgeon, T.J., 2003, 'What really goes on in Silicon Valley? Spatial clustering and dispersal in modular production networks', *Journal of Economic Geography*, 3(2), 199–225.

Sturgeon, T.J. and Gereffi, G., 2009, 'Measuring success in the global economy: International trade, industrial upgrading and business function outsourcing in global value chains', *Transnational Corporations*, 18(2), 1–36.

Sun, S.L., 2009, 'Internationalization strategy of MNEs from emerging economies: The case of Huawei', *Multinational Business Review*, 17(2), 129–156.

Tencent, 2015, 'Tencent annual report 2015', Available at www.tencent.com/zh-cn/articles/1700051460102129.pdf. Accessed 07/18/2017.

Thun, E. and Sturgeon, T. (2017) When global technology meets local standards: reassessing the China's Mobile telecom policy in the age of platform innovation. MIT Industrial Performance Center Working Paper 17-001. Cambridge, MA.

Truong, A., 2015, 'Huawei's R&D spend is massive even by the standards of American tech giants', *Quartz*, March 31, 2015. Available at https://qz.com/374039/huaweis-rd-spend-is-massive-even-by-the-standards-of-american-tech-giants/. Accessed 07/18/2017.

UNCTAD, 2013, 'World investment report 2013: Global value chains: Investment and trade for development', Available at www.cggc.duke.edu/pdfs/2013_UNCTAD_WIR_GVCs_and_Development.pdf. Accessed 07/18/2017.

Wang, W., Chen, Y., Ching, K. and Chu, Y., 2010, 'A case study on the Motorola China's localization strategy', *The Journal of International Management Studies*, 5(1), 54–61.

Wu, D. and Zhao, F., 2007, 'Entry modes for international markets: Case study of Huawei, A Chinese technology enterprise', *International Review of Business Research Papers*, 3(1), 183–196.

Xia, J., 2012a, 'Competition and regulation in China's 3G/4G mobile communications industry – institutions, governance, and telecom SOEs', *Telecommunications Policy*, 36(7), 403–421.

Xia, J., 2012b, 'Reprint of: Competition and regulation in China's 3G/4G mobile communications industry – institutions, governance, and telecom SOEs', *Telecommunications Policy*, 36(10–11), 798–816.

Xia, J., 2012c, 'China's telecommunications industry in the era of 3G and beyond: Market, technology, and institutions', *Telecommunications Policy*, 36(10–11), 793–797.

Xiao, W., 2002, *Enterprise Leaders That Influence China's Economy*, Shenyang, Shengyang Press Ltd.

Xing, Y. and Detert, N., 2010, 'How the iPhone widens the United States trade deficit with the People's Republic of China', Available at www.adbi.org/files/2010.12.14. wp257.iphone.widens.us.trade.deficit.prc.pdf. Accessed 07/18/2017.

Yang, C., 2007, 'Divergent hybrid capitalisms in China: Hong Kong and Taiwanese electronics clusters in Dongguan', *Economic Geography*, 83(4), 395–420.

Yang, C., 2014a, 'Market rebalancing of global production networks in the Post-Washington Consensus globalizing era: Transformation of export-oriented development in China', *Review of International Political Economy*, 21(1), 130–156.

Yang, C., 2014b, 'State-led technological innovation of domestic firms in Shenzhen, China: Evidence from liquid crystal display (LCD) industry', *Cities*, 38, 1–10.

Yang, C.F., Pai, C.C. and Lee, Z.Y., 2012, 'Performance assessment of the top ten TFT-LCD manufacturers', *International Journal of Electronic Business Management*, 10(2), 85–100.

5 China's evolving role in Apple's GVC

A micro view

Using Apple's 2015 published list of supplier companies and their subsidiaries, this chapter analyzes how one of the world's most significant lead technology companies and its network of suppliers have become increasingly embedded in China's ICT industry. To be specific, it will first make the case for examining Apple's supply chain both globally and in China within the context of global value chain thinking generally. Next it will look in detail at the mapping of Apple's supply chain of component suppliers both globally and within China. Finally, it will trace the evolution of Asia's evolving value chains and look in particular at China's role in the ICT GVC, including the rise of China's local brand company, Xiaomi. In examining this detailed case study of Apple's supply chain, it is useful to bear in mind that Apple, albeit one of the most significant ICT companies globally, is but one of many major global technology companies, together with an extensive ecosystem of both foreign and Chinese supplier companies that constitute that part of the ICT GVC, which is located in China.

Introduction

With the accelerating process of globalization, the geography of the GVC in the ICT sector has been changing in recent years as the center of gravity of production, and to some extent innovation, has been shifting away from the more developed regions of the world to emerging regions in Asia and particularly in China. Much of this relocation of elements of the ICT global value chain results from the increased fragmentation of production through outsourcing by global lead technology companies of non-core functions to other companies, and in many cases to offshoring an increasing range of activities to lower cost locations. MNCs and local companies play a very important role in the process of offshoring. The pattern of this evolving geography of production continues to change over time as markets in Asia become more significant, and also as the capabilities of supplier companies within Asia improves.

In addition to tracing the evolving geography of the ICT global value chain, the particular attention of scholars has been given to the benefits or otherwise of increasing integration of emerging countries in these value chains as the number of supplier companies become concentrated in these regions as part of the local ICT ecosystem. While bearing in mind that many suppliers are not Chinese companies, this process of increasing integration can be a double-edged sword for local companies in emerging countries. Some scholars see this integration of emerging regions in a positive light, with local supplier companies improving their capabilities over time and in some cases becoming significant competitors of lead companies from more developed regions. Sun et al. (2013) note that while the theory suggests a positive impact on suppliers in developing countries, this impact must work through indigenous absorptive capability. Others present a more negative evaluation, suggesting that participation in the supply chains of lead technology companies can result in a subservient relationship which can prevent supplier companies from becoming more innovative and independent.

As a lead firm, Apple plays a vital role in the global ICT network. Satariano and Burrows (2011) explain how Apple has obtained competitive advantage and much higher profit margins in their closed ecosystem compared to rival companies by exerting control over nearly every piece of the supply chain from design to retail store. Although this study focuses more on the assembly of hardware in China, it should be remembered that much of the value of Apple products is derived from the software platform and design that the company creates in the U.S. Jacobides and MacDuffie (2013) regard Apple as an extreme example of a system integrator company with inordinate control in the manufacturing process. It fosters competition within its supply chain by breaking up component processing steps across multiple vendors, which helps Apple preserve product secrecy since suppliers are not sure how the components will be finally used. Janoski et al. (2014) add that Apple prevents its suppliers from growing significant market power by keeping them dependent and by switching key suppliers frequently.

On the other hand, it has been suggested that Apple's asymmetric power in the GVC may have been reduced with its increased focus on China's domestic market in the post-crisis period, as major contract manufacturing companies like Foxconn increase their influence in relation to the location of production (Yang, 2013). Some, however, like Clelland (2014), dispute Cooke's (2013) claim that Apple does not perform as a 'global controller' within the ICT GVC, and they argue that its exploitation of labor highlights some negative dimensions, including its monopolistic role within the GVC. Although there is little doubt that Apple and other major lead companies continue to exercise considerable power within the GVC, the hidden nature of their operations as a result of extensive outsourcing to major contract manufacturers like Foxconn, makes it difficult to identify them in the official trade statistics. Meanwhile, it is worth noting that China is an important market for Apple's product, and the performance of the Chinese market does influence Apple's overall performance.

This chapter will focus at the micro-level on the increasingly important role of China in the ICT global value chain, primarily as one of the major centers of production of sophisticated electronic equipment such as PCs, laptops, tablet computers and smartphones. The terms 'supply chain' and 'value chain' are used interchangeably in this chapter, as the supply chain is related to the value chain, but it is more connected to industry and engineering and involves activities such as procurement and logistics. As mentioned above, value chain analysis, which originated with Porter (1985), examines how companies organize and locate different functions and activities to benefit from the comparative advantage of different regions (World Trade Organization, 2013).

In particular, by analyzing Apple's supply chain, both globally and in China, this chapter seeks to examine how one of the world's most significant ICT companies has been exploiting the comparative advantage of China in recent years to increase its competitiveness globally. By becoming the major global center of production, assembly and testing for ICT products such as smartphones, tablets and laptop computers, China has succeeded in attracting global lead companies involved in ICT together with their core and non-core suppliers. By mapping both the global networks and the networks within China of Apple's supply chain, insights are provided into the significance for China and Chinese companies of increased absorption in the ICT GVC.

The key question to be explored is to what extent has China benefitted from the increased involvement of MNCs like Apple's supply chain in the country? To what extent have Chinese companies become involved in Apple's supply chain, what range of functions are they responsible for, and what do they learn from Apple's supply chain? Meanwhile, this chapter also investigates the rise of Chinese local brand company Xiaomi, as a consequence of China's involvement in the GVC. It is useful to remember that while this chapter, for practical reasons, focuses on the specifics of Apple's supply chain, many of the supplier companies involved are also suppliers to many other major technology companies.

Methodology and data

By analyzing Apple's model, we explain how the company exercises considerable control over the manufacturing process and exploits modularization through coordinating activities in the value chain. Although many suppliers for lead companies like Apple are located in emerging markets like China, because the center of gravity of production has shifted there, many core component suppliers are also leading technology companies from advanced regions, which increases the foreign dominance of the GVC. The potential, therefore, for 'catch up' among emerging economy companies, can be unequally distributed and depends on how widely diffused the necessary sophisticated technical and managerial capabilities required for dealing with increasingly complex functions are (Lee and Gereffi, 2015).

The list of suppliers and classification

An important starting point for this chapter is Apple's list of supplier companies, globally and particularly those located in China, which provides the name and location of each supplier. This facilitates an analysis of the geography of supplier companies both globally and within China and the identification of significant clusters of Apple suppliers in particular Chinese locations. Apple suppliers are classified into three groupings similar to that suggested by the smiling curve. Core component suppliers provide high value-added components, while non-core suppliers provide low value-added components, and 'other suppliers' provide a range of production services including assembly and testing, foundry, packaging and printing.

The bill of materials (BOM) is a useful framework for distinguishing between different types of supplier companies. The BOM provides a comprehensive list of raw materials, components and assemblies required to build or manufacture a product, and it can be illustrated in a hierarchical format, with the topmost level showing the end product, and the bottom levels displaying individual components and materials. Apple produces a range of products such as the iPhone and iPad, with each product having a specific BOM for the range of components provided by supplier companies.

Apple's suppliers can be classified as high and low value-added components, according to the BOM of Apple products. In the case of the iPad Air, for example, the BOM is $270, with a display costing $77 being the most expensive component. The BOM for the iPhone 6 is $196, with a display at $45 being the most expensive component (Jones, 2014). Hence the display is regarded as a core component of Apple products. The BOM is used in this chapter, therefore, as a general framework for classifying supplier companies, supplying components to Apple across their range of products even though specific information on the value-added contribution of each component may be lacking.

Second, in the case of several products, components in the BOM are divided into three categories. Core components include display, printed circuit board (PCB), integrated circuit (IC)/discrete device, optical module, electroacoustic component, internal memory and hard disk/CD-ROM. Non-core components include connector/function/structure, peripheral devices, battery and passive devices, while a third category of 'Others' includes foundry/original design manufacturing (ODM)/ original equipment manufacturing (OEM), packaging and printing and others. The connector/function/structure group includes electronic connectors, electronic functional components and electronic structural components. These components are soldered together on a PCB to create an electronic circuit with a particular function such as an amplifier, radio receiver, oscillator or wireless. Among the main electronic components are resistors, capacitors, transistors, diodes, operational amplifiers, resistor arrays and logic gates.

Research method: social network analysis and location quotient

To illustrate the global distribution of component suppliers, use is made of social network analysis (SNA), with country/economy of origin and country/economy of location being the key nodes in the network. SNA, which emerged as a key technique in modern sociology, is the process of investigating social structures through the use of networks and graph theories. In this chapter, SNA is used to investigate the outsourcing structure of Apple's supply chain. Within the outsourcing network, countries/economies are the nodes, and the outsourcing relationships between origin and destination are the ties. The linkages between destination location and the direction of linkages illustrate the countries of origin and the destination locations, while the significance of a particular country in the network is reflected not only by the number of suppliers originating in it, but also by the number of connections between them and other locations. The origin-location networks are visualized through UCINET – a software program in which nodes are represented as points, and ties are represented as lines.

The position of a country in the network can be measured by the degree of centrality. In the case of the origin-location network as a directed network, two separate measures of the degree of centrality can be defined, namely in-degree and out-degree. Accordingly, in-degree is a count of the number of outsourcing ties directed to a country while out-degree is the number of outsourcing ties that the country directs to others. Mapping Apple's supply chain in this manner distinguishes between those locations in which much of the intellectual property associated with the products originate, and the locations to which various functions in the production process have been outsourced and offshored.

While mapping the geography of linkages within Apple's supply chain globally provides an overview of outsourcing and offshoring arrangements within the GVC, we make use of the location quotient (LQ) to analyze the geographical distribution of Apple's production activities within China. The LQ is a valuable tool for quantifying how 'concentrated' a particular industry is in a location/ region relative to the national distribution, or how 'unique' a particular region is in comparison to the national average. It can highlight those regions in a country in which a particular activity may be over-represented, under-represented or actually reflects the national average.

The LQ is used to identify the key concentrations of subsidiary suppliers in China at a provincial and city level and to compare the distributions of the three categories of subsidiaries used in the study. In this chapter, X is the number of one kind of subsidiary suppliers in a location, and Y is the total number of all subsidiary suppliers in that location. X/Y is then the 'concentration' of the type of suppliers in that location. If X' and Y' are similar data points for some larger reference region, like a country, then the LQ or relative concentration of the kind of suppliers in that location is similar to that of the country $(X/Y)/(X'/Y')$. In order to simplify the process, the LQ can be measured by dividing the regional share of a particular category of suppliers in the country by the regional share of total suppliers in the country.

Data

In addition to Apple's list of suppliers, extensive web searching was used to identify the key components being supplied by the supplier companies. While much of the supply chain is likely to remain relatively stable from year to year, Apple is also likely to replace suppliers from time to time, depending on their performance. A database of supplier companies in Apple's global value chain based on this threefold classification was complied, connecting particular companies with components based on the threefold classification of their value-added.

Apple's list of suppliers provided company names and addresses, while additional information was derived through internet searches. Through an extensive search of supplier websites it was possible to specify the component provided by each supplier. It was necessary to match product components to Apple suppliers to specify their position in the global value chain. In the case of display, for example, the key companies in Apple's list of suppliers included Japan Display Inc, LG Display Co., Ltd., Sharp Corporation and another 21 companies. Hon Hai Precision Industry Co., Ltd (Foxconn), Pegatron, Flextronics International Ltd and six other companies provided foundry and OEM/ODM services to Apple.

Further, by specifying the country of origin and the country of location of each of the subsidiaries, and specifying the provincial and city location of subsidiaries located in China, it was possible to track both the global spread of Apple's GVC and the particular role played by China within that GVC. The firm-level database allows an analysis of the role of different company types within Apple's GVC, with the location of supplier companies illustrating the spatial structure of outsourcing and offshoring in Apple's GVC.

China's role in Apple's global value chain

Although Apple's network of supplier companies is examined specifically, both globally and within China, and therefore in a direct manner its supply chain, the current investigation is conceptualized within the framework of the global value chain which seeks to track the range of activities involved in producing a product or a range of products. It also examines the role of Apple which has significant influence in shaping the trajectory of the technology and also in coordinating the role of supplier companies in the supply chain (Lee and Gereffi, 2015).

Among the tactics used by Apple to exercise power in the GVC are exclusive agreements with equipment manufacturers such as high-end drills; making prepayments to key suppliers which can limit the options of competitor companies; obtaining discounts on parts, manufacturing capacity and air freight; keeping their engineers close to the manufacturing operations to tweak the process when necessary; and by insisting that many key suppliers keep two weeks of inventory within a mile of assembly plants in Asia (Satariano and Burrows, 2011). Apple regularly flies large numbers of their engineers from the U.S. to spend time in the production facilities of contract manufacturers like Foxconn and Pegatron to ensure that the production process reaches the high levels required by the company

The geographical distribution of Apple's suppliers

In the 2015 list of suppliers (see Table 5.1), Apple had 198 companies and 759 subsidiaries, 336 – or 44.2 percent – of which were located in China. Of these, 48 percent of companies and 47 percent of subsidiaries were core component suppliers, while 37.8 percent of companies and 38.4 percent of subsidiaries were

Table 5.1 Number of companies and subsidiaries by type

Types	Companies (Number)	Total Subsidiaries (Number)	Subsidiaries in China (Number)	Subsidiaries in China (Percent)
Core components				
Display	24	76	32	42.1
PCB	16	40	20	50
ICs	35	189	33	17.5
Optical	8	17	8	47.1
Electroacoustic	7	18	13	72.2
Internal Memory	3	11	3	27.3
Hard Disk/CD Rom	2	5	3	60
Total	95	356	112	31.1
Non-core components				
Connector	50	152	91	59.9
Peripheral devices	10	27	21	77.8
Battery	7	29	12	41.4
Passive devices	8	84	23	27.4
Total	75	292	147	50.3
Others components				
Foundry, ODM/OEM	9	54	43	79.6
Packaging/ Printing	11	36	24	66.7
Others	8	21	10	47.6
Total	28	111	77	
Total	198	759	336	44.2

Data sources: Authors' research based on Apple's 2015 list of suppliers

non-core component suppliers. In the third grouping of 'others' were 14.1 percent of companies and 14.6 percent of subsidiaries. Of the core component subsidiaries, 31.1 percent were located in China, compared with 50.3 percent of non-core and 69.3 percent of the others group. While the general trend is for more high value-added activities to be located outside of China, this is not true for each of the core component categories. Thus, in the case of integrated circuits, which is the largest category of supplier companies with 35 companies and 189 subsidiaries, only 16.9 percent of the subsidiaries were in China.

While the majority of companies and their subsidiaries originated in a relatively small number of countries, the subsidiaries are widely distributed globally in 30 countries, with China being the most significant location, having 44.2 percent of the total. Japan comes in second with 17.1 percent, varying from 15.1 percent of core suppliers to 23.2 percent of non-core, and 7.2 percent of others. The U.S. is the only other country with almost 10 percent of all subsidiaries, varying from 9.6 percent of core, to 14.3 percent of non-core and 3.7 percent of 'others'. Korea and Taiwan each had less than 5 percent of the subsidiaries and many other countries had less than 1.0 percent, suggesting that with the general shift of the ICT GVC toward China, many of Apple's supplier subsidiaries, who also in many cases supply other technology companies, have an increasing proportion of their activity located in China. In fact, only 33.1 percent of all subsidiaries were located in developed market economies (including U.S., Europe, Israel and Japan), 44.2 percent in China and 22.6 percent in other Asian and mainly Central American locations.

Of the 198 companies in Apple's supply chain, 14 were Chinese and of the 759 subsidiaries, 29 were Chinese. Of the 14 Chinese companies, five were core component suppliers and eight of the 29 subsidiaries were core component suppliers. Among the core Chinese companies, there was one display, two PCB companies with three subsidiaries, and two electroacoustic component companies with four subsidiaries. This suggests a small beginning for Chinese companies in supplying core components to Apple, but it does point to what could be a greater potential for involvement over time. Among the more numerous non-core companies, there were five connector companies with 10 subsidiaries and three battery companies with six subsidiaries. Finally there was one packaging and printing company in the third grouping of 'others'. Although the overall contribution of Chinese companies to Apple's supply chain is modest, the fact that even a small number of Chinese companies have achieved the status of becoming Apple suppliers against the global competition is a significant development.

The origin-location network of Apple's core suppliers

Because Apple's product supply is significantly dependent on suppliers of core components, these companies are central to its competitive advantage. The relational network between countries of origin and destination location of the 356 core component supplier subsidiaries appear in figure 5.1.

The 759 supplier subsidiaries originated from 16 different countries, while their operations were located in 30 countries. Three countries/economies of origin accounted for 80.2 percent of the total, and 32.7 percent were Japanese, 28.5 percent were the U.S. and 19.0 percent were Taiwanese. Of the remainder, 6.5 percent were European and 7.5 percent were Asian, of which only 3.95 percent were from Mainland China. Thus, while both the Japanese and Taiwanese contributions ensured a strong Asian presence, most of the subsidiaries originated in developed market economies. Taking the 391 subsidiaries that are supplying core components (display, PCB, integrated circuits, optical modules, electroacoustic components, internal memory and hard disk/CD Rom), 40.4 percent are U.S. company subsidiaries, 26.8 percent are Japanese, 10.7 percent are Taiwanese and 9.2 percent are Korean, together accounting for 87.1 percent of the total. Subsidiaries from Europe account for 8.0 percent, while the remaining

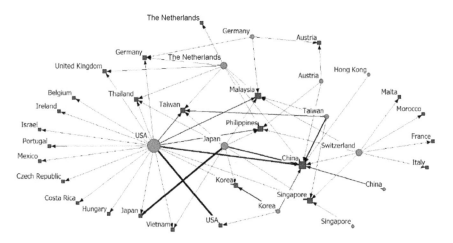

Figure 5.1 The origin-location network of core component supplier subsidiaries

Note: The circles represent countries of origin and the boxes represent location countries. The size of circles and boxes reflects the in-degree or out-degree of each country; the width of links indicates the number of subsidiary connections between countries; the arrows indicate the direction from origin to location. China means Mainland China, excluding Hongkong, Macao and Taiwan.

1.2 percent is from Hong Kong and Singapore. Only 8 (2.2 percent) of the core component subsidiaries were from Mainland China.

The U.S., with 141 subsidiaries originating in it, is dominant as a country of origin, mainly because of its strength in the semiconductor industry, with its main destination linkages for subsidiaries being the U.S. itself and China, and a wide range of other destination countries in both developed and less-developed countries. This reflects partly a desire for core component companies to retain key functions in the U.S., but it also reflects the evolution of U.S. foreign invest-ment over time, initially in more developed regions such as Western Europe, and later to Eastern European countries and later again to Asia and Latin America. The distribution of location countries most likely reflects strategic thinking in relation to intellectual property conditions in different locations, but with an increasing need to be close to the growing center of gravity of production in China. While the geography of supplier companies is likely to change over time as regions in emerging nations become more competitive, the current pattern is a reflection, to some extent, of an asymmetrical relationship between regions that are rich in generating intellectual property and regions that are more consumers and producers.

In all there were 51 U.S. core component companies and 217 subsidiaries supplying Apple and 72 (33.1 percent) of the subsidiaries were in China. While U.S. companies are represented in all categories of suppliers, the two major areas for U.S. companies and their subsidiaries are ICs with 22 companies and 117 subsidiaries, and connector components with 11 companies and 43 subsidiaries. Although 21 of the 117 U.S. IC subsidiaries were in China, 48 were in the U.S. The only other U.S. subsidiary suppliers of the total 217 to be located in the U.S. were the one optical module supplier and one of the two internal memory subsidiaries. Many of the U.S. supplier companies are well known integrated circuit brands, such as AMD, Analog Devices, Broadcom, Fairchild Semiconductor, Intel, Nvidia, Skyworks and Texas Instruments. Considering the recent focus in U.S. political debates on the role of assembly operations in China for Apple and other such companies, our data highlights the significant input by a large number of U.S. core component companies into the products of Apple and related companies and the much greater value-added accruing to these companies as a result. A significant technology gap continues to exist between Chinese companies and those in the U.S. in core technology fields such as semiconductors.

The role played by European nodes in the network of core component suppliers is striking, with the Netherlands, Switzerland and Austria exhibiting a strong background in semiconductors having connections with quite a few network countries. The German company Infineon, which supplies Apple with baseband chips, does so from outside China despite having a plant in China. A second German semiconductor company, Robert Bosch, also supplies Apple from outside China. The Dutch semiconductor company NXP has nine supplier subsidiaries, two of which are in China, and supplies Apple with near-field communications chips for contactless payments. Apple accounted for around 25 percent of NXP's royalty payments in 2014, and in December, 2015, it completed a merger with U.S. company Freescale Semiconductor, which is also an Apple supplier. ST Microelectronics, headquartered in Switzerland, has 11 supplier subsidiaries, one of which is in China. In addition to the 32 core subsidiaries from these nodes, there were also 22 non-core subsidiaries. Although some researchers have suggested a significant shift in the center of gravity of innovation toward Asia in recent years, accompanying the major shift in ICT production, the continued role of developed country technology companies in contributing key intellectual property in the form of core components to Apple products suggests that it may take some years before Chinese companies will replace these key suppliers. In other words, most core component suppliers have not yet shifted to China, and the contribution of the Chinese as key suppliers to Apple is also small.

After the U.S. and the European nodes comes Japan with 98, or 27.5 percent of core subsidiaries originating there, 33 of which were in China. The smaller size of Japan's node, despite its large number of subsidiaries, reflects the fact that so many are located in Japan. While being strong also in non-core components, Japan had nine core component companies with 47 subsidiaries, 11 of which were in China. Of these, four were IC companies with 33 subsidiaries, 15 of which were in China; two were PCB companies with 11 subsidiaries with three in China. With 60 of 76 display subsidiaries, China and Japan were the key locations, despite there being only one Chinese display company. Japan is very strong in display companies with well-known brands such as Japan Display (four subsidiaries), Sharp (seven subsidiaries), and Toshiba (seven subsidiaries). The high value-added nature of this component is reflected in the fact that of the 47

Japanese subsidiaries, 32 were in Japan and only 11 in China. The reluctance to locate subsidiaries in China is reflected in Figure 5.1 with the preference for locating in Japan, but also in a number of other Asian locations. However, there is also a tendency for companies to locate at least one of their subsidiaries in China, which may be involved in some aspects of production and testing of products and allows for just-in-time delivery to final assembly locations. A recent report on the semiconductor sector in China refers to the practice of 'dislocated purchasing' whereby companies in China purchase chips outside to be transhipped to China for use and consumption (PWC, 2015).

Finally, the most significant economy of origin of subsidiaries is Taiwan, with 39 core component subsidiaries, 27 of which are in China. There were 16 PCB subsidiaries, nine optical and eight display, and three each in ICs and electroacoustic components. Unlike both the U.S. and the European nodes, Taiwan's strongest link was with China. Two major Korean companies, Samsung and LG dominated the Korean contribution accounting for 31 of the 43 subsidiaries. Among these were Samsung's two display subsidiaries, eight integrated circuit and seven passive device subsidiaries, and LG had six display subsidiaries, four optical and four battery subsidiaries. Despite the intense rivalry between Samsung and Apple, and despite major legal battles over intellectual property infringement, Samsung continues to be one of Apple's most significant supplier companies.

The origin-location network of Apple's non-core and other suppliers

Besides core suppliers, non-core and other suppliers are also important parts of Apple's supply chain, despite their relatively lower value-added. Figure 5.2 illustrates the network of non-core supplier component companies. Of the 292

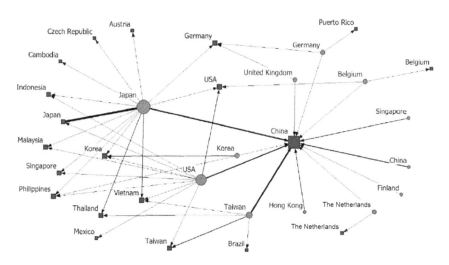

Figure 5.2 The origin-location network of non-core component supplier subsidiaries

Note: See Figure 5.1

non-core subsidiaries (connector, peripheral devices, battery and passive devices), 45.5 percent were Japanese, 17.8 percent were Taiwanese and 17.4 percent were U.S., accounting for 80.7 percent. Of the remainder, 4.7 percent were European and 14.3 percent were Asian, of which 5.4 percent were Chinese. This indicates that more than half of non-core component suppliers have moved their manufacture to China, but there are a few Chinese companies.

While Japan was the primary country of origin of non-core subsidiaries, 23.3 percent of all non-core subsidiaries were located in Japan, suggesting a strong tendency to locate in the home country. Japan is strong in connector components, with 10 companies and 43 subsidiaries, 15 of which were in China. The second major area is passive components, which can be divided into resistors, inductors and capacitors, with capacitors being the most significant globally by value. This area is dominated by the Japanese, with six of the eight supplier companies and 73 of the 84 subsidiaries, and no Chinese company involved. Although 23 of all 84 subsidiaries are in China, in the case of the 73 Japanese subsidiaries, 19 were in China and 35 in Japan. Among the most significant companies are Murata Manufacturing from Japan and Samsung Electro-Mechanics from Korea. Thus, while Japan's non-core component second major location is China, there is a wide dispersion of subsidiaries throughout Asia and a few in Europe.

The pattern of U.S. non-core component supplier locations shows the strongest connection with China, but with many linkages throughout low-cost locations in Asia. Taiwan's linkages are primarily with China, then Taiwan itself and a few other low-cost locations. While Japan is the key node in which non-core subsidiaries originate and disperse to other locations, China is the primary node to which non-core subsidiaries move from many different locations, with Taiwan, Japan and the U.S. being the key countries/economies of origin. Although, overall 50.3 percent of non-core component suppliers were in China, only 23 – or 27.2 percent – of the 84 subsidiaries supplying passive devices were in China.

Figure 5.3 looks at the origin and location of the 111 supplier companies in the 'other' category, which includes foundry, ODM/OEM, packaging and printing and others, and not surprisingly, 69.3 percent of this third category was in China. Three economies of origin, including Taiwan with 48.6 percent, the U.S. with 21.6 percent and Japan with 16.2 percent, together account for 86.4 percent of the total. Although Apple outsources limited assembly work in the U.S., the primary location for final assembly is China, receiving contributions from supplier subsidiaries in various countries. Taiwanese companies, particularly Foxconn, with 22 subsidiaries in China, and Pegatron, with eight subsidiaries in China, dominate final assembly. In 2014, the quarterly contract value for Foxconn was $18 billion and $3.6 billion for Pegatron, with both companies getting more than 41 percent of their revenue from Apple (Satariano and Burrows, 2014). Also, while having only one of its five subsidiaries in China, the Taiwan Semiconductor Manufacturing company (TSMC) was the sole foundry supplier to Apple, and Taiwanese companies also contributed strongly in packaging and printing.

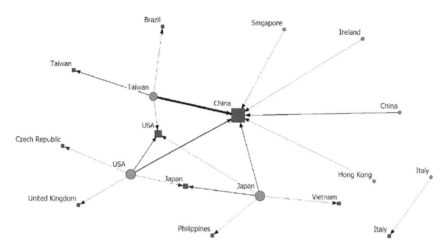

Figure 5.3 The origin-location network of other component supplier subsidiaries
Notes: See Figure 5.1

Apple's supplier subsidiaries in China

Initially, China's interest in attracting technology companies like Apple to invest in China included a range of expected benefits such as contributing to employment growth, the development of skills and increasing high-technology exports with the hope that having such an ecosystem of high caliber technology companies and their suppliers in China would generate technology transfer to local companies.

The problem with the latter objective is that companies involved in supplying high-technology components, such as semiconductors, have every reason to seek to prevent potential competitors, no matter whether Chinese or non-Chinese companies from acquiring their IP. As the ICT global value chain has evolved over time, different countries such as Japan, Korea and Taiwan emerged as important sources of key electronic components, and in each case companies from particular countries sought to prevent all other companies from acquiring their intellectual property. The dilemma for many Apple suppliers is the tension between the advantages for being located in China's major cities of ICT production and the need to protect their intellectual property or competitive advantage.

Locations of Apple's suppliers in China

Having examined the global distribution of Apple suppliers and contextualized that part of its supply chain located in China, we will now look in some detail at the geography of Apple suppliers within China. It is to be expected that this will reflect the recent evolution of the ICT global value chain in China which has been examined by a number of scholars. Initially, much of the activity was located in the Pearl River Delta (PRD) region, particularly between Shenzhen and Dongguan. Another major concentration of supplier companies emerged more recently in the Yangtze River Delta (YRD) region, particularly between Shanghai and Suzhou, partly reflecting a shift of some activity from the PRD. More recently again, there has been a shift of activity inland to lower cost cities, led to some extent by major assemblers like Foxconn, seeking to achieve greater competitiveness and to overcome significant labor problems, including negative publicity associated with suicides in Shenzhen.

Table 5.2 lists the final assembly locations for Apple products in China and shows the dominant role of Foxconn in this sector. In practice, although 44.1 percent of the 759 subsidiaries are in China, the proportion varies by country/economy of origin, from 79.3 percent of Taiwanese to only 26.5 percent of Japanese, which had the highest number of subsidiaries overall (Table 5.3). Even the U.S., with the second largest number of subsidiaries, had 32.8 percent in China.

The proportion also varies according to type of subsidiary, from 31.1 percent core components, 50.3 percent of non-core and 69.3 percent of others, and again this varies according to country of origin. The high proportion of Taiwanese operations in Mainland China is not surprising, since Taiwanese companies led the relocation of the ICT sector to Mainland China and play a dominant role in final assembly. While the usual pattern is for a higher proportion of non-core subsidiaries to be located in China relative to core component subsidiaries, this is reversed in the case of Korea, although the numbers involved are small.

Table 5.2 Final assembly locations of Apple products in China

City	Province	Company	Product
Shenzhen	Guangdong	BYD	accessories
		Foxconn	iPad
		Foxconn	iPhone
		Foxconn	Mac
		Foxconn	iPod
Shanghai		Foxconn	accessories
		Foxconn	iPad
		Pagatron	iPhone
		Inventec Corp	iPod
		Quanta Computer	Mac
Taiyuan	Shanxi	Foxconn	iPhone
		Pegatron	iPad
Kunshan	Jiangsu	Pegatron	iPhone
Changshu	Jiangsu	Quanta Computer	iPod
Chengdu	Sichuan	Foxconn	iPad

Source: Apple Supplier List 2015. Note this table does not include all ODM/OEM supplier companies in the complete list such as, for example, Foxconn in Kunshan.

Table 5.3 The share of subsidiaries in China by economy origin

Economy origin	Core		Non-core		Others		Total Subsidiaries	
	All	% in China	All	% in China	All	% in China	All	% in China
The U.S.	141	22.7	51	52.9	24	50	216	32.8
Europe	33	12.1	14	42.9	4	75	51	25.5
Japan	98	23.5	133	27.8	18	33.3	249	26.5
Taiwan	39	69.2	52	82.7	54	83.3	145	79.3
Korea	32	40.6	11	27.3			43	37.2
Hong Kong	4	100	6	100	4	100	14	100
Singapore	1		9	100	2	100	12	91.6
China	8	100	16	100	5	100	29	100
Total	356		292		111		759	44.1

Source: Apple Supplier List 2015

In some cases, decisions on where to locate particular functions will reflect this strategy, and companies from some countries may be more cautious in their decision-making than others. With the growing shift, however, of much of the production, assembly and testing of electronic products to China, it has become increasingly difficult to keep key component suppliers at a distance from the location of production and assembly. In some cases the location of particular technology suppliers outside China may reflect state policies outside China preventing the exporting of the most recent technology processes to China. This may happen, for example, in the case of semiconductors, a core component in Apple products, under the guise that they might be used for military purposes. Ernst (2014a, 16) points out that Intel, Samsung and TSMC, which are the three big semiconductor fabricators, who account for 60 percent of capital expenditure globally, are the only companies with leading edge process technologies to build next generation facilities. Yet China's new semiconductor strategy is partly based on the hope that with a 800 million market for smartphones, the demand pull of the mobile sector will help to upgrade the local industry. Actually, despite China having spent many billions of dollars of state-led investment, China's domestic production of semiconductors accounts for less than 13 percent of the country's demand, and its ability to design and produce this critical input remains seriously constrained (Ernst, 2016).

LQs for major locations in China

While the 'others' category, mainly associated with final assembly, was the most likely to be located in China, it was the smallest grouping with 77 subsidiaries, but some of these facilities, including Foxconn's major assembly operations, employed in some cases hundreds of thousands of workers. The 336 subsidiaries were distributed widely in 57 different cities, but the main concentrations were

Table 5.4 Location quotients for major concentrations of subsidiaries in China

Province	City	% Total	% Core	% Non-core	% Others	LQ Core	LQ Non-C	LQ Others
Shanghai		13.4	9.9	13.6	18.2	0.7	1.0	1.4
Jiangsu	Wuxi	5.4	9.0	4.1	2.6	1.7	0.7	0.5
	Suzhou	9.5	13.5	8.8	5.2	1.4	0.9	0.5
	Kunshan	8.4	4.5	10.2	10.4	0.5	1.2	1.2
	Total	28.7	33.3	29.9	19.4	1.2	1.0	0.7
Guangdong	Dongguan	14.6	11.7	17.7	13.0	0.8	1.2	0.9
	Guangzhou	3.6	6.3	2.7	1.3	1.7	0.7	0.4
	Shenzhen	11.6	7.2	12.2	16.9	0.6	1	1.4
	Total	37.7	31.5	40.8	36.3	0.8	1.1	1.0
Other Provinces		20.2	25.2	15.6	26.0	1.2	0.8	1.3
Total		100	100	100	100			

Sources: Authors' research

along the eastern seaboard, particularly around Shanghai-Suzhou and Shenzhen-Dongguan, which have been well-established centers of ICT activity for many years (Table 5.4). There was less than 1 percent of subsidiaries in 42 of the 57 cities. Outside the main concentrations in an additional 33 cities, 20.2 percent of subsidiaries were located. The shift away from the major concentrations along the eastern seaboard has been in progress for some time, with Foxconn in particular moving major operations away from Shenzhen to inland cities such as Zhengzhou and Taiyuan with lower costs, attractive incentives and closer to the labor supply.

Table 5.4 illustrates the LQs of the major concentrations and outliers of the three types of subsidiaries, while also showing details for cities having 3 percent or more of all subsidiaries. Shanghai, together with the neighboring province of Jiangsu, account for more than 42 percent of all subsidiaries, with the overall profile showing a slight over-representation of core and non-core subsidiaries and an under-representation of others. Within this grouping there is some variation with Shanghai and Kunshan having higher LQs for others. Foxconn has a major assembly operation in Kunshan which has been producing iPods since 2009, while Taiwanese ODMs Foxconn, Inventec, Pegatron and Quanta Computer all assemble products for Apple in Shanghai.

Guangdong province had 37.7 percent of subsidiaries, which together with the Shanghai-Jiangsu province concentration accounted for almost 80 percent of all subsidiaries in China. The two key cities in Guangdong were Dongguan with 14.6 percent and Shenzhen with 11.6 percent of subsidiaries. Although Shenzhen's LQ for 'others' was 1.4, which reflects its ongoing importance as an assembly center, overall Guangdong's importance in this area with 36 percent of all others subsidiaries appears to have diminished somewhat, with the shift to the interior of China reflected in the 1.3 location quotient for Other Provinces for the 'others' category.

Although many studies have commented on the major shift or relocation of production from the earlier concentration of mainly Taiwanese companies and their suppliers in Guangdong in the PRD region to Jiangsu in the YRD region, apparently seeking a more sophisticated production environment, few studies have analyzed more recent shifts to the interior regions of China. Yang and He (2017), however, have presented more recent data, supported by company interviews, which reveal a reduction in the contribution of Hong Kong/Macao/ Taiwanese companies in total electronics production in Guangdong from 72.7 percent in 1998 to 40.9 percent in 2009, with their contribution to exports dropping in the same period from 82.5 percent to 40.9 percent. The share by domestic firms in Guangdong during this period increased from 23.1 percent to 43.9 percent, and their share of exports from 32.7 percent to 68.8 percent, revealing a significant shift in the overall profile of electronics production in Guangdong province, particularly the PRD region during this period.

Among these outlier assembly locations are operations such as Foxconn's iPad plant in Chengdu (Sichuan province), employing 20,000, and both Foxconn's iPhone plant, employing 79,000, and Pegatron's iPad plant in Taiyuan (Shanxi province). Foxconn's largest iPhone assembly plant, accounting for 70 percent of production and employing 200,000, is in Zhengzhou in Henan province, where it comprises about 60 percent of industrial output. Having obtained considerable labor subsidies and tax incentives from the local government, Foxconn relocated some of its assembly activity from Shenzhen to Henan. A recent report by the *New York Times* revealed how subsidies in excess of $1.5 billion have been provided by the local government together with flexible bureaucratic arrangements to facilitate Foxconn's largest production facility of the iPhone to sell the final products to Apple for domestic consumption (Barboza, 2016).

While the LQ values in Table 5.4 do not reveal any major differences between core and non-core component subsidiaries in terms of spatial concentrations, there is some evidence of over-representation of core component subsidiaries in smaller concentrations like Wuxi (Jiangsu province) and Guangzhou (Guangdong province). Chan et al. (2013) note Apple's increased ability to pressure Foxconn to accept lower margins while at the same time acceding to Apple's demands for technical changes and large orders. Considering the enormous scale of Foxconn, with over one million employees, scholars like Sinkovics et al. (2014) wonder whether such companies are merely catching up technologically or are in fact changing the rules of the game globally. Because of the technology gap between Foxconn and other smaller contract manufacturers, it appears that Foxconn will continue to dominate assembly work for Apple for some time to come.

Apple's evolving relationship with China

Despite its relative hiddenness in China behind its main contract manufacturers, Apple continues to exercise considerable power and control within the GVC in terms of prices, standards and the location of activities, but also through investing in equipment in its supplier companies for its exclusive use, and also having its own engineers monitoring production. While Apple's supply chain has been consistently ranked as one of the best in the world, Froud et al. (2014) argues that rather than the supply chain being its main source of advantage, the shareholder value of Apple's financialized business model plays out in the supply chain by using its contract power to shift cost control and risk to its Chinese suppliers, taking profit from their already tight margins and hindering the development of their Asian subcontractors. Rather than Foxconn benefitting from any significant shift in the locus of power, its position within the GVC remains subordinate and dependent while it bears much of the burden of adjusting to fast moving competition.

Increased attention has recently been given to the possibilities of reshoring production activities by companies like Apple back to the U.S. (see The Washington Post, 2016). A more important question, however, is how and when that part of the ICT activity in China will move further up the value chain as it becomes more involved in IP-generating activity. It should be remembered that no ICT company in China, however powerful, is an isolated operation. Many of the key companies are closely interconnected, being either customers or suppliers of each other. So when the question of reshoring value chains such as Apple's in China arises, it should be posed in terms of how Apple might disentangle itself from China's high density ICT ecosystem. Since this ecosystem is unlikely to relocate outside of China in the short- to medium-term, this would make it very difficult for any individual company to disconnect from the network of key suppliers. Thus, while much of the IP used in producing Apple products is generated outside of China, increasingly much of the world's production of electronics devices is concentrated within China.

Indeed, there are few places in the world where the needs of Apple's production could be met on the same scale and with such flexibility as in China. In terms of the future of ICT companies like Apple, which are focused on internet services and ecommerce, China, according to Alibaba's Jack Ma, will experience solid growth for another 20 years. Here you have 800 million (and growing) subscribers to smartphones, one of the largest scale and most dynamic mobile markets anywhere. The technology may still be largely developed outside of China, but China's market will play an important role in shaping how the technology responds to the needs of users. The China market reflects a high level of smartphone-intensive usage, spanning all age groups, with increasing dependence on highly innovative ecommerce platforms such as WeChat, which has 768 million daily users (Minter, 2017).

So while Apple plays a dominant role in the mobile sector, capturing 91 percent of smartphone operating profits both globally and in China, compared with 2.4 percent for Huawei and 2.2 percent for Oppo and Vivo, three Chinese smartphone manufacturers (Dou, 2017), China will play a unique role in shaping future developments. Apple's closed model of locking in customers to cream off high margins is very much the opposite of what China wants to bring about, which is a more affordable model for products and services. It will be interesting to track the extent to which China's powerful state can squeeze more from Apple for the consumer's sake. Yet the irony is that, because of protectionism and state security issues, the internet sector is the most controlled one in China with some of Apple's services being blocked. This is partly why Apple is already beginning to lose ground in the China market besides other reasons such as less innovation, market saturation and the rise of local brands, and they may well have to face the dilemma faced by other companies such as Google in relation to how much it is prepared to compromise to ensure its future in China. The recent announcement by Apple to set up R&D activity in China would appear to be an attempt to develop a more favorable relationship with the state.

Most ICT companies feel they have no choice but to grin and bear whatever pressure is applied by the state in China in order to continue growing in the market and ensure their ability to compete globally. Like Motorola, Nokia, Alcatel Lucent and other major technology companies, Apple has benefitted greatly from China to date, both as a competitive production location and in terms of market growth. But a tipping point may come when China's dependence on Apple decreases, although the company still contributes significantly to China's GDP and export performance. China's impatience with playing a subservient role in the ICT global value chain is reflected in its relatively premature push for technology autonomy, and it could have definite repercussions for companies like Apple in China.

Apple to date has had the best of both worlds. It relies on IP developed outside of China while benefiting from the comparative advantage of production in China. There are growing signs that Beijing may demand more from Apple, and there are many historical precedents of the Chinese state squeezing more from MNCs. China's rapidly growing and large scale market, which is vital for the continuing dominant role of companies like Apple, continues to be a significant leverage for the Chinese state in the bargaining process for greater technology upgrading.

Beyond Apple: China's role in the ICT GVC

By examining in detail the geography/location of Apple's supply chain, the results provide additional insights to the research to date on how one of the most significant global technology companies, together with its supplier companies, has evolved and how it exploits the advantages of China. Importantly, it is necessary to explain the rationale behind this geography, and why some functions are mainly located either within our outside China.

The gap of China and Chinese companies

Data analysis shows that a greater proportion of core component suppliers such as semiconductor companies are found outside of China, while an increasing number of non-core supplier companies are located in China. Many of Apple's supplier companies are major global technology companies in their own right and in many cases supply other ICT companies. If China is to benefit from having an increasing proportion of Apple's supply chain, and its associated ecosystem located within the country, there should be a growing substitution by Chinese companies of non-Chinese suppliers over time, and to some extent the supplier functions should increase in sophistication from non-core to core components. When focusing primarily on the production aspect of Apple's activities in China, the domestic market for Apple is growing in significance, not only for their range of products, but also for the wide range of services and applications provided by the company, which also includes a growing range of Chinese applications.

For more than 30 years, China has been heavily reliant on foreign investing companies to transfer technology to local companies. Although there is no unanimous agreement about the benefits and disadvantages of this heavy reliance on foreign technology, Chinese policymakers are increasingly focusing on developing their own technology through a policy of 'indigenous innovation' and are seeking increased technological autonomy from sources of technology outside China (Grimes and Sun, 2014). This is partly related to growing dissatisfaction with the apparent low rates of technology transfer through the former reliance on creating joint JVs between foreign and Chinese companies. However, political and ideological factors have also become important in recent years as China has grown in global significance, and concerns about state security relating to technology generally, particularly telecommunications, have become more important (Yang, 2015).

China's share of global ICT exports grew from 2.1 percent in 1996 to 30 percent in 2012, making it the world's leading exporter of ICT products (Ezell and Atkinson, 2014). China's own domestic market for ICT products and services has also grown significantly, with important implications for the new shift from over-reliance on an export model toward promoting domestic consumption in the post-2008 international financial crisis period. This has also had implications for foreign investor companies in China, which see China's growing domestic market of great significance to their own development, but they are experiencing growing competition from Chinese technology companies supported by China's government giving preference to local companies, products and services particularly in the public procurement market.

The MI phenomenon in China

Despite this changing business environment, which many would regard as a natural evolution in a huge country which has grown greatly in economic significance, many global lead companies continue to see China as an important location, both in terms of production and also as a market, even though the policy environment may reflect considerable 'structured uncertainty' (Breznitz and Murphree, 2011). Notwithstanding China's impressive performance in technology catch-up in recent years, and the fact that a small number of significant Chinese technology companies such as Huawei, Xiaomi, Lenovo and ZTE have developed international brands, global lead technology companies from outside China continue to dominate the technology sector, mainly because of their continued control over key intellectual property in areas like semiconductors and software architecture.

Xiaomi Inc, founded in April 2010 by Lei Jun, is a privately owned Chinese electronics company headquartered in Beijing. Lei Jun, the company's founder and CEO, had been working at Kingsoft as an engineer after graduating from Wuhan University in 1991 and became the CEO of the company in 1998. In 2000, Lei founded Joyo.com, an online bookstore, which was eventually sold for $75 million to Amazon.com in 2004. His founding team at Xiaomi included former Chinese executives from Microsoft, Google, Motorola and Kingsoft. 'Xiaomi' means 'Millet' in Chinese. The 'MI' in its logo stands for 'Mobile Internet' or 'Mission Impossible' (Xiaomi website). Indeed, Xiaomi's rise is attributed to Lei's entrepreneurial spirit and experiences and other founder's work experiences in MNCs, resulting in a kind of inward international knowledge spillover.

Xiaomi officially launched its first Android-based firmware MIUI in August 2010. The Xiaomi Mi1 smartphone was announced in August 2011. Since the release of its first smartphone, Xiaomi has gained market share in Mainland China and expanded into developing a wider range of consumer electronics, including a smart home device ecosystem. However, it is still primarily a smartphone maker and the world's largest one. Despite Xiaomi's spectacular success in China's market, Ernst (2014a) is skeptical about its long-term potential because of its dependence on foreign companies for core technologies like applications processors and systems platforms. He also questions whether China has a sufficient portfolio of core technologies and the necessary ecosystem to become a lead market for mobile devices. Brandt and Thun (2011) suggest that the rapid evolution in technology in the handset industry makes the process of local firms catching up extremely difficult. Nevertheless, Chinese brands are increasingly dominating the domestic market, with major global brands like Apple begging to lose market share.

The background to Xiaomi's rapid development is the change in the global smartphone market and the rise of Chinese makers (see Table 5.5). Chinese smartphone makers together shipped 539 million units in 2015, while Samsung

Table 5.5 Top 10 smartphone vendors based on global market share

Ranking	2014		2015		2016	
	Company	*Market (%)*	*Company*	*Market (%)*	*Company*	*Market (%)*
1	Samsung	27.8	Samsung	24.8	Samsung	22.2
2	Apple	16.4	Apple	17.5	Apple	16.8
3	Lenovo+Moto	7.9	Huawei	8.4	Huawei	9.3
4	Huawei	6.2	Xiaomi	5.6	Lenovo	6.1
5	LG	5.4	Lenovo	5.4	Xiaomi	5.8
6	Xiaomi	5.2	LG	5.3	LG	5.0
7	Coolpad	4.2	TCL	4.0	TCL	4.0
8	Sony	3.9	OPPO	3.8	OPPO	3.9
9	TCL	3.3	BBK/ VIVO	3.3	BBK/ VIVO	3.4
10	ZTE	3.1	ZTE	3.1	ZTE	3.1
11	Others	16.6	Others	18.8	Others	20.3

Source: TrendForce, Jan., 2016

Note: Data are preliminary and subject to change. 2016 data is estimated.

and Apple together shipped a total of 547 million units, indicating the close match between Chinese vendors collectively and the top two global brands. Chinese smartphone brands made big gains worldwide in 2015, with their market share reaching a new high of over 40 percent (Trendforce, 2016). Chinese smartphone makers also took seven of the top 10 spots in the 2015 worldwide vendor ranking. Huawei in particular edged out Lenovo for the first time to become the No. 3 vendor globally and the leading vendor in China.

Xiaomi's advantages

Xiaomi has quickly become one of the most important forces in the global smartphone market, becoming the third largest vendor in China (Table 5.6) and attracting great attention from scholars and business people. In fact, according to McKinsey's report, Xiaomi is a typical case of customer-focused innovation (McKinsey Global Institute, 2015). It shows that the power of China's massive and dynamic consumer market to rapidly commercialize new products and services should not be underestimated. Following the concept of customer-focused innovation, there are several reasons to explain the MI phenomenon.

First, solving consumer problems by customer feedback is the model of interactive innovation, or user-oriented innovation, employed by Xiaomi. Generally, there are two modes of innovation. One, the Science, Technology and Innovation (STI) mode is based on the production and use of codified scientific and technical knowledge. The other, the Doing, Using and Interacting (DUI) mode, relies on informal processes of learning and experience-based know-how (Jensen et al., 2007). Clearly, Xiaomi's innovation follows the DUI mode. Xiaomi listens closely to customer feedback, having them test upcoming features themselves, and builds an extensive online community (http://bbs.xiaomi.cn/). In practice, Xiaomi follows the process known as 'design as you build'. Xiaomi's product managers spend a lot of time browsing through the company's user forums. Then, if a suggestion is picked up, it will be quickly transferred to the engineers. Therefore, features can turn from mere concept to shipping products

Table 5.6 Top five Chinese smartphone vendors based on market share

Ranking	2014		2015		2016	
	Company	Market (%)	Company	Market (%)	Company	Market (%)
1	Lenovo+Moto	19.8	Huawei	20.0	Huawei	20.9
2	Huawei	15.6	Xiaomi	13.3	Lenovo	13.7
3	Xiaomi	13.2	Lenovo	13	Xiaomi	13
4	Coolpad	10.5	TCL	9.6	TCL	9
5	TCL	8.4	OPPO	9.1	OPPO	8.9
6	Others	32.5	Others	34.9	Others	34.5

Note: Data are preliminary and subject to change. 2016 data is estimated.

Source: TrendForce, Jan., 2016

within a week. The company then ships a new batch of phones out every week on Tuesday at noon Beijing time, containing the new software builds and possible minor hardware tweaks.

Second, adopting a cost leadership strategy facilitates the provision of 'good enough' products. According to Porter's generic strategies, strategy should target either cost leadership, differentiation or focus (Porter, 1980). Porter claimed that a company must only choose one of the three or otherwise risk wasting precious resources. In selling the Xiaomi smartphone, the company adopted the cost leadership strategy, which is very unlike that of other smartphone makers such as Samsung and Apple. Xiaomi prices the phone almost at the BOM prices, and sees hardware sales as a means of delivering software and services in the long-term. To further reduce overhead costs, Xiaomi does not own any physical stores, selling exclusively from its online store. However, this strategy is causing the company to lose ground against competitors as the market expands toward lower-tier cities in China, with lower levels of online purchasing. It also did away with traditional advertising and relies on social networking services and word-of-mouth to publicize its products. 'Good enough' products still work for lower-income consumers, but in an increasingly affluent China, innovators must create 'cheaper and better' products to win new mainstream customers.

Third, China's massive and dynamic consumer market also helps explain the MI phenomenon. It is worth noting that Xiaomi is but one of a group of companies that have emerged in China. Since seven Chinese companies were among the global top 10 smartphone makers in 2015, it is necessary to consider the national competitiveness of this industry in China. Porter's National Diamond framework suggests that demand conditions in the domestic market provide the primary driver for growth, innovation and quality improvement (Porter, 1990). Xiaomi's greatest successes to date depend, to some degree, on China's massive and dynamic smartphone market. China has become the world's largest market for smartphones, personal computers, air conditioners, refrigerators, microwaves and home laundry appliances. In addition, Chinese companies have a better understanding of consumer needs in the domestic market than foreign companies.

Xiaomi's challenges

Using a similar method to that used in analyzing Apple's supply chain, it is not surprising to find that Xiaomi's suppliers are mainly located in Taiwan, Korea, Japan and Guangdong province (see Table 5.7). Of these, Taiwan and Shenzhen are the two most important locations for suppliers. Although Qualcomm, Corning and SanDisk are U.S. suppliers, they have manufacturing bases in Mainland China. Several Chinese companies like FATO and BOE also participate in the value chain as core suppliers. For central parts such as chips, CPU, camera and memory, it is dependent on U.S., Japanese and Taiwanese companies, and the products are manufactured by Foxconn and Inventec. According to its suppliers, Xiaomi faces several development challenges in the future.

Table 5.7 Xiaomi suppliers list

Core	Suppliers	Non-core	Suppliers	Others	Suppliers
Chip and CPU	Qualcomm (U.S.), MediaTek (Taiwan), NVDIA (Taiwan), Elite Semiconductor Memory Technology (ESMT) (Taiwan)	Battery	LG (Korean), Sunwoda (Shenzhen) Desay Battery (Shenzhen)	OEM	Inventec (Taiwan)
Camera	SONY (Japan), Largan Precision (Taiwan)	Glass	Corning (U.S.), Lens Tech (Shenzhen)	ODM	Foxcomm (Taiwan)
Memory	SanDisk (U.S.) Elpida (Japan)	Components	TDK(Japan) Janus (Dongwan)		
Touch screen	Synaptics (U.S.), Wally Electronics (Nanjing), O-film (Shenzhen), Laibao High-tech (Shenzhen), Sharp (Japan)	Coil/ inductor	Sunlord (Shenzhen)		
Panel	BOE (Beijin), AU Optronics (Taiwan)	Mobile power	Zowee (Shenzhen)		
PCB	FATO (Leqin, Zhejiang)				

Source: Authors' research

First, Xiaomi's deficiencies in intellectual property rights seriously restrict its profit and internationalization. Xiaomi adopted the DUI model to solve consumer problems. As we know, the smartphone is a knowledge-intensive product, and building IP ownership through R&D investment is central to the company's competitiveness. According to a report released by patent litigation consulting firm LexInnova in May, 2015, Xiaomi had 101 U.S. patent applications with only two granted patents. IP deficiencies not only reduce profit levels because of the need to pay royalties and license fees but also the competitiveness of the company's products.

For the same reason, Xiaomi has been unable to make significant headway in international markets. A major obstacle to Xiaomi's overseas expansion plan is the lack of intellectual property, and this problem actually resulted in several of the vendor's smartphone models being banned in India. Xiaomi's position in the domestic market is also under threat, as other Chinese vendors with R&D capabilities adopt the same sales strategy it developed. For example, Huawei has invested heavily in R&D in recent years and as a result has been able to expand into foreign markets while avoiding patent litigations with competitors. It has also been able to match major international brands in product quality and features.

Second, Xiaomi's development is dependent on the suppliers of processors. Xiaomi's supply chain system is copied from Apple, and it is constantly under pressure to imitate this global brand, but Apple has several other competitive advantages, such as R&D, design, brand and marketing. Since chips and processors are the most highly valued smartphone components, Xiaomi's product development is heavily dependent on suppliers like Qualcomm and NVIDIA. In 2014, Qualcomm was hit with a record fine, exceeding $1 billion in a Chinese antitrust probe, and NVIDIA decided to pull out of the mobile phone market, creating considerable problems for Xiaomi's supply chain. As chips form a major obstacle for Xiaomi's future development, the company is planning to develop its own chip. To date, Huawei is the only Chinese smartphone company with its own semiconductor subsidiary, HiSilicon, while Xiaomi, Lenovo, ZTE and other vendors are dependent on their suppliers. Thus, Huawei is able to make its own mobile processors and accumulate intellectual property related to mobile chipsets. Huawei currently reserves its in-house mobile processors, the Kirin series, for its high-end smartphones while continuing to collaborate with Qualcomm and MediaTek for products aimed at the mid-range and low-end markets.

Third, as mentioned above, Xiaomi attempts to copy Apple's supply chain, but unlike Apple, which has the highest quality products, it offers products with high-cost-performance ratios. As a start-up entering an increasingly mature and competitive market, it is difficult for Xiaomi to attract top suppliers of critical components, since the company has no brand, no factory and no record of sales, let alone high levels of profit. Apple already sources components from 90 of the top 100 global suppliers, investing in their factories to help them buy necessary machinery, while Xiaomi simply produces cheap imitations of Apple products. Some big suppliers previously had bad experiences with Chinese tech companies over-extending themselves and eventually going bankrupt. In order to provide products with high-cost-performance ratios, Xiaomi must push down supplier prices, with large shipments being their bargaining chip. Xiaomi's main production center is in South China, with a large proportion of its suppliers from Guangdong and Zhejiang provinces.

Xiaomi's deficiencies in intellectual property ownership are reflected in other Chinese brands such as ZTE, which relies on U.S. chip companies like Qualcomm, Broadcom and Intel for 34 percent of inputs for handsets and networking equipment in China (Culpan, 2016). This dependence was highlighted recently when the U.S. Commerce Department accused the company of breaking U.S. rules regarding the Export Administration Regulations (EAR) and the Iranian Transactions and Sanctions Regulations (ITSR) on sales of equipment to Iran and North Korea, something which not only resulted in a record high combined civil and criminal penalty of $1.19 billion, but also with serious consequences for its U.S. chip suppliers and disruption of its supply chain.

No pain, no gain

While the evolving geography/location of Xiaomi's global value chain reflects the increased ability of Asian companies to develop global technology brands, it is important to focus on those companies which continue to play a significant role in the trajectory of the technology itself. In the PC era, companies like Microsoft and Intel had considerable control within the ICT GVC. Both of these companies, however, have been challenged by developments in the mobile era, with companies like Apple, Google and Samsung growing in significance. Apart from the few global brands emerging in China, much of the development has been focused on developing lower cost imitation products for the domestic market such as those found in the Shanzai mobile phone sector. This sector of low-cost phones is reliant on a common architecture and depends on others to develop the standard, while innovating in an incremental manner on the margins (Tang et al., 2016).

Nevertheless, in facilitating the emergence of outlying regions, Cooke (2013, 1325) argues that a displacement by a 'territorial innovation system' (TIS) of the traditional global production network, associated with PC and laptop production by Western multinational companies is taking place, with the result that, while the West continues to dominate in software, systems, services and 'apps', Asia has become the main center for engineering design and hardware. Cooke (2013, 1333) also argues that a major shift occurred in Apple suppliers from the U.S. and Europe to Asia in the transition between iPhone 3G and iPhone 4S.

Fragmentation of global value chains has been facilitated by the modularization of technology production, allowing core and non-core functions to be located in the most competitive regions. While China has increasingly benefited from this changing geography, the danger of 'lock-in' to lower value-added functions such as assembly has been a considerable concern among policymakers. Ernst (2014b) argues that Taiwan's PC industry's participation in GPNs impeded rather than fostered innovation because the dominant supplier companies Microsoft and Intel, who reaped most of the benefits, controlled the architecture. An additional danger arising from not upgrading local capabilities is that such lower cost functions can easily be relocated to other regions. There is increasing interest among major assemblers like Foxconn, who have already regionalized some of their production to Brazil, in investing in large facilities in India, for example, where the local market is also growing.

Understanding China's evolving role in the ICT GVC

Apple's supply chain is a good illustration of the advantages and disadvantages for China arising from its integration in the ICT GVC. To some extent China seeks to emulate the success achieved by its Asian neighbors, particularly Japan, South Korea and Taiwan, and to some extent the Xiaomi case study reflects some of this success.

Benchmarking spillovers from neighbors

East Asian countries have achieved varying levels of success in advancing their technology sectors, which to some extent was influenced by considerable levels of state intervention in the market. Somewhat different approaches have been adopted in these countries, with different outcomes and levels of success. The evolving demand-supply relationship between the U.S. and Asia has led to Asian economies being structured in accordance with their respective comparative advantages, and over time, economic roles within East Asia have evolved, leading to a regional clustering of supply chains based on close industrial interconnections (WTO, 2013). Asia's global value chains began to evolve in the 1980s, with Japan investing $300 billion in emerging Asia, of which $100 billion was invested in China, with 23,000 Japanese companies today employing 10 million Chinese workers (West, 2015). Korea became an important location for smartphone components, including high value-added memory, LCD panels and semiconductors, retaining much of the supply chain locally, and with major ICT companies like Samsung emerging, partly with the help of state policy.

In the case of Taiwan, state policy strongly promoted the semiconductor sector, and Taiwan became an important center of fabless production for major global technology companies. However, because of inadequate proprietary R&D capacity, Taiwan has struggled to compete for high-value components, and it is a major supplier of low-value passive components such as resistors, inductors and capacitors (APEC Policy Support Unit, 2013). Much of the production, assembly and testing activity was later relocated to Mainland China, and Taiwanese companies have played a leading role in the development of the ICT sector in Mainland China, particularly in supplying global technology companies, and also as major assemblers of ICT products. As China became increasingly competitive as an ICT production center, much of the global ICT production activity relocated there over time, initially to the eastern urban seaboard and more recently to inland locations. More recently again, lower cost locations beyond China such as Vietnam have become attractive for ICT companies.

Learning from FDI

As a later developer than other Asian locations, much of Chinese involvement is happening at a stage when major technological advances have been achieved in relation to the Internet, smartphones, ecommerce and cloud computing. To some extent China's early involvement in the ICT sector was closely related to its dependence on foreign technology and FDI to help China develop this sector.

A number of studies have been carried out on China's ICT sector, looking both at the effects of FDI on the sector and also the potential for technology transfer and local firm upgrading (Yang, 2013, 2015; Breznitz and Murphree, 2011; Sun et al., 2013). The extensive work of Yang (2013, 2015) on Taiwanese involvement in the evolution of the ICT GVC, particularly in the PRD region, has been based on extensive company interviewing and has highlighted the challenges facing Chinese companies from gaining access to Taiwanese-dominated supplier networks. In a study of Taiwan's machine tool industry in China, however, it was suggested that the relationship between Taiwanese machine tool makers and their Taiwanese suppliers was changing with some level of preference for doing business with local Chinese companies rather than with those run by fellow nationals. Some studies by focusing only on Chinese supplier companies, in a sector in which many key suppliers are non-Chinese companies, and by conceptualizing the flow of technology transfer only from lead firms to 'developing country' supplier firms, fail to grasp the full complexity of China's ICT GVC, which is relatively globalized (Sun et al., 2013).

As mentioned before, because of this continued dominance by non-Chinese companies of the sector, more than 80 percent of China's high-technology exports are from foreign invested firms who continue to exploit China's comparative advantage as a significant ICT production, assembly and testing center (Grimes and Sun, 2014). The example of Xiaomi is illustrative of China's technological weaknesses, particularly in the area of semiconductors. Although more than 50 percent of all semiconductors globally are consumed in China, mainly in the production of high-tech products, Chinese companies, which are two generations behind the most recent technology, only produce around 12 percent of the demand (PWC, 2015). While foreign investment and the integration of China's high-technology sector in the ICT global value chain has contributed significantly to economic growth in China, some question whether such integration will have positive effects in the long-term. Baldwin (2012) suggests that such integration can lead to a more superficial form of development than was achieved in developed regions earlier in history, partly because of low levels of technology transfer in the GVC model, but also because of how technological change could transform locational requirements of industry over time.

Technological autonomy

China has also invested heavily in science and technology and R&D in a sustained effort to catch up with more developed regions. With the determination of the Chinese state to achieve technological autonomy in targeted sectors such as telecommunications closely associated with state security and political control within China, and with the significant progress made by its own companies in recent years, Chinese policy has shifted in the direction of indigenous innovation since 2006, including the development of intellectual property within China and the promotion of domestic technology standards.

Due to the increasing improvement of indigenous R&D and technology capability, Chinese companies have developed a certain level of absorption capability. While noting that involvement in subcontracting with foreign or domestic lead firms should provide learning opportunities for local firms, Sun et al. (2013) concluded that keeping the balance between autonomy and subcontracting is challenging, with suppliers and lead firms having asymmetrical power relationships. The increasing focus, however, by both Chinese and foreign companies on the growing domestic market for high-technology products is contributing to significant growth in the local ICT sector (Ezell and Atkinson, 2014). Yet national statistics reveal high levels of foreign involvement in both the importing and exporting of high-technology goods, with a continued high level of dependence on export processing of intermediate goods (OECD, 2012).

While heavy R&D investment provides an increasingly attractive investment environment for foreign technology companies in terms of the supply of science and technology skills and infrastructure, such companies are beginning to find a much less enthusiastic acceptance in China and are facing much greater competition from local companies than previously for access to the local market. While it is useful to consider this growing competition from Chinese companies, which is of considerable interest from a Chinese policy perspective, it should be remembered that much of the intense competition both globally and within China is between global lead technology companies, whatever their country of origin.

One element of this competition relates to the protection of intellectual property in China, and while much attention is given to threats from local Chinese companies in acquiring the IP of foreign investors, such fears are more general in nature, with a considerable lack of trust between Japanese multinationals and Taiwanese firms in the electronics sector (Edgington and Hayter, 2012). Weak protection of intellectual property in China, related to the immature state of the legal system may make it difficult for Chinese firms to gain access to Western technology, and while increased productivity in low-tech and middle-technology areas could be achieved, moving further up the value chain was not guaranteed.

Xiaomi Vs Huawei

Manufacturing capability underlying indigenous technology, after all, is the point of development. As mentioned above, Xiaomi always describes itself as a mobile internet business rather than as a smartphone manufacturer. The traditional mobile phone manufacturer is interested in a combination of increasing, or at least maintaining, market share whilst selling products at a high enough margin in order to turn a profit for shareholders. Xiaomi, however, has adopted a different approach: it sells smartphones and other consumer electronics products at a very low margin, with some of its profit being derived from services (Steele, 2015). Thus, while Xiaomi adopted Apple as a role model for phone production, Google provides its business model.

Our argument is that if Xiaomi wishes to sell electronics products to consumers, it must be a manufacturing firm in the first instance, while also benefiting from software products and services like other smartphone companies. As a relatively new company, however, it is lacking in manufacturing capabilities and will need a long time to accumulate needed strengths in technology, branding and supplier relationships. Certainly, technology purchase or license is a rapid way to get IP. While having a good relationship with Qualcomm as its third largest customer, it is seeking to reduce this dependence by developing its own smartphone chip. This indicates that the basis of benefiting from software products and services is hardware manufacturing.

The value-added of manufacturing comes mainly from ownership of indigenous technologies or IP, rather than from low-cost labor. Because of its significant deficit in patents, the company risks being sued by other companies with larger patent portfolios. Xiaomi has already experienced considerable opposition in its efforts to expand in the Indian market, where it was sued by Ericsson who claimed it had infringed its wireless technology and had refused to discuss license fees for years. It also faces the risk of litigation from patent trolls like Unwired Planet, a U.S. company that specializes in targeting companies like Xiaomi. Two years ago, this former internet services company bought 2,185 patents from Ericsson, and it has since sued a number of companies, including Apple, Google and Samsung (Olson, 2015).

Unlike Xiaomi, Huawei is a successful manufacturer of communications equipment in the first instance, and from its strong background in manufacturing telecoms equipment has also become a successful manufacturer of smartphones. In 2017, Huawei released two flagship smartphones, the P9 and the Mate 9 with great fanfare from the international media. The P9 became China's flagship smartphone, seeking to capture the best features of both Apple and Samsung products. Perlow (2016), however, while acknowledging that Apple and Samsung continued to be the premium brands globally, suggest that it was not clear if this would still be the case within five years. The smartphone market in China is experiencing considerable shifts, with local brands increasing their popularity. Huawei is currently the third largest smartphone manufacturer in the world and is determined to improve its technology in order to displace global brands like Apple (Reuters, 2016).

However, according to the latest research from Strategy Analytics, a Boston based research institution, Apple captures record 91 percent share of global smartphone profits in Q3 2016 (see Table 5.8). An efficient supply chain, sleek

Table 5.8 Global smartphone operating profit share in Q3 2016

Global Smartphone Profit by Vendor	Operating Profit (US $, Billions)	Operating Profit Share (%)
Apple	$8.5	91.0%
Huawei	$0.2	2.4%
Vivo	$0.2	2.2%
OPPO	$0.2	2.2%
Others	$0.2	2.2%
Total	$9.4	100.0%

Source: Strategy Analytics. www.strategyanalytics.com/strategy-analytics/news/strategy-analytics-press-releases/strategy-analytics-press-release/2016/11/22/strategy-analytics-apple-captures-record-91-percent-share-of-global-smartphone-profits-in-q3–2016#.WMNriPl6_0p.

Note: Numbers are rounded. The data table includes global smartphone hardware profit only. Profit is defined as realized operating profit.

products and effective marketing have been among the main drivers of Huawei's robust profitability. Huawei, Vivo and OPPO, three Chinese vendors, are the most profitable smartphone vendors globally, but they are still a long way behind Apple. This indicates that there is a great gap between the leading company like Apple and others in the profitability or value-added.

In terms of the number of devices sold globally in 2015, Huawei faces stiff opposition from Samsung which shipped 75.3 million, which is a 20.1 percent market share, and Apple which sold 45.5 million, representing a 12 percent market share. While learning from Xiaomi how to increase customer loyalty, Huawei's success is firmly based on R&D and internationalization. With its ability to produce products along each point of the wireless communications spectrum, there are few companies that can match its technical strengths (Cendrowski, 2017). In addition to its technical strengths, Huawei has also developed a division of labor within the company whereby each employee acts as a unit within the system, and it also employs an innovative rotating CEO regime and an employee stock ownership incentive scheme which seeks to promote a culture of sharing responsibilities and benefits, as a series of institutional changes. Indeed, technological innovation and institutional change are an interactive process; institutional change could promote technological innovation and technological innovation also could lead to institutional change.

In 2012, Huawei overtook Ericsson to become the world's largest telecommunications equipment company, and in 2014, with 170,000 employees worldwide, it generated $5.5 billion in profits from its sales in 170 countries. It is the only Chinese company of the 91 listed on the Fortune 500 Global list earning more revenue abroad than in China. In their book, *Dedication: The Foundations of Huawei's HR Management*, Huang (2016) provides useful insights into its management system. Whilst the research and development and the technology that results from it are core drivers of Huawei's success, the company's remarkable growth was also determined by its human resource strategy. This is based on a 'customer-first' approach, the belief that obtaining opportunities comes through hard work and, above all, 'a dedication to do the best in anything we do' (De Cremer and Tao, 2015). Through its original incentive system, employees are encouraged to feel ownership of the company and to have a mentality to act like a boss, creating a culture of dedication that has become the bedrock of its growth.

Lastly, it is possible that Huawei's smartphone shipments may outpace those of Apple to make it the second largest smartphone producer within two years or so. This would not mean, however, that Huawei had replaced Apple, or that it had earned anything like Apple's revenue. For this to happen, both Huawei and other Chinese smartphone companies will need to transition from their customer-oriented model to one that is more strongly based on science, making them a leader rather than a follower and resulting in significantly more value-added. Cendrowski (2017), however, notes the significant support which Huawei receives from government policy, such as financial aid from China Development Bank which allows Huawei to provide loans to its customers in Africa and

Latin America to purchase equipment. He also explains the important benefits of Huawei's business model whereby telecoms carrier companies that buy Huawei's network receive discounted devices. A major challenge facing Huawei's global progress, however, is the political opposition it faces in selling network equipment in the U.S. and other markets under the guise of being a security threat.

References

APEC Policy Support Unit, 2013, *Global Supply Chain Operation in the APEC Region: Case Study of the Electrical and Electronics Industry*, Singapore, APEC Policy Support Unit.

Baldwin, R., 2012, 'Global supply chains: Why they emerged, why they matter, and where they are going', Available at http://graduateinstitute.ch/files/live/sites/iheid/files/sites/ctei/shared/CTEI/working_papers/CTEI-2012-13.pdf. Accessed 07/18/2017.

Barboza, D., 2016, 'How China built "iPhone city" with billions in perks to Apple's partner', Available at www.nytimes.com/2016/12/29/technology/apple-iphone-china-foxconn.html?smid=tw-share. Accessed 07/18/2017.

Brandt, L. and Thun, E., 2011, 'Going mobile in China: Shifting value chains and upgrading in the mobile telecom sector', *International Journal of Technological Learning, Innovation and Development*, 4(1–3), 148–180.

Breznitz, D. and Murphree, M., 2011, *Run of the Red Queen*, New Haven, Yale University Press.

Cendrowski, S., 2017, 'Is the world big enough for Huawei?' Available at http://fortune.com/huawei-china-smartphone/?iid=sr-link1. Accessed 07/18/2017.

Chan, J., Pun, N. and Selden, M., 2013, 'The politics of global production: Apple, Foxconn and China's new working class', *Work and Employment*, 28(2), 100–115.

Clelland, D., 2014, 'The core of the Apple: Dark value and degrees of monopoly in global commodity chains', *Journal of World-Systems Research*, 20(1), 82–111.

Cooke, P., 2013, 'Qualitative analysis and comparison of firm and system incumbents in the new ICT global innovation network', *European Planning Studies*, 21(9), 1323–1340.

Culpan, T., 2016, 'ZTE ban could backfire', Available at www.bloomberg.com/gadfly/articles/2016-03-07/a-u-s-ban-on-sales-to-china-s-zte-could-backfire. Accessed 07/18/2017.

De Cremer, D. and Tao, T., 2015. 'Huawei's Culture Is the Key to Its Success', Available at https://hbr.org/2015/06/huaweis-culture-is-the-key-to-its-success. Accessed 10/26/2017.

Dou, E., 2017, 'Cheaper rivals eat away at Apple sales in China', Available at www.wsj.com/articles/cheaper-rivals-eat-away-at-apple-sales-in-china-1485924305. Accessed 07/18/2017.

Edgington, D.W. and Hayter, R., 2012, 'New relationships between Japanese and Taiwanese electronics firms', *Environment and Planning A*, 44(1), 68–88.

Ernst, D., 2014a, 'From catching up to forging ahead? China's prospects in semiconductors', *East-West Center Working Papers Innovation and Economic Growth Series*, 1.

Ernst, D., 2014b, 'Trade and innovation in global networks – regional policy implications', *East-West Center Working Papers Economics Series*, 137.

Ernst, D., 2016, 'China's bold strategy for semiconductors – zero-sum game or catalyst for cooperation?' *East-West Center Working Papers: Innovation and Economic Growth Series*, 9.

Ezell, S.J. and Atkinson, R.D., 2014, 'How ITA expansion benefits the Chinese and global economies ITIF', Available at www2.itif.org/2014-ita-expansion-benefits-chinese-global-economies.pdf. Accessed 07/18/2017.

Froud, J., et al., 2014, 'Financialization across the Pacific: Manufacturing cost ratios, supply chains and power', *Critical Perspectives on Accounting*, 25(1), 46–57.

Grimes, S. and Sun, Y., 2014, 'Implications of China's on-going dependence on foreign technology', *Geoforum*, 54, 59–69.

Jacobides, M.G. and MacDuffie, J.P., 2013, 'How to drive value your way', Available at https://hbr.org/2013/07/how-to-drive-value-your-way. Accessed 07/18/2017.

Janoski, T., Luke, D. and Oliver, C., 2014, *The Causes of Structural Unemployment*, Cambridge, Polity Press.

Jensen, M.B., Johnson, B., Lorenz, E. and Lundvall, B.Å., 2007, 'Forms of knowledge and modes of innovation', *Research Policy*, 36, 680–693.

Jones, C., 2014, 'Apple's iPhone 6 teardown and other costs analysis', Available at www.forbes.com/sites/chuckjones/2014/09/24/apples-iphone-6-teardown-and-other-costs-analysis/. Accessed 07/18/2017.

Lee, J. and Gereffi, G., 2015, 'Global value chains, rising power firms and economic and social upgrading', *Critical Perspectives on International Business*, 11(3/4), 319–339.

The McKinsey Global Institute, 2015, 'The China effect on global innovation', Available at www.mckinseychina.com/the-china-effect-on-global-innovation/. Accessed 07/18/2017.

Minter, A., 2017, 'WeChat's app revolution', Available at www.bloomberg.com/view/articles/2017-01-19/wechat-s-app-revolution. Accessed 07/18/2017.

OECD, 2012, *China in Focus: Lesson and Challenges*, Paris, OECD.

Olson, P., 2015, 'Xiaomi may have a major patent problem', Available at www.forbes.com/sites/parmyolson/2015/01/29/xiaomi-patent-problem/#28355c8322ec. Accessed 07/18/2017.

Perlow, J., 2016, 'Huawei P9: China's flagship smartphone serves up Apple and Samsung's secret sauce', Available at www.zdnet.com/article/huawei-p9-chinas-flagship-smartphone-serves-up-apple-and-samsungs-secret-sauce/. Accessed 07/18/2017.

Porter, M.E., 1980, *Competitive Strategy*, New York, The Free Press.

Porter, M.E., 1985, *The Competitive Advantage: Creating and Sustaining Superior Performance*, New York, The Free Press.

Porter, M.E., 1990, *The Competitive Advantage of Nations*, New York, The Free Press.

PWC, 2015, 'China's impact on the semiconductor industry – 2015 update', Available at www.pwc.com/gx/en/industries/technology/chinas-impact-on-semiconductor-industry.html. Accessed 07/18/2017.

Reuters, 2016, 'China's Huawei wants to beat Apple in smartphones in two years', Available at http://fortune.com/2016/11/04/huawei-apple-smartphones-china-samsung/. Accessed 07/18/2017.

Satariano, A. and Burrows, P., 2011, 'Apple's supply chain secret? Hoard Lasers', *Technology*, 4, 50.

Satariano, A. and Burrows, P., 2014, 'There's a downside to making parts for Apple', Available at www.bloomberg.com/bw/articles/2014-09-18/some-apple-suppliers-get-cut-off-must-scramble-for-new-business. Accessed 07/18/2017.

Sinkovics, R.R., Nadvi, K. and Zhang, Y.Z., 2014, 'Rising powers from emerging markets – The changing face of international business', *International Business Review*, 23, 675–679.

Steele, D., 2015, 'Xiaomi's careful supply chain management keeps prices low', Available at www.androidheadlines.com/2015/05/xiaomis-careful-supply-chain-management-keeps-prices-low.html. Accessed 07/18/2017.

Sun, Y., Zhou, Y., Lin, G.C.S. and Wei, D., 2013, 'Subcontracting and supplier innovativeness in a developing economy: Evidence from China's information and communication technology industry', *Regional Studies*, 4(10), 1766–1784.

Tang, L., Murphree, M. and Breznitz, D., 2016, 'Structured uncertainty: A pilot study on innovation in China's mobile phone handset industry', *Journal of Technology Transfer*, 41(5), 1168-1194.

Trendforce, 2016, 'TrendForce says Huawei led the global rise of Chinese smartphone brands in 2015 by shipping over 100 million units to take No. 3 worldwide', Available at http://press.trendforce.com/node/view/2265.html#m83PqTARJtafb7yo.99. Accessed 07/18/2017.

The Washington Post, 2016, 'Trump's demand that Apple must make iPhones in the U.S. actually isn't that crazy', Available at www.washingtonpost.com/news/innovations/wp/2016/05/17/trumps-demand-that-apple-must-make-iphones-in-the-u-s-actually-isnt-that-crazy/. Accessed 08/12/2016.

Huang, W., 2016, *Dedication: The Foundations of Huawei's Human Resource Management*, London, LID Publishing.

West, J., 2015, 'Asia's global value chains', Available at www.asiancenturyinstitute.com/index.php?option=com_content&view=article&id=918:asia-s-global-value-chains-part-1&catid=9:economy&Itemid=111. Accessed 07/18/2017.

World Trade Organisation, 2013, 'Trade patterns and global value chains in East Asia: From trade in goods to trade in tasks', Available at www.wto.org/english/res_e/booksp_e/stat_tradepat_globvalchains_e.pdf. Accessed 07/18/2017.

Yang, C., 2013, 'From strategic coupling to recoupling and decoupling: Restructuring global production networks and regional evolution in China', *European Planning Studies*, 21(7), 1046–1063.

Yang, C., 2015, 'Government policy change and evolution of regional innovation systems in China: Evidence from strategic emerging industries in Shenzhen', *Environment and Planning C: Government and Policy*, 33(3), 661–682.

Yang, C. and He, C., 2017, 'Transformation of China's 'world factory': Production, relocation and export evolution of the electronics firms', *Tijdschrift voor Economische en Sociale Geografie*, 108(5), 571–591.

6 Conclusions and discussions
China's advance and challenges

This chapter generalizes some conclusions based on the above analysis and recommendations for China's future development within the context of opportunities and challenges. First, it summarizes several conclusions based on our research, which enrich our understanding of the role of globalization and innovation in China's economic development. Second, it summarizes our research's contribution and new findings, particularly the application of the GVC approach and two sides of China's ICT development in the GVC. Finally, it is clear that anti-globalization is a challenge to a latecomer country like China in seeking to upgrade its position in the GVC. It presents several recommendations for China's policymakers and business community on how to increase higher value-added products, and also for Western policymakers and CEOs on the opportunities and challenges facing China's technological upgrading.

Tensions between China's globalization and autonomy

Using a variety of methodologies at different scales, this study has sought to provide insights into China's integration into a more globalized economy and particularly into the ICT GVC. An important challenge for China arising from this integration is the extent to which it continues to be dependent on key foreign technologies and how it might acquire greater IP ownership, more influence in determining the technology trajectory and greater value-added from those GVC functions located in China. A fundamental question therefore is whether GVC participation is helping China to transition its economy from the low value-added activities associated with being the 'world's factory' to higher levels of indigenous innovation and greater technology autonomy. These questions, however, need to be posited in terms of the challenges facing a latecomer nation to achieve upgrading within high-technology sectors such as semiconductors, which are global in nature.

Furthermore, this book also sought to explain some of the reasons why China, despite its increasingly significant involvement in GVCs continues to play a relatively subordinate role. Having failed to achieve significant technology transfer from foreign companies in China through insisting on the establishment of joint ventures with Chinese companies, state policy more recently has focused on the promotion of indigenous innovation, while using its rapidly growing market as a leverage for its relationship with foreign investors. In addition to avoiding falling into the modularity trap of low value-added functions, China's policymakers must achieve the right balance between essential global integration of knowledge development and domestic ownership of IP.

Tension between foreign technology and indigenous innovation

Despite its ongoing dependence on foreign technology, China is determined to transition to an innovation-oriented development model. Our analysis of the changing profile of China's top exporting companies between 2001 and 2012 indicates a dominant, if decreasing, role of foreign invested firms, and the beginnings of the emergence of the private sector's role in exporting. It is also evident that despite their falling numbers and increased scaling, SOEs continue to play a significant role more generally in China's exports. Policymakers are well aware that if China is to transition from playing a relatively subordinate role within global value chains, it must focus on developing a more innovative and globally competitive development model. There are some signs, however, that China's progress could be slowed down by its opting for a more inward model of technology autonomy within a relatively protected large domestic market.

First, during this transition period from its dependence on export-led growth based on FDI to a greater emphasis on indigenous innovation and domestic consumption, it is necessary to consider both trade activity and developments within the domestic economy to evaluate the extent to which Chinese companies have achieved some level of technological upgrading. Ordinary trade, which is primarily composed of lower technology labor-intensive activity and of which Chinese companies account for two-thirds of the activity, has grown significantly, with a growing involvement of foreign companies who are increasingly turning their attention to the domestic economy. Processing trade, on the other hand, accounting for at least half of China's trade activity, and based on the importation of parts and components for final assembly in China, continues to be dominated by foreign companies, particularly in the high-technology sectors. Evidence of the dominant role of Taiwanese companies and particularly of Foxconn in China's electronics sector is striking, but even in the case of these 'foreign' companies, their role as low-cost assemblers in Mainland China continues to be a subordinate one within the value chains of the lead technology companies.

Second, China's policymakers continue their efforts to steer this enormous country toward some form of hybrid market economy by developing a more sustainable model based around indigenous innovation and domestic consumption rather than the export-led growth model based on FDI which has predominated to date. The impatient push toward technology autonomy, which could be argued to be partly driven by nationalistic and political factors, but also by the unsustainable nature of the traditional model, may, however, prove to be somewhat premature. With demographic change reducing labor supply, and significant levels of environmental problems associated with its 'world factory' model, China is under pressure to shift its comparative advantage to more knowledge-based activities. Policy tensions continue, however, between its nationalistic push for indigenous innovation within the confines of its own borders and the challenge to become more competitively innovative within global value chains in which an important component of its economic activity has become embedded.

Third, the managers of foreign subsidiaries in China provided an impressively nuanced perspective on China's new indigenous innovation policy and transition. Their companies in China are facing the challenges of competing for greater market share against increasingly competitive local companies, who receive significant support from Chinese policy interventions such as domestic standards and the public procurement market regulation. These managers showed a deep understanding of China's need to move its development model further up the value chain in order to reduce dependence on foreign technology. The overall impression gained from these interviews suggested that the best way forward for both the Chinese state and indeed for foreign multinationals was a greater willingness for more give-and-take in that relationship. There was an appreciation that China would continue to depend on the contribution of foreign companies in strategic sectors for a considerable time to come, but the best way for foreign companies to increase their market share in China was to collaborate as much as possible with the state in order to help it achieve its stated objectives.

Tensions between technology dependence and industrial upgrading

Indeed, China continues to depend significantly on foreign technology, and the ICT sector is no exception. Nevertheless, an important part of China's ICT industrial upgrading will involve considerable assimilation of foreign technology, and this major shift from technology dependence to greater autonomy will involve a long-term process.

First, Western companies together with companies from Japan, Korea and Taiwan continue to dominate the upper reaches of the ICT GVC, and despite locating much of their production activity in China, they have succeeded in avoiding any major leakage of intellectual property to local competitors. Because of the importance of intellectual property and innovation in controlling the technological trajectory of the ICT sector, the role played by high value-added component companies in areas like semiconductors and hard disk drives, and more recently applications processors for mobile devices is crucial. Apart from the dominant role of Korean and Taiwanese companies in the TFT-LCD display area, Western companies continue to play an important role as component suppliers, with Samsung being both a significant own brand company as well as a major supplier. Apart from Foxconn in the OEM/ODM sector, Samsung, with its rather exceptional in-house production model, is the other company that dominates trade data across the whole spectrum of activity. The lack of technological progress to date by mainland companies in generating significant inputs from indigenous innovation is obvious. Among the implications of this foreign dominance is the extent to which major global technology corporations can exploit the comparative advantages of China while continuing to ensure its subordinate role in the GVC. While some progress has been made to date in promoting indigenous innovation by Chinese firms, policymakers have begun to appreciate the limits of a growth path driven by policy-induced high-tech exports.

Second, although the technological trajectory of the ICT GVC continues to be controlled by foreign companies, the significant shift in ICT production to Mainland China raises questions about the future evolution of the GVC, and whether a tipping point has been reached in relation to China's possible indispensable role in its development. Despite a poor performance in achieving any significant control in either ICT assembly or in the supply of key components to companies like Apple, a small number of Chinese companies have become highly successful global brands. While questions continue to be raised about the extent of state regulation of China's domestic market, and bearing in mind their reliance to some extent on the capabilities of foreign suppliers, the significant progress made by these Chinese brands should be acknowledged. Over time, Chinese companies have succeeded in dislodging significant Western companies that were initially highly successful in China from the lists of top ICT traders in China. While conceptualizations of relationships between the Chinese state and foreign investors, however, may tend to emphasize the obvious tensions that can arise in the bargaining process, our data analysis, including company interviews, suggests a more nuanced and complex relationship.

Third, the challenge for Chinese policymakers is to find the right balance between China's ongoing dependence on foreign technology and the collaborative role it needs to develop with major technology corporations in its deepening involvement in the ICT GVC. In pushing for technical standards based on indigenous innovation, China faces demands for compliance with international norms both from abroad and from within the country, while attempting to achieve a certain level of autonomy for the development of Chinese firms (Wang et al., 2014). To some extent, the main beneficiaries of this enormous shift in the center of gravity of ICT production have been Taiwanese companies, and in particular Foxconn, which by far is the world leader in contract manufacturing for global technology companies. These OEM/ODM companies, however, operate under a regime of very tight control with their major clients, who also ensure that profit margins are razor thin. Meanwhile, the considerable strides made by Chinese companies, which is reflected in their ability to compete globally, is further attested to by our research. But rather than falling into a simplistic binary model of foreign and mainland companies, our research suggests a more nuanced picture of significant interconnections between many types of companies through client relationships, joint ventures and mergers and acquisitions.

The willingness of global technology companies such as Intel and Qualcomm to develop partnerships with Chinese companies, in order to ensure market access in China, is an indication of the ongoing bargaining relationship between a powerful state with a huge market and the need of technology leaders to maintain their dominance in the market. Ghemawat and Hout (2016) highlight a number of important differences between Western companies, whose capabilities are mainly 'upstream' and who continue to dominate the high-tech sector in China and Chinese companies, whose capabilities are mainly 'downstream'. While having made important progress in sectors such as the Internet and telecommunications, they point to deficiencies in Chinese companies in areas such as deep knowledge of customers' technical needs, software development and managing global supply chains. While the Western company model is to source components globally, China continues to be influenced by an historical preoccupation with self-sufficiency.

Tension between ecosystem embedding and value-adding

Despite the poor performance by Chinese companies in adding value in the ICT sector, a significantly rich ecosystem of ICT companies like Apple have been attracted to locate in China. Our research indicates that 44 percent of all company subsidiaries supplying Apple with components globally are located in China, which is a good reflection of the extent to which the center of gravity of both Apple's and the ICT GVC more generally has shifted to China in recent years. It should be remembered that while some Apple suppliers, particularly its most significant contract manufacturer Foxconn, obtain between 40 percent and 50 percent of their revenue from Apple, in many cases such major supplier companies are lead technology companies in their own right, supplying many other major global lead companies. Almost 80 percent of Apple's 336 supplier subsidiaries in China are to be found in two key concentrations, Shanghai/Jiangsu province and Guangdong province in the south, with the remaining 20 percent scattered widely in outlier locations in the interior, reflecting the more recent shift, particularly by the major contract manufacturer Foxconn, to lower cost locations closer to migrant labor.

While many of Apple's core suppliers continue to be located outside the mainland, China has succeeded in attracting a rich ecosystem of ICT companies to locate some of their activities in China, and Apple's supply chain is clearly an important element in that ecosystem. While it is not surprising that the category of activity mainly associated with final assembly had the highest presence in China, the general pattern was for a higher proportion of non-core component supplier subsidiaries to be located in China relative to core components. However, this pattern is somewhat qualified depending on the particular components in question and also the country of origin of suppliers. In the case of integrated circuits, one of the largest categories of component suppliers, there was a distinct under-representation in China, and in the case of all categories of Japanese suppliers, there was a very strong tendency not to locate in China. Thus, while one could argue that factors such as strategies to protect intellectual property were important in explaining locational patterns, there would also appear to be strong cultural differences at work. Taiwanese supplier companies were the most likely group to locate in China, with some reluctance to locate core component subsidiaries there.

Second, low labor cost is still a primary, though declining, competitive advantage for Mainland China. Foxconn's rise since 2001 has been particularly associated with Apple's business model of outsourcing 100 percent of its production to China, while they also ensure no leakage of intellectual property by stringently controlling its contract manufacturers and supplier companies. Contrary to some suggestions, there appears to be little evidence of any major shift in the asymmetrical relationships between lead companies like Apple and major contract manufacturers in recent times. Since 2008, the relocation of assembly activity away from dominant locations like Shenzhen has not yet been followed by any significant relocation of other types of suppliers, although each outlier location often has some other component suppliers present. The relative ease with which Foxconn's enormous operations have been able to relocate to inland locations, made attractive by plentiful labor and significant local government subsidies and tax incentives, might suggest that the long-term sustainability of these assembly operations could be open to question. But the enormous scale, flexibility and advantages in relation to the risk management of such huge operations may be very difficult to replicate in other low-cost locations. As major contract manufacturers make greater use of robotics in their assembly operations, the geography of such operations globally may well be more strongly influenced by proximity to the market.

Third, to some extent the success of Chinese brands is exaggerated by the invisibility of major global brands such as Apple, whose production is masked by OEM/ODM company trade. The success of these Chinese brands, however, raises interesting questions about the ability of indigenous companies in an exceptionally rapidly growing market of enormous scale, to displace formerly successful brands in what is, for them, a very different marketplace. While China has had some level of success in establishing a number of key international companies in the ICT sector, their dependence on foreign companies for key technologies, design and architecture qualifies their level of success to date and significantly reduces their profit margins. The recent push for indigenous and autonomous technology development by Chinese policymakers reflects their ongoing unease with predominantly low value-added functions being located in China and the consequent low levels of benefits to China. The very modest contribution by Chinese suppliers to Apple's supply chain in China reflects China's relatively immature state in local technology development. But the way forward for China may best be served by deepening its integration with lead technology companies, irrespective of nationality, if it is to make more significant progress in deepening its acquisition of core intellectual property in the ICT sector.

Contributions and findings

The topicality of this book is highlighted by the current political debate about international trade and the benefits or losses associated with globalization, with Trump's election campaign rhetoric about reshoring the production of Apple products to the U.S. having considerable appeal to electoral groups that have experienced the negative impact of globalization. Few politicians will make the effort to explain the complexities of global value chains, whereby those U.S.

citizens who can afford to invest in technology companies like Apple, in their quest for higher dividend payments, place significant pressure on management to locate functions in the most competitive global regions, which in turn may result in fellow citizens losing their employment.

Applying the GVC approach to China's ICT globalization

The main theoretical and methodological framework we employ in seeking to analyze China's integration into a more globalized economy is the GVC. But as a prelude, we trace a number of economic and management theories which have grappled with key concepts such as competitiveness, comparative advantage and productivity. Many of these earlier theories, which still retain considerable relevance, were used more widely in comparing the performance of different national or domestic economies through trade. Trump's investment and trade protection policies are based on these traditional theories, which do not clarify a country's value contribution to products.

While such comparisons remain important both in terms of economic theory and for policy formulation, a more globalized economic landscape based on fragmented production and increased interdependence between world regions has resulted in more recent frameworks such as global value chains, which seek to overcome the limitations of traditional trade theory and trade data. To some extent, the confused political discourse about international trade which has emerged in recent times reflects the more traditional understanding of competition between nations based on outcomes such as trade surpluses and deficits.

The GVC approach seeks to determine how value is created and captured by a more fragmented pattern of production globally. Meanwhile, the value-added by the fragmented unit of production, location or company is an effective indicator when measuring national competitiveness. It is in this sense that this book seeks to elucidate both the impacts on China by its integration into the ICT GVC and China's increased impact on other regions. This book seeks to explain how ICT manufacturing has been increasingly offshored to locations in China and how China has become a major global location for the assembly of ICT products. It also explains, however, that the benefits accruing to China are relatively modest, since much of the intellectual property which creates the key components of these products is derived from developed country companies, with Chinese companies playing only a modest role to date.

China's foreign dependency in the ICT sector

China's role within the ICT GVC to date remains a subordinate one, even with its input into the assembly of products, which is the key function located in China being dominated by Taiwanese companies. For more than 10 years, Chinese policymakers, fully aware of the unsustainability of China's 'world factory' model, based on low-cost labor and other incentives to attract global technology companies, have sought to transition its economic model toward greater levels of indigenous innovation. This policy transition, however, faces many challenges compared to the relatively easier task of initially attracting FDI to China to benefit from its competitive factors of production. The post-2008 crisis period has highlighted China's precarious dependence on an export-led economic model with its high-tech sectors dominated by foreign companies. The significant drop in global demand for Chinese exports, the decline in the labor force and the challenges of environmental degradation are among the factors that have converged demanding a significant shift in policy direction.

While it is clear that foreign investment in China has played an important role in helping to develop China's own technology sector, with China continuing to depend significantly on foreign sources of technology, it has also made huge strides in investing in its own R&D and innovation in recent years. This enormous investment, coupled with its rapidly growing market, has made China an increasingly attractive location not only for the production of ICT products, but also for market expansion by foreign technology companies. Over time, however, since China's initial policy objective of gaining technology transfer for market access has not produced the required results, a greater focus on indigenous innovation has emerged, with a range of policies to promote the expansion of domestic companies at the expense of foreign companies within the domestic market.

In addition, China's globalization is different from that of Japan in the 1980s. Among the top exporters from China to the U.S., more than 80 percent are owned by companies outside of the mainland, which means that China is primarily an assembly location of imported components to be exported as products. Most of Japan's big exporters in the 1980s were Japanese, and Japan added most of the value to exported products. Our empirical results, however, indicate that China in recent years adds less value to its exports than Japan and other developed countries. Clearly, China's rise is more complex than that of Japan in the 1980s. China's globalization results from inward FDI and being an export platform for foreign companies, whereas Japan's globalization resulted from exporting products based on licensed technology. An additional major difference between the two countries, however, is China's market size.

When Japan invested in and exported to the U.S. in the 1980s, President Ronald Reagan increased tariffs on Japanese products including motorcycles and TVs, and this resulted in a stronger yen via the Plaza Accord in 1985. While China's situation is different to that of Japan, it could face considerable risks. China is currently the biggest trade partner of the U.S., accounting for about 21 percent of the total, which is similar to that of Japan in the mid-1980s, and the U.S. is also China's principal investment partner. But China's development path is likely to be quite different to that of Japan. One reason for this is the role played by non-Chinese companies such as Quanta Computers and Foxconn, both Taiwanese companies, in exporting to the U.S.

Our empirical investigation of the evolution of China's ICT sector in the 12 years after WTO accession reveals the continued dominance of foreign companies in the categories of own brands, component suppliers and assembly operations, with a major shift toward final assembly in China during that period.

The weakness of China's technology sector in intellectual property ownership is revealed in the low levels of involvement by Chinese companies as component suppliers and in assembly operations. This weakness is also reflected in the aggregate data measuring value-added in high-technology exports, which continued to be dominated by global companies and their manufacturing contractors.

China's indigenous advance in the ICT sector

Although China has clearly benefited from increased integration into the global economy, its relatively subordinate role within the ICT GVC to date in low value-added functions like assembly has provided it with greater determination to shape its future relationships within the GVC, or if one likes, to seek to determine its future globalization more on its own terms. While most late-developing countries have found it exceptionally difficult to change the 'rules of the game', China's enormous market leverage, together with its particular political economy, may be a sufficient combination to at least ameliorate the relatively asymmetrical relationship between IP weak regions and those which significantly impact the technology trajectory. Whether it is by an aggressive outward FDI policy to acquire missing technology capabilities from non-Chinese companies, or through controlling how its own internet market at home will evolve by restricting non-Chinese companies' involvement, China's policymakers are always proactive in seeking the best advantages for developing their own indigenous technology sector.

Our analysis also reveals the emergence of Chinese brand companies such as Huawei and ZTE, which were beginning to replace well known global brands. In addition to China's policymakers' concerns about the dangers of falling into the low value-added modularity trap within the ICT GVC, they are also concerned about the national security dangers associated with high levels of dependence on foreign technology sources. Hence their recent significant investment in building their own semiconductor sector, which includes a recent focus on acquiring foreign technology companies. While there is little doubt that the determined policy focus of China, backed up by significant investment, will yield results in the long-term, some scholars have expressed skepticism about late-developing countries seeking to boost their technological prowess without being significantly embedded in global knowledge networks. Partly for domestic political reasons, China's policy formulation continues to reflect tensions between the need for such global integration and the desire for national autonomy.

Late-developer nations like China have the capacity to leapfrog certain elements of technological development. In China's case, its enormous internet-based consumer market, coupled with its rapidly growing middle-class population has the potential for creating some disruption in the evolution of ecommerce markets and ecosystems. The impressive performance of Tencent's WeChat in developing a sophisticated range of mobile services capable of responding to China's rapidly evolving internet market is evidence of this potential. But such developments, albeit by private companies in an intensely competitive market, are taking place within the relatively protected boundaries of China, while evidence of internationalization capabilities remains restricted to a relatively few major Chinese companies such as Huawei. So despite the relative progress in a number of areas, a critical question is whether China can overcome the limitations of IP deficiencies in critical technologies like semiconductors by creating high levels of innovation in such areas as internet business platforms and ecosystems. In tracking China's evolving role in the ICT GVC at various levels, this book highlights how such IP weaknesses have resulted in asymmetrical relationships within the GVC, reflecting the relatively low value-added nature of activities located in China.

While our analysis has highlighted some successful elements in the ICT GVC in China, particularly the rise of Chinese brands such as Huawei, ZTE, Xiaomi and the highly competitive BAT internet companies, in most cases China's domestic market has played a key role in their development. In some cases, such as Xiaomi, IP deficiencies have created barriers to internationalization, and Chinese companies have frequently begun internationalization in less-developed country markets with relatively weak IPR regimes. Huawei's successful internationalization, apart from the political obstacles it has faced particularly in the U.S., but also elsewhere, has been relatively exceptional.

Thus, while Chinese technology companies need to follow Huawei's successful example in expanding internationally, foreign technology companies in China, which have benefitted very significantly from both the comparative advantage of assembling products in China and from their share in the Chinese domestic market, may face considerable obstacles to increasing that market share in the future. Chinese policymakers are determined to increase the value-added of their own companies within China and extract significant technological advantages from foreign technology companies whose future global competitiveness is dependent on exploiting China's advantages.

China's future globalization

There is little doubt that China's increased role in the ICT GVC was greatly facilitated by the opening of its market to foreign investment, which coincided with WTO accession and increased offshoring of manufacturing to emerging countries. While many agree that China has benefitted greatly from integrating into the global economy, its participation has also had a profound impact on the landscape of global economics, including contributing to significant tension with developed countries such as the U.S.

As developed economies increased their wealth, much of the manufacturing of textiles, shoes, furniture and basic consumer electronics was offshored to more competitive locations. ICT manufacturing migrated from the U.S. to Japan, then from Japan to South Korea and Taiwan, and more recently to China. This industrial migration has been gradual over many decades, and it will continue as new locations develop competitive capabilities and attractive cost structures. It is in this sense that we can say that globalization is driven by both developed economies and emerging economies like Mainland China. In order to maintain international competitive advantage, developed economies have been forced to shift from labor-intensive industries to capital- and knowledge/technology-intensive industries due to increasing labor costs.

In fact, our research shows that value creation and contribution to the ICT GVC by Chinese companies is modest, with companies from developed economies contributing most of the value-added and gaining most of the benefits by continuing to exercise significant control. With the expansion of the international division of labor through globalization, a greater divide in the distribution of added value has followed. The offshoring of manufacturing has not been as extensive as many scholars and policymakers believe, and there has been considerable misunderstanding of the role played by China in expanding global value chains. Autor et al. (2016), while acknowledging the positive benefits for consumers in the U.S. from trade with China, have provided empirical evidence of the substantial adjustment costs, such as high levels of unemployment, that have affected local labor markets in the U.S., dependent on industries with high levels of exposure to competition from China. On the other hand, China's concern relates to the predominantly low skilled employment opportunities associated with low value added tasks which resulted from globalisation.

The current political outcry in major regions of the U.S. that have suffered most from the restructuring associated with manufacturing offshoring has resulted in strong protectionist reactions to international trade, particularly with China. Our case study of Apple's supply chain, however, suggests that the changing nature of global supply chains makes it difficult to interpret the implications of trade data since they fail to specify which locations benefit most from trade (Morrison, 2017).

Yet, in addition to manufacturing offshoring, employment loss in developed economies has also resulted from improvements in productivity. Some would argue that without the positive gains to developed country companies through offshoring to China, employment losses in some regions may have been greater, but the restructuring of some regions with heavy losses from the closure of labor-intensive industries may also have been under-estimated. China's contribution to global value chains has not only been in terms of providing low-cost labor, but also through the provision of one of the world's largest concentrations of science and engineering graduates and an increasingly attractive market for developed country MNCs. Our study explains how China is but one – though very important – node in what is, in many cases, quite complex global value chains. The complexity of these value chains, which contributes greatly to international interdependence between companies, their subsidiaries and the locations in which they operate, is well illustrated by our detailed case study of Apple's supply chain in China. As Moretti (2012) argued, a company's innovation success depends on the entire ecosystem that surrounds it, and it is necessary to move not just one company but an entire ecosystem. This logic suggest that the competitiveness of a nation's manufactured exports will increasingly depend on the local availability of a broad range of excellent, reasonably priced components and services.

When we return to the starting point of this book, it is worth noting that Donald Trump, who has now become President of the U.S., promised his supporters that he would force Apple to manufacture its hardware in the U.S. instead of looking to overseas labor. Already he has pulled the U.S. out of the Trans Pacific Partnership, which sought to develop a single market among 12 countries in the Pacific Ocean but did not include China. Apart from the U.S., UK voters have supported Brexit, which will result in Britain leaving the European single market. Despite the enormous benefits which these two major economies have gained from globalization in recent decades, a groundswell of political opinion has reacted to the considerable negative consequences for some groups of workers in particular industries and regions.

Despite these momentous developments, it will be difficult to reverse the process of globalization, and with China's accession to the WTO it is inconceivable that any major reversal of that process will take shape. Although China is but one link in the global value chains of many companies, because of its size it is quite an important link; yet, it continues to play a subservient role in terms of value creation and benefits accruing to China. Rather than seeing China's emergence as an economic power which threatens the influence of other countries, China's participation in the global value chains of production such as ICT should be seen as a positive contribution toward international collaboration and interdependence. While China's participation in a more globalized economy will continue to be characterized by strong competition between nations, the successful development of China's own economy will be a major contribution to peaceful coexistence and mutual benefit.

Coinciding with a strong anti-globalization wave of trade protectionism and populism affecting some Western countries, China launched its Belt and Road Initiative in 2013. This four trillion dollar infrastructure development programme is designed to provide greater connectivity between China, Central Asia and Europe over the next 30 to 40 years. Thus China is seeking to promote globalization between emerging and developed countries. With the center of gravity of economic activity shifting towards emerging nations, China's Belt and Road Initiative seeks to create greater integration between both the BRIC countries (Brazil, Russia, India, China and South Africa) and the E7 countries (China, India, Brazil, Mexico, Russia, Indonesia and Turkey). Thus, rather than retreating from globalization, China's strategy is to promote greater integration between these regions.

It is clear that the recent stage of globalisation in which China became more integrated into the global economy has resulted in negative outcomes for both developed and emerging economies. The current anti-globalization reaction sweeping the world, with a shift towards trade protectionism, is unlikely to provide solutions to the challenges facing developed regions. On a more positive note, there is a considerable gap between the Trump campaign rhetoric and the actual policy development to date, and while many in the UK may be having second thoughts about the wisdom of the Brexit decision, the French electorate have shown themselves to be more wary of following the British example.

References

Autor, D.H., Dorn, D. and Hanson, G.H., 2016, 'The China shock: Learning from labour-market adjustment to large changes in trade', *Annual Review of Economics*, 8(1), 205–240.

Ghemawat, P. and Hout, T., 2016, 'Can china's companies conquer the world?' *Foreign Affairs*, 95, 211–224.Moretti, E., 2012, *The New Geography of Jobs*, Boston, MA, Houghton Mifflin Harcourt.

Morrison, W.M., 2017, *China-U.S. Trade Issues*, Congressional Research Service Reports,

August 26, 2017. Congressional Research Service, Library of Congress, Washington, D.C. Available at https://fas.org/sgp/crs/row/RL33536.pdf. Accessed 10/29/2017.

Wang, P., Kwak, J. and Lee, H., 2014, 'The latecomer strategy for global ICT standardization: Indigenous innovation and its dilemma', *Telecommunications Policy*, 38(10), 933–943.

Index

For Product Safety Concerns and Information please contact our EU
representative GPSR@taylorandfrancis.com
Taylor & Francis Verlag GmbH, Kaufingerstraße 24, 80331 München, Germany

www.ingramcontent.com/pod-product-compliance
Ingram Content Group UK Ltd.
Pitfield, Milton Keynes, MK11 3LW, UK
UKHW020951180425
457613UK00019B/622